ABOUT THIS PUBLICATION

FOR SERVICE ASSISTANCE

Customer Service Department
704.898.0770

North Carolina General Statues is published by The Muliti-Media Group of Greater Charlotte in Charlotte, North Carolina. Copyright 2015 by the Multi-Media Group of Greater Charlotte. This book or parts thereof may not be reproduced in any form, stored in a retrieval system, or transmitted in any form by any means—electronic, mechanical, photocopy, recording or otherwise—without prior written permission of the publisher, except as provided by United States of America copyright law.

The records required by U.S. Code 2257(a) through (c) and the pertinent regulations 28 C.F.R. Cli. 1, Part 75 with respect to this publication and all materials associated with such records are maintained by The Multi-Media Group of Greater Charlotte, Publisher and available for review by Attorney General.

www.visionbooks.org

Copyright © 2015 by MMGGC
All rights reserved!

TID: 5031859
ISBN (10) digit: 1502599651
ISBN (13) digit: 978-1502599650

123-4-56789-01239-Paperback
123-4-56789-01239-Hardback

First Edition

090520140547

Printed in the United States of America

2015 EDITION

North Carolina Criminal Law And Procedure-Pamphlet # 24

Printed In conjunction with the Administration of the Courts

North Carolina Criminal Law and Procedure
Pamphlet Reference Guide

Chapters	Pamphlet
Chapter 1 Civil Procedure	1
Chapter 1 Civil Procedure (Continue)	2
Chapter 1A Rules of Civil Procedure	2
Chapter 1B Contribution.	2
Chapter 1C Enforcement of Judgments.	2
Chapter 1D Punitive Damages.	2
Chapter 1E Eastern Band of Cherokee Indians.	2
Chapter 1F North Carolina Uniform Interstate Depositions and Discovery Act.	2
Chapter 2 - Clerk of Superior Court [Repealed and Transferred.]	3
Chapter 3 - Commissioners of Affidavits and Deeds [Repealed.]	3
Chapter 4 - Common Law	3
Chapter 5 - Contempt [Repealed.]	3
Chapter 5A - Contempt	3
Chapter 6 - Liability for Court Costs	3
Chapter 7 - Courts [Repealed and Transferred.]	3
Chapter 7A – Judicial Department	3
Chapter 7A – Continuation (Judicial Department)	4
Chapter 7A – Continuation (Judicial Department)	5
Chapter 7B - Juvenile Code	5
Chapter 8 - Evidence	6
Chapter 8A - Interpreters for Deaf Persons [Recodified.]	6
Chapter 8B - Interpreters for Deaf Persons	6
Chapter 8C - Evidence Code	6
Chapter 9 - Jurors	6
Chapter 10 - Notaries [Repealed.]	6
Chapter 10A - Notaries [Recodified.]	6
Chapter 10B - Notaries	6
Chapter 11 - Oaths	6
Chapter 12 - Statutory Construction	6
Chapter 13 - Citizenship Restored	6
Chapter 14 - Criminal Law	7
Chapter 14 –Criminal Law (Continuation)	8
Chapter 15 - Criminal Procedure	9
Chapter 15A - Criminal Procedure Act (Continuation)	10
Chapter 15A - Criminal Procedure Act (Continuation)	11
Chapter 15B - Victims Compensation	11
Chapter 15C - Address Confidentiality Program	11
Chapter 16 - Gaming Contracts and Futures	11
Chapter 17 - Habeas Corpus	11

Chapter 17A - Law-Enforcement Officers [Recodified.]	11
Chapter 17B - North Carolina Criminal Justice Education and Training System [Recodified.] Chapter 17C - North Carolina Criminal Justice Education and Training Standards Commission	11
	11
Chapter 17D - North Carolina Justice Academy	11
Chapter 17E - North Carolina Sheriffs' Education and Training Standards Commission	11
Chapter 18 - Regulation of Intoxicating Liquors [Repealed.]	12
Chapter 18A - Regulation of Intoxicating Liquors [Repealed.]	12
Chapter 18B - Regulation of Alcoholic Beverages	12
Chapter 18C - North Carolina State Lottery	12
Chapter 19 - Offenses against Public Morals	12
Chapter 19A - Protection of Animals	12
Chapter 20 - Motor Vehicles	13
Chapter 20 - Motor Vehicles (Continuation)	14
Chapter 20 - Motor Vehicles (Continuation)	15
Chapter 20 - Motor Vehicles (Continuation)	16
Chapter 21 - Bills of Lading	17
Chapter 22 - Contracts Requiring Writing	17
Chapter 22A - Signatures	17
Chapter 22B - Contracts Against Public Policy	17
Chapter 22C - Payments to Subcontractors	17
Chapter 23 - Debtor and Creditor	17
Chapter 24 – Interest	17
Chapter 25 – Uniform Commercial Code	18
Chapter 25 – Uniform Commercial Code (Continuation)	19
Chapter 25A – Retail Installment Sales Act	20
Chapter 25B - Credit	20
Chapter 25C - Sales of Artwork	20
Chapter 26 - Suretyship	20
Chapter 27 - Warehouse Receipts [Repealed.]	20
Chapter 28 - Administration [Repealed.]	20
Chapter 28A - Administration of Decedents' Estates	20
Chapter 28B - Estates of Absentees in Military Service	20
Chapter 28C - Estates of Missing Persons	20
Chapter 29 - Intestate Succession	21
Chapter 30 - Surviving Spouses	21
Chapter 31 - Wills	21
Chapter 31A - Acts Barring Property Rights	21
Chapter 31B - Renunciation of Property and Renunciation of Fiduciary Powers Act	21
Chapter 31C - Uniform Disposition of Community Property Rights at Death Act	21
Chapter 32 - Fiduciaries	21
Chapter 32A - Powers of Attorney	21
Chapter 33 - Guardian and Ward [Repealed and Recodified.]	21

Chapter 33A - North Carolina Uniform Transfers to Minors Act	21
Chapter 33B - North Carolina Uniform Custodial Trust Act	21
Chapter 34 - Veterans' Guardianship Act	22
Chapter 35 - Sterilization Procedures	22
Chapter 35A - Incompetency and Guardianship	22
Chapter 36 - Trusts and Trustees [Repealed.]	22
Chapter 36A - Trusts and Trustees	22
Chapter 36B - Uniform Management of Institutional Funds Act [Repealed.]	22
Chapter 36C - North Carolina Uniform Trust Code	22
Chapter 36D - North Carolina Community Third Party Trusts, Pooled Trusts	23
Chapter 36E - Uniform Prudent Management of Institutional Funds Act	23
Chapter 37 - Allocation of Principal and Income [Repealed.]	23
Chapter 37A - Uniform Principal and Income Act	23
Chapter 38 - Boundaries	23
Chapter 38A - Landowner Liability	23
Chapter 38B - Trespasser Responsibility	23
Chapter 39 - Conveyances	23
Chapter 39A - Transfer Fee Covenants Prohibited	23
Chapter 40 - Eminent Domain [Repealed.]	23
Chapter 40A - Eminent Domain	23
Chapter 41 - Estates	23
Chapter 41A - State Fair Housing Act	23
Chapter 42 - Landlord and Tenant	23
Chapter 42A - Vacation Rental Act	23
Chapter 43 - Land Registration	23
Chapter 44 - Liens	24
Chapter 44A - Statutory Liens and Charges	24
Chapter 45 - Mortgages and Deeds of Trust	24
Chapter 45A - Good Funds Settlement Act	24
Chapter 46 - Partition	24
Chapter 47 - Probate and Registration	25
Chapter 47A - Unit Ownership	25
Chapter 47B - Real Property Marketable Title Act	25
Chapter 47C - North Carolina Condominium Act	25
Chapter 47D - Notice of Settlement Act [Expired.]	25
Chapter 47E - Residential Property Disclosure Act	25
Chapter 47F - North Carolina Planned Community Act	25
Chapter 47G - Option to Purchase Contracts	25
Chapter 47H - Contracts for Deed	25
Chapter 48 - Adoptions +	26
Chapter 48A - Minors	26
Chapter 49 - Bastardy	26
Chapter 49A - Rights of Children	26
Chapter 50 - Divorce and Alimony	26

Chapter 50A - Uniform Child-Custody Jurisdiction and Enforcement Act	26
Chapter 50B - Domestic Violence	26
Chapter 50C - Civil No-Contact Orders	26
Chapter 51 - Marriage	26
Chapter 52 - Powers and Liabilities of Married Persons	27
Chapter 52A - Uniform Reciprocal Enforcement of Support Act [Repealed.]	27
Chapter 52B - Uniform Premarital Agreement Act	27
Chapter 52C - Uniform Interstate Family Support Act	27
Chapter 53 - Banks	27
Chapter 53A - Business Development Corporations and North Carolina Capital Resource Corporations	28
Chapter 53B - Financial Privacy Act	28
Chapter 54 - Cooperative Organizations	28
Chapter 54A - Capital Stock Savings and Loan Associations [Repealed.]	28
Chapter 54B - Savings and Loan Associations	29
Chapter 54C - Savings Banks	29
Chapter 55 - North Carolina Business Corporation Act	30
Chapter 55A - North Carolina Nonprofit Corporation Act	31
Chapter 55B - Professional Corporation Act	31
Chapter 55C - Foreign Trade Zones	31
Chapter 55D - Filings, Names, and Registered Agents for Corporations, Nonprofit Corporations, and Partnerships	31
Chapter 56 - Electric, Telegraph and Power Companies [Repealed.]	31
Chapter 57 - Hospital, Medical and Dental Service Corporations [Recodified.]	31
Chapter 57A - Health Maintenance Organization Act [Recodified.]	31
Chapter 57B - Health Maintenance Organization Act [Recodified.]	31
Chapter 57C - North Carolina Limited Liability Company Act.	31
Chapter 58 - Insurance.	32
Chapter 58 - Insurance (Continuation)	33
Chapter 58 - Insurance (Continuation)	34
Chapter 58 - Insurance (Continuation)	35
Chapter 58 - Insurance (Continuation)	36
Chapter 58 - Insurance (Continuation)	37
Chapter 58 - Insurance (Continuation)	38
Chapter 58A - North Carolina Health Insurance Trust Commission [Recodified.]	38
Chapter 59 - Partnership.	39
Chapter 59B - Uniform Unincorporated Nonprofit Association Act.	39
Chapter 60 - Railroads and Other Carriers [Repealed and Transferred.]	39
Chapter 61 - Religious Societies	39
Chapter 62 - Public Utilities	39

Chapter 62 - Public Utilities (Continuation)	40
Chapter 62A - Public Safety Telephone Service And Wireless Telephone Service	40
Chapter 63 - Aeronautics	40
Chapter 63A - North Carolina Global TransPark Authority	40
Chapter 64 - Aliens	40
Chapter 65 – Cemeteries	40
Chapter 66 - Commerce and Business	41
Chapter 67 - Dogs	41
Chapter 68 - Fences and Stock Law	41
Chapter 69 - Fire Protection	41
Chapter 70 - Indian Antiquities, Archaeological Resources and Unmarked Human Skeletal Remains Protection	42
Chapter 71 - Indians [Repealed.]	42
Chapter 71A - Indians	42
Chapter 72 - Inns, Hotels and Restaurants	42
Chapter 73 - Mills	42
Chapter 74 - Mines and Quarries	42
Chapter 74A - Company Police [Repealed.]	42
Chapter 74B - Private Protective Services Act [Repealed.]	42
Chapter 74C - Private Protective Services	42
Chapter 74D - Alarm Systems	42
Chapter 74E - Company Police Act	42
Chapter 74F - Locksmith Licensing Act	42
Chapter 74G - Campus Police Act	42
Chapter 75 - Monopolies, Trusts and Consumer Protection	42
Chapter 75A - Boating and Water Safety	43
Chapter 75B - Discrimination in Business	43
Chapter 75C - Motion Picture Fair Competition Act	43
Chapter 75D - Racketeer Influenced and Corrupt Organizations	43
Chapter 75E - Unlawful Activities in Connection With Certain Corporate Transactions	43
Chapter 76 - Navigation	43
Chapter 76A - Navigation and Pilotage Commissions	43
Chapter 77 - Rivers, Creeks, and Coastal Waters	43
Chapter 78 - Securities Law [Repealed.]	43
Chapter 78A - North Carolina Securities Act	43
Chapter 78B - Tender Offer Disclosure Act [Repealed.]	43
Chapter 78C - Investment Advisers	43
Chapter 78D - Commodities Act	43
Chapter 79 - Strays [Repealed.]	43
Chapter 80 - Trademarks, Brands, etc.	44
Chapter 81 - Weights and Measures [Recodified.]	44
Chapter 81A - Weights and Measures Act of 1975.	44
Chapter 82 - Wrecks [Repealed.]	44
Chapter 83 - Architects [Recodified.]	44

Chapter 83A - Architects	44
Chapter 84 - Attorneys-at-Law	44
Chapter 84A - Foreign Legal Consultants	44
Chapter 85 - Auctions and Auctioneers [Repealed.]	44
Chapter 85A - Bail Bondsmen and Runners [Recodified.]	44
Chapter 85B - Auctions and Auctioneers	44
Chapter 85C - Bail Bondsmen and Runners [Recodified.]	44
Chapter 86 - Barbers [Recodified.]	44
Chapter 86A - Barbers	44
Chapter 87 - Contractors	44
Chapter 88 - Cosmetic Art [Repealed.]	44
Chapter 88A - Electrolysis Practice Act	44
Chapter 88B - Cosmetic Art	45
Chapter 89 - Engineering and Land Surveying [Recodified.]	45
Chapter 89A - Landscape Architects	45
Chapter 89B - Foresters	45
Chapter 89C - Engineering and Land Surveying	45
Chapter 89D - Landscape Contractors	45
Chapter 89E - Geologists Licensing Act	45
Chapter 89F - North Carolina Soil Scientist Licensing Act	45
Chapter 89G - Irrigation Contractors	45
Chapter 90 - Medicine and Allied Occupations	45
Chapter 90 - Medicine and Allied Occupations (Continuation)	46
Chapter 90 - Medicine and Allied Occupations (Continuation)	47
Chapter 90 - Medicine and Allied Occupations (Continuation)	48
Chapter 90A - Sanitarians and Water and Wastewater Treatment Facility Operators	48
Chapter 90B - Social Worker Certification and Licensure Act	48
Chapter 90C - North Carolina Recreational Therapy Licensure Act	48
Chapter 90D - Interpreters and Transliterators	48
Chapter 91 - Pawnbrokers [Repealed.]	48
Chapter 91A - Pawnbrokers Modernization Act of 1989	48
Chapter 92 - Photographers [Deleted.]	48
Chapter 93 - Certified Public Accountants	48
Chapter 93A - Real Estate License Law	49
Chapter 93B - Occupational Licensing Boards	49
Chapter 93C - Watchmakers [Repealed.]	49
Chapter 93D - North Carolina State Hearing Aid Dealers and Fitters Board.	49
Chapter 93E - North Carolina Appraisers Act	49
Chapter 94 - Apprenticeship	49
Chapter 95 - Department of Labor and Labor Regulations	49
Chapter 95 - Department of Labor and Labor Regulations (Continuation)	50
Chapter 96 - Employment Security	50
Chapter 97 - Workers' Compensation Act	50
Chapter 97 - Workers' Compensation Act (Continuation)	51

Chapter 98 - Burnt and Lost Records	51
Chapter 99 - Libel and Slander	51
Chapter 99A - Civil Remedies for Criminal Actions	51
Chapter 99B - Products Liability	51
Chapter 99C - Actions Relating to Winter Sports Safety and Accidents	51
Chapter 99D - Civil Rights	51
Chapter 99E - Special Liability Provisions	51
Chapter 100 - Monuments, Memorials and Parks	51
Chapter 101 - Names of Persons	51
Chapter 102 - Official Survey Base	51
Chapter 103 - Sundays, Holidays and Special Days	51
Chapter 104 - United States Lands	51
Chapter 104A - Degrees of Kinship	51
Chapter 104B - Hurricanes or Other Acts of Nature	51
Chapter 104C - Atomic Energy, Radioactivity and Ionizing Radiation [Repealed and Recodified.]	51
Chapter 104D - Southern States Energy Compact	51
Chapter 104E - North Carolina Radiation Protection Act	51
Chapter 104F - Southeast Interstate Low-Level Radioactive Waste Management Compact [Repealed]	51
Chapter 104G - North Carolina Low-Level Radioactive Waste Management Authority Act of 1987 [Repealed]	51
Chapter 105 - Taxation	51
Chapter 105 - Taxation (Continuation)	52
Chapter 105 - Taxation (Continuation)	53
Chapter 105 - Taxation (Continuation)	54
Chapter 105A - Setoff Debt Collection Act	55
Chapter 105B - Defaulted Student Loan Recovery Act	55
Chapter 106 - Agriculture	55
Chapter 106 - Agriculture (Continue)	56
Chapter 106 - Agriculture (Continue)	57
Chapter 107 - Agricultural Development Districts [Repealed.]	57
Chapter 108 - Social Services [Repealed and Recodified.]	57
Chapter 108A - Social Services	57
Chapter 108B - Community Action Programs	58
Chapter 108C Medicaid and Health Choice Provider Requirements.	58
Chapter 108D Medicaid Managed Care for Behavioral Health Services.	58
Chapter 109 - Bonds [Recodified.]	58
Chapter 110 - Child Welfare	58
Chapter 111 - Aid to the Blind	58
Chapter 112 - Confederate Homes and Pensions [Repealed.]	58
Chapter 113 - Conservation and Development	58
Chapter 113 - Conservation and Development (Continuation)	59

Chapter 113A - Pollution Control and Environment	59
Chapter 113A - Pollution Control and Environment (Continuation)	60
Chapter 113B - North Carolina Energy Policy Act of 1975	60
Chapter 114 - Department of Justice	60
Chapter 115 - Elementary and Secondary Education [Repealed.]	60
Chapter 115A - Community Colleges, Technical Institutes, and Industrial Education Centers [Repealed.]	60
Chapter 115B - Tuition and Fee Waivers	60
Chapter 115C - Elementary and Secondary Education	60
Chapter 115C - Elementary and Secondary Education (Continuation)	61
Chapter 115C - Elementary and Secondary Education (Continuation)	62
Chapter 115C - Elementary and Secondary Education (Continuation)	63
Chapter 115D - Community Colleges	63
Chapter 115E - Private Educational Facilities Finance Act [Recodified]	63
Chapter 116 - Higher Education	63
Chapter 116 - Higher Education (Continuation)	63
Chapter 116A - Escheats and Abandoned Property [Repealed.]	64
Chapter 116B - Escheats and Abandoned Property	64
Chapter 116C - Continuum of Education Programs	64
Chapter 116D - Higher Education Bonds	64
Chapter 117 - Electrification	64
Chapter 118 - Firemen's and Rescue Squad Workers' Relief and Pension Funds [Recodified.]	64
Chapter 118A - Firemen's Death Benefit Act [Repealed.]	64
Chapter 118B - Members of a Rescue Squad Death Benefit Act [Repealed.]	64
Chapter 119 - Gasoline and Oil Inspection and Regulation	64
Chapter 120 - General Assembly	65
Chapter 120 - General Assembly (Continuation)	66
Chapter 120 - General Assembly (Continuation)	67
Chapter 120C - Lobbying	67
Chapter 121 - Archives and History	67
Chapter 122 - Hospitals for the Mentally Disordered [Repealed.]	67
Chapter 122A - North Carolina Housing Finance Agency	67
Chapter 122B - North Carolina Agricultural Facilities Finance Act [Repealed.]	67
Chapter 122C - Mental Health, Developmental Disabilities, and Substance Abuse Act of 1985	67
Chapter 122C - Mental Health, Developmental Disabilities, and Substance Abuse Act of 1985 (Continuation)	68
Chapter 122D - North Carolina Agricultural Finance Act	68

Chapter 122E - North Carolina Housing Trust and Oil Overcharge Act	68
Chapter 123 - Impeachment	69
Chapter 123A - Industrial Development [Repealed.]	69
Chapter 124 - Internal Improvements	69
Chapter 125 - Libraries	69
Chapter 126 - State Personnel System	69
Chapter 127 - Militia [Repealed.]	69
Chapter 127A - Militia	69
Chapter 127B - Military Affairs	69
Chapter 127C - Advisory Commission on Military Affairs	69
Chapter 128 - Offices and Public Officers	69
Chapter 128 - Offices and Public Officers (Continuation)	70
Chapter 129 - Public Buildings and Grounds	70
Chapter 130 - Public Health [Repealed.]	70
Chapter 130A - Public Health	70
Chapter 130A - Public Health (Continuation)	71
Chapter 130A - Public Health (Continuation)	72
Chapter 130B - Hazardous Waste Management Commission [Repealed.]	72
Chapter 131 - Public Hospitals [Repealed.]	72
Chapter 131A - Health Care Facilities Finance Act	72
Chapter 131B - Licensing of Ambulatory Surgical Facilities [Repealed.]	72
Chapter 131C - Charitable Solicitation Licensure Act [Repealed.]	72
Chapter 131D - Inspection and Licensing of Facilities	72
Chapter 131E - Health Care Facilities and Services	72
Chapter 131E - Health Care Facilities and Services (Continuation)	73
Chapter 131F - Solicitation of Contributions	73
Chapter 132 - Public Records	73
Chapter 133 - Public Works	74
Chapter 134 - Youth Development [Recodified.]	74
Chapter 134A - Youth Services [Repealed.]	74
Chapter 135 - Retirement System for Teachers and State Employees; Social Security; Health Insurance Program for Children	74
Chapter 135 - Retirement System for Teachers and State Employees; Social Security; Health Insurance Program for Children	75
Chapter 136 - Transportation	75
Chapter 136 - Transportation (Continuation)	76
Chapter 137 - Rural Rehabilitation [Repealed.]	76
Chapter 138 - Salaries, Fees and Allowances	76
Chapter 138A - State Government Ethics Act	76
Chapter 139 - Soil and Water Conservation Districts	76

Chapter 140 - State Art Museum; Symphony and Art Societies	76
Chapter 140A - State Awards System	76
Chapter 141 - State Boundaries	76
Chapter 142 - State Debt	76
Chapter 143 - State Departments, Institutions, and Commissions	77
Chapter 143 - State Departments, Institutions, and Commissions (Continuation)	78
Chapter 143 - State Departments, Institutions, and Commissions (Continuation)	79
Chapter 143 - State Departments, Institutions, and Commissions (Continuation)	80
Chapter 143A - State Government Reorganization	80
Chapter 143B - Executive Organization Act of 1973	80
Chapter 143B - Executive Organization Act of 1973 (Continuation)	81
Chapter 143B - Executive Organization Act of 1973 (Continuation)	82
Chapter 143C - State Budget Act	83
Chapter 143D - The State Governmental Accountability and Internal Control Act	83
Chapter 144 - State Flag, Official Governmental Flags, Motto, and Colors	83
Chapter 145 - State Symbols and Other Official Adoptions.	83
Chapter 146 - State Lands	83
Chapter 147 - State Officers	83
Chapter 148 - State Prison System	84
Chapter 149 - State Song and Toast	84
Chapter 150 - Uniform Revocation of Licenses [Repealed.]	84
Chapter 150A - Administrative Procedure Act [Recodified.]	84
Chapter 150B - Administrative Procedure Act	84
Chapter 151 - Constables [Repealed.]	84
Chapter 152 - Coroners	84
Chapter 152A - County Medical Examiner [Repealed.]	84
Chapter 152A - County Medical Examiner [Repealed.] (Continuation)	85
Chapter 153 - Counties and County Commissioners [Repealed.]	85
Chapter 153A - Counties	85
Chapter 153B - Mountain Resources Planning Act	85
Chapter 153C - Uwharrie Regional Resources Act	85
Chapter 154 - County Surveyor [Repealed.]	85
Chapter 155 - County Treasurer [Repealed.]	85
Chapter 156 - Drainage	85
Chapter 156 – Drainage (Continuation)	86

Chapter 157 - Housing Authorities and Projects	86
Chapter 157A - Historic Properties Commissions [Transferred.]	86
Chapter 158 - Local Development	86
Chapter 159 - Local Government Finance	86
Chapter 159 - Local Government Finance (Continuation)	87
Chapter 159A - Pollution Abatement and Industrial Facilities Financing Act [Unconstitutional.]	87
Chapter 159B - Joint Municipal Electric Power and Energy Act	87
Chapter 159C - Industrial and Pollution Control Facilities Financing Act	87
Chapter 159D - The North Carolina Capital Facilities Financing Act	87
Chapter 159E - Registered Public Obligations Act	87
Chapter 159F - North Carolina Energy Development Authority [Repealed.]	87
Chapter 159G - Water Infrastructure	87
Chapter 159H - [Reserved.]	87
Chapter 159I - Solid Waste Management Loan Program and Local Government Special Obligation Bonds	87
Chapter 160 - Municipal Corporations [Repealed And Transferred.]	87
Chapter 160A - Cities and Towns	88
Chapter 160A - Cities and Towns (Continuation)	89
Chapter 160B - Consolidated City-County Act	89
Chapter 160C - Baseball Park Districts [Repealed.]	90
Chapter 161 - Register of Deeds	90
Chapter 162 - Sheriff	90
Chapter 162A - Water and Sewer Systems	90
Chapter 162B Continuity of Local Government in Emergency.	90
Chapter 163 Elections and Election Laws.	90
Chapter 163 Elections and Election Laws. (Continuation)	91
Chapter 164 Concerning the General Statutes of North Carolina.	92
Chapter 165 Veterans.	92
Chapter 166 Civil Preparedness Agencies [Repealed.]	92
Chapter 166A North Carolina Emergency Management Act.	92
Chapter 167 State Civil Air Patrol [Repealed.]	92
Chapter 168 Persons with Disabilities.	92
Chapter 168A Persons With Disabilities Protection Act.	92

Chapter 44.

Liens.

Article 1.

Mechanics', Laborers', and Materialmen's Liens.

§ 44-1. Repealed by Session Laws 1969, c. 1112, s. 4.

§§ 44-2 through 44-5. Repealed by Session Laws 1967, c. 1029, s. 2.

Article 1A.

Wage Liens.

§ 44-5.1. Wages for two months' lien on assets.

In case of the insolvency of a corporation, partnership or individual, all persons doing labor or service of whatever character in its regular employment have a lien upon the assets thereof for the amount of wages due to them for all labor, work, and services rendered within two months next preceding the date when proceedings in insolvency were actually instituted and begun against the corporation, partnership or individual, which lien is prior to all other liens that can be acquired against such assets: Provided, that the lien created by this section shall not apply to multiple unit dwellings, apartment houses, or other buildings for family occupancy except as to labor performed on the premises upon which the lien is claimed. This section shall not apply to any single unit family dwelling. (1901, c. 2, s. 87; Rev., s. 1206; C.S., s. 1197; 1937, c. 223; 1943, c. 501; 1955, c. 1345, s. 4.)

Article 2.

Subcontractors', etc., Liens and Rights against Owners.

§ 44-6. Repealed by Session Laws 1971, c. 880, s. 2.

§ 44-7. Repealed by Session Laws 1943, c. 543.

§§ 44-8 through 44-13. Repealed by Session Laws 1971, c. 880, s. 2.

§ 44-14. Repealed by Session Laws 1973, c. 1194, s. 6.

Article 3.

Liens on Vessels.

§§ 44-15 through 44-27. Repealed by Session Laws 1967, c. 1029, s. 2.

Article 4.

Warehouse Storage Liens.

§§ 44-28 through 44-29. Repealed by Session Laws 1967, c. 562, s. 6.

Article 5.

Liens of Hotel, Boarding and Lodging House Keeper.

§§ 44-30 through 44-32. Repealed by Session Laws 1967, c. 1029, s. 2.

Article 6.

Liens of Livery Stable Keepers.

§§ 44-33 through 44-35. Repealed by Session Laws 1967, c. 1029, s. 2.

Article 7.

Liens on Colts, Calves and Pigs.

§§ 44-36 through 44-37.1. Repealed by Session Laws 1967, c. 1029, s. 2.

Article 8.

Perfecting, Recording, Enforcing and Discharging Liens.

§ 44-38. Claim of lien to be filed; place of filing.

All claims shall be filed in the office of the clerk of superior court in the county where the labor has been performed or the materials furnished, specifying in detail the materials furnished or the labor performed, and the time thereof. If the parties interested make a special contract for such labor performed, or if such material and labor are specified in writing, in such cases it shall be decided agreeably to the terms of the contract, provided the terms of such contract do not affect the lien for such labor performed or materials furnished. (1869-70, c. 206, s. 4; 1876-7, c. 53, s. 1; Code, s. 1784; Rev., s. 2026; C.S., s. 2469; 1971, c. 1185, s. 4.)

§ 44-38.1. Repealed by Session Laws 1967, c. 562, s. 7.

§§ 44-39 through 44-46. Repealed by Session Laws 1969, c. 1112, s. 4.

§ 44-47. Repealed by Session Laws 1971, c. 1185, s. 5.

§ 44-48. Discharge of liens.

All liens created by this Chapter may be discharged as follows:

(1) By filing with the clerk a receipt or acknowledgment, signed by the claimant, that the lien has been paid or discharged.

(2) By depositing with the clerk money equal to the amount of the claim, which money shall be held by said officer for the benefit of the claimant.

(3) By an entry in the lien docket that the action on the part of the claimant to enforce the lien has been dismissed, or a judgment rendered against the claimant in such action.

(4) By a failure of the claimant to commence an action for the enforcement of the lien within six months from the notice of lien filed. (1868-9, c. 117, s. 12; Code, s. 1793; Rev., s. 2033; C.S., s. 2479; 1971, c. 1185, s. 6.)

Article 9.

Liens upon Recoveries for Personal Injuries to Secure Sums Due for Medical Attention, etc.

§ 44-49. Lien created; applicable to persons non sui juris.

(a) From and after March 26, 1935, there is hereby created a lien upon any sums recovered as damages for personal injury in any civil action in this State. This lien is in favor of any person, corporation, State entity, municipal corporation or county to whom the person so recovering, or the person in whose behalf the recovery has been made, may be indebted for any drugs, medical supplies, ambulance services, services rendered by any physician, dentist, nurse, or hospital, or hospital attention or services rendered in connection with the injury in compensation for which the damages have been recovered. Where damages are recovered for and in behalf of minors or persons non compos mentis, the liens shall attach to the sum recovered as fully as if the person were sui juris.

(b)   Notwithstanding subsection (a) of this section, no lien provided for under subsection (a) of this section is valid with respect to any claims whatsoever unless the physician, dentist, nurse, hospital, corporation, or other person entitled to the lien furnishes, without charge to the attorney as a condition precedent to the creation of the lien, upon request to the attorney representing the person in whose behalf the claim for personal injury is made, an itemized statement, hospital record, or medical report for the use of the attorney in the negotiation, settlement, or trial of the claim arising by reason of the personal injury, and a written notice to the attorney of the lien claimed.

(c)   No action shall lie against any clerk of court or any surety on any clerk's bond to recover any claims based upon any lien or liens created under subsection (a) of this section when recovery has been had by the person injured, and no claims against the recovery were filed with the clerk by any person or corporation, and the clerk has otherwise disbursed according to law the money recovered in the action for personal injuries. (1935, c. 121, s. 1; 1947, c. 1027; 1959, c. 800, s. 1; 1967, c. 1204, s. 1; 1969, c. 450, s. 1; 2001-377, s. 1; 2001-487, s. 59.)

§ 44-49.1: Recodified as § 58-3-135 by Session Laws 1995 (Regular Session, 1996), c. 674, s. 1.

§ 44-50. Receiving person charged with duty of retaining funds for purpose stated; evidence; attorney's fees; charges.

A lien as provided under G.S. 44-49 shall also attach upon all funds paid to any person in compensation for or settlement of the injuries, whether in litigation or otherwise. If an attorney represents the injured person, the lien is perfected as provided under G.S. 44-49. Before their disbursement, any person that receives those funds shall retain out of any recovery or any compensation so received a sufficient amount to pay the just and bona fide claims for any drugs, medical supplies, ambulance services, services rendered by any physician, dentist, nurse, or hospital, or hospital attention or services, after having received notice of those claims. Evidence as to the amount of the charges shall be competent in the trial of the action. Nothing in this section or in G.S. 44-49 shall be construed so as to interfere with any amount due for attorney's services. The lien provided for shall in no case, exclusive of attorneys' fees, exceed fifty percent (50%) of the amount of damages recovered. Except as provided in G.S. 44-51, a client's instructions for the disbursement of settlement or judgment proceeds are not binding on the disbursing attorney to the extent that the instructions conflict with the requirements of this Article. (1935, c. 121, s. 2; 1959, c. 800, s. 2; 1969, c. 450, s. 2; 1995 (Reg. Sess., 1996), c. 674, s. 3; 2001-377, s. 2.)

§ 44-50.1. Accounting of disbursements; attorney's fees to enforce lien rights.

(a) Notwithstanding any confidentiality agreement entered into between the injured person and the payor of proceeds as settlement of compensation for injuries, upon the lienholder's written request and the lienholder's written agreement to be bound by any confidentiality agreements regarding the contents of the accounting, any person distributing funds to a lienholder under this Article in an amount less than the amount claimed by that lienholder shall provide to that lienholder a certification with sufficient information to demonstrate that the distribution was pro rata and consistent with this Article. If the person distributing settlement or judgment proceeds is an attorney, the accounting required by this section is not a breach of the attorney-client privilege.

(b) The certification under subsection (a) of this section shall include a statement of all of the following:

(1) The total amount of the settlement.

(2) The total distribution to lienholders, the amount of each lien claimed, and the percentage of each lien paid.

(3) The total attorney's fees.

(c) Nothing in this Article shall be construed to require any person to act contrary to the requirements of the Health Insurance Portability and Accountability Act of 1996, P.L. 104-91, and regulations adopted pursuant to that Act. (2003-309, s. 1.)

§ 44-51. Disputed claims to be settled before payments.

Whenever the sum or amount or amounts demanded for medical services or hospital fees shall be in dispute, nothing in this Article shall have any effect of compelling payment thereof until the claim is fully established and determined, in the manner provided by law: Provided, however, that when any such sums are in dispute the amount of the lien shall in no case exceed the amount of the bills in dispute. (1935, c. 121, s. 3; 1943, c. 543.)

Article 9A.

Liens for Ambulance Service.

§ 44-51.1. Lien on real property of recipient of ambulance service paid for or provided by county or municipality.

There is hereby created a general lien upon the real property of any person who has been furnished ambulance service by a county or municipal agency or at the expense of county or municipal government. The lien created by this section shall continue from the date of filing until satisfied, except that no action to enforce it may be brought more than 10 years after the date on which ambulance service was furnished nor more than three years after the date of recipient's death. Failure to bring action within such times shall be a complete bar against any recovery and shall extinguish the lien. (1969, c. 684.)

§ 44-51.2. Filing within 90 days required.

No lien created by G.S. 44-51.1 shall be valid but from the time of filing in the office of the clerk of superior court a statement containing the name and address of the person against whom the lien is claimed, the name of the county or municipality claiming the lien, the amount of the unpaid charge for ambulance service, and the date and place of furnishing ambulance service for which charges are asserted and the lien claimed. No lien under this Article shall be valid unless filed in accordance with this section within 90 days of the date of the furnishing the ambulance service. (1969, c. 684.)

§ 44-51.3. Discharge of lien.

Liens created by this Article may be discharged as follows:

(1) By filing with the clerk of superior court a receipt or acknowledgment, signed by the county or municipal treasurer, that the lien has been paid or discharged;

(2) By depositing with the clerk of superior court money equal to the amount of the claim, which money shall be held for the benefit of the claimant; or

(3) By an entry in the lien docket that the action on the part of the lien claimant to enforce the lien has been dismissed, or a judgment has been rendered against the claimant in such action. (1969, c. 684.)

Article 9B.

Attachment or Garnishment and Lien for Ambulance Service in Certain Counties.

§ 44-51.4. Attachment or garnishment for county or city ambulance or county or city supported ambulance service.

Whenever ambulance services are provided by a county, by a county-franchised ambulance service supplemented by county funds, or by a municipally owned and operated ambulance service or by an ambulance service supplemented by municipal funds and a recipient of such ambulance services or one legally responsible for the support of a recipient of such services fails to pay charges fixed for such services for a period of 90 days after the rendering of such services, the county or municipality providing the ambulance services, or providing financial support to the ambulance service, may treat the amount due for such services as if it were a tax due to the county or municipality and may proceed to collect the amount due through the use of attachment and garnishment proceedings as set out in G.S. 105-368. (1969, c. 708, s. 1; 1973, c. 1366, s. 1; 1975, c. 595, s. 2; 1991, c. 595.)

§ 44-51.5. General lien for county or city ambulance service.

There is hereby created a general lien upon the real property of any person who has been furnished ambulance service by a county, by a county-franchised ambulance service supplemented by county funds, or municipal agency or at the expense of a county or municipal government or upon the real property of one legally responsible for the support of any person who has been furnished such ambulance service. (1969, c. 708, s. 2; 1973, c. 1366, s. 2.)

§ 44-51.6. Lien to be filed.

No lien created by G.S. 44-51.5 shall be valid but from the time of filing in the office of the clerk of superior court a statement containing the name and address of the person against whom the lien is claimed, the name of the county or municipality claiming the lien, the amount of the unpaid charge for ambulance service, and the date and place of furnishing the ambulance service for which charges are asserted and the lien claimed. No lien under this section shall be valid unless filed after 90 days of the date of the furnishing of ambulance service, and within 180 days of the date of the furnishing of ambulance service. (1969, c. 708, s. 3.)

§ 44-51.7. Discharging lien.

Liens created by G.S. 44-51.5 may be discharged as follows:

(1)   By filing with the clerk of superior court a receipt of acknowledgment, signed by the county treasurer, that the lien has been paid or discharged;

(2)   By depositing with the clerk of superior court money equal to the amount of the claim, which money shall be held for the benefit of the claimant; or

(3)   By an entry in the lien docket that the action on the part of the lien claimant to enforce the lien has been dismissed, or a judgment has been rendered against the claimant in such action. (1969, c. 708, s. 4.)

§ 44-51.8. Counties to which Article applies.

The provisions of this Article shall apply only to Alamance, Alexander, Alleghany, Anson, Ashe, Beaufort, Bladen, Brunswick, Buncombe, Burke, Cabarrus, Caldwell, Camden, Carteret, Caswell, Catawba, Chatham, Cherokee, Chowan, Cleveland, Columbus, Craven, Cumberland, Dare, Davidson, Davie, Duplin, Durham, Edgecombe, Forsyth, Franklin, Gaston, Graham, Granville, Greene, Guilford, Halifax, Harnett, Haywood, Henderson, Hertford, Hoke, Hyde, Iredell, Johnston, Jones, Lee, Lenoir, Lincoln, McDowell, Macon, Madison, Mecklenburg, Mitchell, Montgomery, Moore, Nash, New Hanover, Onslow, Orange, Pasquotank, Pender, Person, Pitt, Polk, Randolph, Richmond, Robeson, Rockingham, Rowan, Rutherford, Sampson, Scotland, Stanly, Stokes, Surry, Swain, Transylvania, Tyrrell, Union, Vance, Wake, Warren, Washington, Watauga, Wilkes, Wilson, Yadkin and Yancey Counties. (1969, c. 708, s. 5; c. 1197; 1971, c. 132; 1973, c. 880, s. 1; cc. 887, 894, 907, 1182; 1975, c. 595, s. 1; 1977, cc. 64, 138, 357; 1977, 2nd Sess., cc. 1144, 1157; 1979, c. 452; 1983, cc. 186, 424; 1983 (Reg. Sess., 1984), c. 933; 1985, c. 9; 1985 (Reg. Sess., 1986), c. 936, s. 6; 1987, c. 466; 1995, c. 9, s. 1; 1995 (Reg. Sess., 1996), c. 676, s. 1; 2000-15, s. 3; 2000-107, s. 1.)

Article 10.

Agricultural Liens for Advances.

§§ 44-52 through 44-64: Repealed by Session Laws 1965, c. 700, s. 2.

Article 11.

Uniform Federal Tax Lien Registration Act.

§§ 44-65 through 44-68: Repealed by Session Laws 1969, c. 216.

§§ 44-68.1 through 44-68.7: Repealed by Session Laws 1989 (Reg. Sess., 1990), c. 1047, s. 2.

§ 44-68.8. Reserved for future codification purposes.

§ 44-68.9. Reserved for future codification purposes.

Article 11A.

Uniform Federal Lien Registration Act.

§ 44-68.10. Short title.

This Article may be cited as the Uniform Federal Lien Registration Act. (1989 (Reg. Sess., 1990), c. 1047, s. 1.)

§ 44-68.11. Scope.

This Article applies only to federal tax liens, to other federal liens notices of which under any Act of Congress or any regulation adopted pursuant thereto are required or permitted to be filed in the same manner as notices of federal tax liens, and to notices of federal liens upon real property pursuant to 42 U.S.C. § 9607(l). (1989 (Reg. Sess., 1990), c. 1047, s. 1.)

§ 44-68.12. Place of filing.

(a) Notices of liens, certificates, and other notices affecting federal tax liens or other federal liens must be filed in accordance with this Article.

(b) Notices of liens upon real property for obligations payable to the United States and certificates and notices affecting the liens shall be filed in the office of the clerk of superior court of the county in which the real property subject to the liens is situated.

(c) Notices of federal liens upon personal property, whether tangible or intangible, for obligations payable to the United States and certificates and notices affecting the liens shall be filed as follows:

(1) If the person against whose interest the lien applies is a corporation or a partnership whose principal executive office is in this State, as these entities are defined in the internal revenue laws of the United States, in the office of the Secretary of State;

(2) In all other cases, in the office of the clerk of superior court of the county where the person against whose interest the lien applies resides at the time of filing of the notice of lien. (1989 (Reg. Sess., 1990), c. 1047, s. 1.)

§ 44-68.13. Execution of notices and certificates.

Certification of notices of liens, certificates, or other notices affecting federal liens by the Secretary of the Treasury of the United States or his delegate, or by any official or entity of the United States responsible for filing or certifying of notice of any other lien, entitles them to be filed and no other attestation, certification, or acknowledgement is necessary. (1989 (Reg. Sess., 1990), c. 1047, s. 1.)

§ 44-68.14. Duties of filing officer.

(a) If a notice of federal lien, a refiling of a notice of federal lien, or a notice of revocation of any certificate described in subsection (b) is presented to a filing officer who is:

(1) The Secretary of State, he shall cause the notice to be numbered, maintained, and indexed in accordance with G.S. 25-9-519, as if the notice were a financing statement within the meaning of the Uniform Commercial Code, Chapter 25 of the General Statutes; or

(2) Any other officer described in G.S. 44-68.12, he shall endorse thereon his identification and the date and time of receipt and forthwith file it alphabetically or enter it in an alphabetical index showing the name and address

of the person named in the notice, the date and time of receipt, the title and address of the official or entity certifying the lien, and the total amount appearing on the notice of lien.

(b)   If a certificate of release, nonattachment, discharge, or subordination of any lien is presented to the Secretary of State for filing he shall cause:

(1)   A record of a certificate of release or nonattachment to be numbered, maintained, and indexed as if a record of the certificate were a termination statement within the meaning of the Uniform Commercial Code, Chapter 25 of the General Statutes, but the record of the notice of lien to which the certificate relates may not be removed from the files; and

(2)   A record of a certificate of discharge or subordination to be numbered, maintained, and indexed as if the record of the certificate were a release of collateral within the meaning of the Uniform Commercial Code, Chapter 25 of the General Statutes.

(c)   If a refiled notice of federal lien referred to in subsection (a) or any of the certificates or notices referred to in subsection (b) is presented for filing to any other filing officer specified in G.S. 44-68.12, he shall permanently attach the refiled notice or the certificate to the original notice of lien and enter the refiled notice or the certificate with the date of filing in any alphabetical lien index on the line where the original notice of lien is entered.

(d)   Upon request of any person, the filing officer shall issue his certificate showing whether there is on file, on the date and hour stated therein, any notice of lien or certificate or notice affecting any lien filed under this Article or (reference previous federal tax lien registration act), naming a particular person, and if a notice or certificate is on file, giving the date and hour of filing of each notice or certificate. The fee for a certificate is five dollars ($5.00). Upon request, the filing officer shall furnish a copy of any notice of federal lien, or notice or certificate affecting a federal lien, for a fee of one dollar ($1.00) per page. (Ex. Sess. 1924, c. 44, ss. 2, 3; 1953, c. 1106, ss. 1, 2; 1963, c. 544; 1969, c. 216; 1989 (Reg. Sess., 1990), c. 1047, s. 1; 2000-169, ss. 33, 34.)

§ 44-68.15. Fees.

(a) The fee for filing and indexing each notice of lien or certificate or notice affecting the lien in the Office of the Secretary of State is:

(1) For a lien on real estate, five dollars ($5.00);

(2) For a lien on tangible and intangible personal property, five dollars ($5.00);

(3) For a certificate of discharge or subordination, five dollars ($5.00);

(4) For all other notices, including a certificate of release or nonattachment, five dollars ($5.00).

(b) The fee for filing and indexing each notice of lien or certificate or notice affecting the lien in the office of the Clerk of Superior Court, and the fee for furnishing the certificate or copies provided for in G.S. 44-68.14(d), is as provided in G.S. 7A-308.

(c) The officer shall bill the district directors of internal revenue or other appropriate federal officials on a monthly basis for fees for documents filed by them. (1989 (Reg. Sess., 1990), c. 1047, s. 1.)

§ 44-68.16. Uniformity of application and construction.

This Article shall be applied and construed to effectuate its general purpose to make uniform the law with respect to the subject of this Article among states enacting it. (1989 (Reg. Sess., 1990), c. 1047, s. 1.)

§ 44-68.17. Liens and notices filed before August 1, 1990.

All liens, notices, certificates, releases and refilings filed before August 1, 1990, to which this Article would otherwise apply if such filing occurred on or after August 1, 1990, and any indexes pertaining thereto, shall be transferred to and maintained in the office in which such filing would have been made had the filing occurred on or after August 1, 1990. (1989 (Reg. Sess., 1990), c. 1047, s. 1.)

Article 12.

Liens on Certain Agricultural Products.

§ 44-69. Effective period for lien on leaf tobacco sold in auction warehouse.

No chattel mortgage, agricultural lien, or other lien of any nature upon leaf tobacco shall be effective for any purpose for a longer period than six months after the sale of such tobacco at a regular sale in an auction tobacco warehouse during the regular season for auction sales of tobacco in such warehouse. This section shall not absolve any person from prosecution and punishment for crime. (1943, c. 642, s. 1; 1975, c. 318.)

§ 44-69.1. Effective period for liens on peanuts, cotton and grains.

No chattel mortgage, agricultural lien or other lien of any nature upon peanuts, cotton, soybeans, corn, wheat or other grains shall be effective for any purpose for a longer period than 18 months from the date of sale or the date of delivery to the purchaser, whichever date shall fall last. This section shall not absolve any person from prosecution and punishment for crime. (1955, c. 266; 1975, c. 318.)

§ 44-69.2. Effective period for liens on fruits and vegetables.

No security interest in or lien on fruits and vegetables sold at a regular sale at an auction market at which the Department of Agriculture and Consumer Services furnishes certified inspectors pursuant to Article 17 of Chapter 106 is effective for any purpose more than six months after the date of the sale. This section does not absolve any person from prosecution and punishment for crime. (1981, c. 640, s. 2; 1997-261, s. 109.)

§ 44-69.3. Liens on tangible and intangible assets of milk distributors.

(a) A producer, or an association of producers who supplies milk either through an agreement of sale or on consignment to a distributor shall, upon complying with the provisions of this section, have a lien upon the tangible and intangible assets, including but not limited to the accounts receivable of the distributor to secure payment for such milk. For the purposes of this section, "milk" means the lacteal secretion of cows and includes all skim, butterfat, or other constituents obtained from separation or other process.

(b) The lien claimed by the producer or association of producers must be filed in the office of the clerk of court for the county of the distributor's principal place of business. Provided that if the distributor is not a resident of the State a filing must be made with the clerk of superior court for the county in which the distributor's registered office is located. The clerk shall note the claim of lien on the judgment docket and index the same under the name of the distributor at the time the claim is filed.

(c) A producer or association of producers claiming nonpayment for milk sold to a distributor shall file with the clerk a notarized statement of nonpayment. The statement shall contain at a minimum all of the following information:

(1) The name of the distributor who received the milk.

(2) The date and quantity of milk shipped for which payment has not been received.

(3) Repealed by Session Laws 2004-199, s. 27(f), effective August 17, 2004.

The producer or association of producers shall furnish a copy of the statement as provided by this subsection to the distributor, which shall constitute a notice of claim of lien. The notice shall be served personally by a person authorized by law to serve process or by certified mail. The lien granted by this section shall be effective as of the time it is filed with the clerk of court. Provided the distributor shall have the right to contest the validity of such lien by filing, with the clerk of court and serving on the producer within 10 days after he receives notice that the producer has filed a claim of lien, a notice that the distributor contest the amount due thereunder. In the event the distributor fails to contest the lien or is unsuccessful in obtaining a discharge of the lien, the lien shall be perfected as of the date of filing with the clerk of court.

(d) The lien created by this section may be discharged in any of the following manner:

(1) Repealed by Session Laws 2004-199, s. 27(f), effective August 17, 2004.

(2) By depositing with the clerk of superior court money equal to the amount of the claim, which money shall be held for the benefit of the producer.

(3) By an entry in the lien docket that the action on the part of the lien claimant to enforce the lien has been dismissed or a judgment has been rendered against the claimant in such action.

(4) By filing with the clerk a sworn statement signed by the producer or an official of an association of producers that the lien or claim of lien has been satisfied.

(e) Action to enforce the lien created by this section may be instituted in any court of competent jurisdiction in the county where the lien was filed not later than 90 days following the maturity of the distributor's obligation to pay for the milk. In the event no action to enforce the lien is commenced within the 90-day period the lien created hereby shall no longer be valid. (1985, c. 678, s. 1; 2004-199, s. 27(f).)

Article 13.

Factors' Liens.

§§ 44-70 through 44-76. Repealed by Session Laws 1965, c. 700, s. 2.

Article 14.

Assignment of Accounts Receivable and Liens Thereon.

§§ 44-77 through 44-85. Repealed by Session Laws 1965, c. 700, s. 2.

Article 15.

Liens for Overdue Child Support.

§ 44-86. Lien on real and personal property of person owing past-due child support; definitions; filing required; discharge.

(a) Definitions. - As used in this Article, the terms "designated representative", "obligee", and "obligor" have the meanings given them in G.S. 110-129.

(b) Lien Created. - There is created a general lien upon the real and personal property of any person who is delinquent in the payment of court-ordered child support. For purposes of this section, an obligor is delinquent when arrears under a court-ordered child support obligation equals three months of payments or three thousand dollars ($3,000), whichever occurs first. The amount of the lien shall be determined by a verified statement of child support delinquency prepared in accordance with subsection (c) of this section.

(c) Contents of Statement; Verification. - A verified statement of child support delinquency shall contain the following information:

(1) The caption and file docket number of the case in which child support was ordered;

(2) The date of the order of support;

(3) The amount of the child support obligation established by the order; and

(4) The amount of the arrearage as of the date of the statement.

The statement shall be verified by the designated representative in a IV-D case and by the obligee in a non-IV-D case.

(d) Filing and Perfection of Lien. - The verified statement shall be filed in the office of the clerk of superior court in the county in which the child support was ordered. At the time of filing the verified statement, the designated representative in a IV-D case and the obligee in a non-IV-D case shall serve notice on the obligor that the statement has been filed. The notice shall be served and the return of service filed with the clerk of court in accordance with

Rule 4 of the North Carolina Rules of Civil Procedure. The notice shall specify the manners in which the lien may be discharged. Upon perfection of the lien, as set forth herein, the clerk shall docket and index the statement on the judgment docket. The clerk shall issue a transcript of the docketed statement to the clerk of any other county as requested by the designated representative in a IV-D case or the obligee in a non-IV-D case. The clerk receiving the transcript shall docket and index the transcript. A lien on personal property attaches when the property is seized by the sheriff. A lien on real property attaches when the perfected lien is docketed and indexed on the judgment docket.

(1) IV-D Cases. - In IV-D cases, the filing of a verified statement with the clerk of court by the designated representative shall perfect the lien. The obligor may contest the lien by motion in the cause.

(2) Non-IV-D Cases. - In a non-IV-D case, the notice to the obligor of the filing of the verified statement shall state that the obligor has 30 days from the date of service to request a hearing before a district court judge to contest the validity of the lien. If the obligor fails to contest the lien after 30 days from the time of service, the obligee may make application to the clerk, and the clerk shall record and index the lien on the judgment docket. If the obligee files a petition contesting the validity of the lien, a hearing shall be held before a district court judge to determine whether the lien is valid and proper. In contested cases, the clerk of court shall record and index the lien on the judgment docket only by order of the judge. The docketing of a verified statement in a non-IV-D case shall perfect the lien when duly recorded and indexed.

(e) Lien Superior to Subsequent Liens. - Except as otherwise provided by law, a lien established in accordance with this section shall take priority over all other liens subsequently acquired and shall continue from the date of filing until discharged in accordance with G.S. 44-87.

(f) Execution on the Lien. - A designated representative in a IV-D case, after 30 days from the docketing of the perfected lien, or an obligee in a non-IV-D case, after docketing the perfected lien, may enforce the lien in the same manner as for a civil judgment.

(g) Liens Arising Out-of-State. - This State shall accord full faith and credit to child support liens arising in another state when the child support enforcement agency, party, or other entity seeking to enforce the lien complies with the requirements relating to recording and serving child support liens as set forth in this Article and with the requirements relating to the enforcement of foreign judgments as set forth in Chapter 1C of the General Statutes. (1997-433, s. 7; 1998-17, s. 1.)

§ 44-87. Discharge of lien; penalty for failure to discharge.

(a) Liens created by this Article may be discharged as follows:

(1) By the designated representative in IV-D cases, or by the obligee in non-IV-D cases, filing with the clerk of superior court an acknowledgment that the obligor has satisfied the full amount of the lien;

(2) By depositing with the clerk of superior court money equal to the amount of the claim and filing a petition in the cause requesting a district court judge to determine the validity of the lien. The money shall not be disbursed except by order of a district court judge following the hearing on the merits; or

(3) By an entry in the judgment docket book that the action on the part of the lien claimant to enforce the lien has been dismissed, or a judgment has been rendered against the claimant in such action.

(b) An obligee in a non-IV-D case who has received payment in full for a delinquent child support obligation which is the basis for the lien shall, within 30 days of receipt of payment, file with the clerk of court an acknowledgment that the obligor has satisfied the full amount of the lien and that the lien is discharged. If the lienholder fails to timely file the acknowledgment, the obligor may, after serving notice on the obligee, file an action in district court to discharge the lien. If in an action filed by the obligor to discharge the lien, the court discharges the lien and finds that the obligee failed to timely file an acknowledgment discharging the lien, then the court may allow the prevailing party to recover reasonable attorneys' fees to be taxed as court costs against the obligee. (1997-433, s. 7; 1998-17, s. 1.)

Chapter 44A.

Statutory Liens and Charges.

Article 1.

Possessory Liens on Personal Property.

§ 44A-1. Definitions.

As used in this Article:

(1)   "Legal possessor" means

a.   Any person entrusted with possession of personal property by an owner thereof, or

b.   Any person in possession of personal property and entitled thereto by operation of law.

(2)   "Lienor" means any person entitled to a lien under this Article.

(2a)   "Motor Vehicle" has the meaning provided in G.S. 20-4.01.

(3)   "Owner" means

a.   Any person having legal title to the property, or

b.   A lessee of the person having legal title, or

c.   A debtor entrusted with possession of the property by a secured party, or

d.   A secured party entitled to possession, or

e.   Any person entrusted with possession of the property by his employer or principal who is an owner under any of the above.

(4)   "Secured party" means a person holding a security interest.

(5)   "Security interest" means any interest in personal property which interest is subject to the provisions of Article 9 of the Uniform Commercial Code, or any other interest intended to create security in real or personal property.

(6)   "Vessel" has the meaning provided in G.S. 75A-2. (1967, c. 1029, s. 1; 1991, c. 731, s. 1.)

§ 44A-2. Persons entitled to lien on personal property.

(a)   Any person who tows, alters, repairs, stores, services, treats, or improves personal property other than a motor vehicle or an aircraft in the ordinary course of his business pursuant to an express or implied contract with an owner or legal possessor of the personal property has a lien upon the property. The amount of the lien shall be the lesser of

(1)   The reasonable charges for the services and materials; or

(2)   The contract price; or

(3)   One hundred dollars ($100.00) if the lienor has dealt with a legal possessor who is not an owner.

This lien shall have priority over perfected and unperfected security interests.

(b)   Any person engaged in the business of operating a hotel, motel, or boardinghouse has a lien upon all baggage, vehicles and other personal property brought upon his premises by a guest or boarder who is an owner thereof to the extent of reasonable charges for the room, accommodations and other items or services furnished at the request of the guest or boarder. This lien shall not have priority over any security interest in the property which is perfected at the time the guest or boarder brings the property to said hotel, motel or boardinghouse.

(c)   Any person engaged in the business of boarding animals has a lien on the animals boarded for reasonable charges for such boarding which are contracted for with an owner or legal possessor of the animal. This lien shall have priority over perfected and unperfected security interests.

(d)   Any person who repairs, services, tows, or stores motor vehicles in the ordinary course of the person's business pursuant to an express or implied contract with an owner or legal possessor of the motor vehicle, except for a motor vehicle seized pursuant to G.S. 20-28.3, has a lien upon the motor vehicle for reasonable charges for such repairs, servicing, towing, storing, or for the rental of one or more substitute vehicles provided during the repair, servicing, or storage. This lien shall have priority over perfected and unperfected security interests. Payment for towing and storing a motor vehicle seized pursuant to G.S. 20-28.3 shall be as provided for in G.S. 20-28.2 through G.S. 20-28.5.

(e) Any lessor of nonresidential demised premises has a lien on all furniture, furnishings, trade fixtures, equipment and other personal property to which the tenant has legal title and which remains on the demised premises if (i) the tenant has vacated the premises for 21 or more days after the paid rental period has expired, and (ii) the lessor has a lawful claim for damages against the tenant. If the tenant has vacated the premises for 21 or more days after the expiration of the paid rental period, or if the lessor has received a judgment for possession of the premises which is executable and the tenant has vacated the premises, then all property remaining on the premises may be removed and placed in storage. If the total value of all property remaining on the premises is less than one hundred dollars ($100.00), then it shall be deemed abandoned five days after the tenant has vacated the premises, and the lessor may remove it and may donate it to any charitable institution or organization. Provided, the lessor shall not have a lien if there is an agreement between the lessor or his agent and the tenant that the lessor shall not have a lien. This lien shall be for the amount of any rents which were due the lessor at the time the tenant vacated the premises and for the time, up to 60 days, from the vacating of the premises to the date of sale; and for any sums necessary to repair damages to the premises caused by the tenant, normal wear and tear excepted; and for reasonable costs and expenses of sale. The lien created by this subsection shall be enforced by sale at public sale pursuant to the provisions of G.S. 44A-4(e). This lien shall not have priority over any security interest in the property which is perfected at the time the lessor acquires this lien.

(e1) This Article shall not apply to liens created by storage of personal property at a self-service storage facility.

(e2) Any lessor of a space for a manufactured home as defined in G.S. 143-143.9(6) has a lien on all furniture, furnishings, and other personal property including the manufactured home titled in the name of the tenant if (i) the manufactured home remains on the demised premises 21 days after the lessor is placed in lawful possession by writ of possession and (ii) the lessor has a lawful claim for damages against the tenant. If the lessor has received a judgment for possession of the premises which has been executed, then all property remaining on the premises may be removed and placed in storage. Prior to the expiration of the 21-day period, the landlord shall release possession of the personal property and manufactured home to the tenant during regular business hours or at a time mutually agreed upon. This lien shall be for the amount of any rents which were due the lessor at the time the tenant vacated the premises and for the time, up to 60 days, from the vacating of the premises to the date of sale; and for any sums necessary to repair damages to the premises caused by the tenant, normal wear and tear excepted; and for reasonable costs and expenses of the sale. The lien created by this subsection shall be enforced by public sale under G.S. 44A-4(e). The landlord may begin the advertisement for sale process immediately upon execution of the writ of possession by the sheriff, but may not conduct the sale until the lien has attached. This lien shall not have any priority over any security interest in the property that is perfected at the time the lessor acquires this lien. The lessor shall not have a lien under this subsection if there is an agreement between the lessor or the lessor's agent and the tenant that the lessor shall not have a lien.

(f) Any person who improves any textile goods in the ordinary course of his business pursuant to an express or implied contract with the owner or legal possessor of such goods shall have a lien upon all goods of such owner or possessor in his possession for improvement. The amount of such lien shall be for the entire unpaid contracted charges owed such person for improvement of said goods including any amount owed for improvement of goods, the possession of which may have been relinquished, and such lien shall have priority over perfected and unperfected security interests. "Goods" as used herein includes any textile goods, yarns or products of natural or man-made fibers or combination thereof. "Improve" as used herein shall be construed to include processing, fabricating or treating by throwing, spinning, knitting, dyeing, finishing, fabricating or otherwise.

(g) Any person who fabricates, casts, or otherwise makes a mold or who uses a mold to manufacture, assemble, or otherwise make a product pursuant to an express or implied contract with the owner of such mold shall have a lien upon the mold. For a lien to arise under this subsection, there must exist written evidence that the parties understood that a lien could be applied against the mold, with the evidence being in the form either of a written contract or a separate written statement provided by the potential holder of the lien under this subsection to the owner of the mold prior to the fabrication or use of the mold. The written contract or separate written statement must describe generally the amount of the potential lien as set forth in this subsection. The amount of the lien under this subsection shall equal the total of (i) any unpaid contracted charges due from the owner of the mold for making the mold, plus (ii) any unpaid contracted charges for all products made with the mold. The lien under this subsection shall not have priority over any security interest in the mold which is perfected at the time the person acquires this lien. As used in this subsection, the word "mold" shall include a mold, die, form, or pattern.

(h) Any landlord of nonresidential property, including any storage or self-storage space, in which potentially confidential materials, as that term is defined in G.S. 42-14.4(a), remain after the landlord has obtained possession of the property must provide notice to the North Carolina State Bar and comply with the provisions of G.S. 42-14.4, if the landlord has actual knowledge that the former tenant is an attorney. Potentially confidential materials shall not be the subject of a lien under the provisions of this Article. (1967, c. 1029, s. 1; 1971, cc. 261, 403; c. 544, s. 1; c. 1197; 1973, c. 1298, s. 1; 1975, c. 461; 1981, c. 566, s. 2; c. 682, s. 9; 1981 (Reg. Sess., 1982), c. 1275, s. 2; 1995, c. 460, s. 9; c. 480, s. 1; 1995 (Reg. Sess., 1996), c. 744, s. 1; 1998-182, s. 14; 1999-278, s. 5; 2006-222, s. 1.2; 2012-76, s. 2.)

§ 44A-3. When lien arises and terminates.

Liens conferred under this Article arise only when the lienor acquires possession of the property and terminate and become unenforceable when the lienor voluntarily relinquishes the possession of the property upon which a lien might be claimed, or when an owner, his agent, a legal possessor or any other person having a security or other interest in the property tenders prior to sale the amount secured by the lien plus reasonable storage, boarding and other expenses incurred by the lienor. The reacquisition of possession of property voluntarily relinquished shall not reinstate the lien. Liens conferred under this Article do not terminate when the lienor involuntarily relinquishes the possession of the property. (1967, c. 1029, s. 1; 1991, c. 344, s. 3, c. 731, s. 2.)

§ 44A-4. Enforcement of lien by sale.

(a) Enforcement by Sale. - If the charges for which the lien is claimed under this Article remain unpaid or unsatisfied for 30 days or, in the case of towing and storage charges on a motor vehicle, 10 days following the maturity of the obligation to pay any such charges, the lienor may enforce the lien by public or private sale as provided in this section. The lienor may bring an action on the debt in any court of competent jurisdiction at any time following maturity of the obligation. Failure of the lienor to bring such action within a 180-day period following the commencement of storage shall constitute a waiver of any right to collect storage charges which accrue after such period. Provided that when property is placed in storage pursuant to an express contract of storage, the lien shall continue and the lienor may bring an action to collect storage charges and enforce his lien at any time within 120 days following default on the obligation to pay storage charges.

The owner or person with whom the lienor dealt may at any time following the maturity of the obligation bring an action in any court of competent jurisdiction as by law provided. If in any such action the owner or other party requests immediate possession of the property and pays the amount of the lien asserted into the clerk of the court in which such action is pending, the clerk shall issue an order to the lienor to relinquish possession of the property to the owner or other party. The request for immediate possession may be made in the complaint, which shall also set forth the amount of the asserted lien and the portion thereof which is not in dispute, if any. If within three days after service of the summons and complaint, as the number of days is computed in G.S. 1A-1, Rule 6, the lienor does not file a contrary statement of the amount of the lien at the time of the filing of the complaint, the amount set forth in the complaint shall be deemed to be the amount of the asserted lien. The clerk may at any time disburse to the lienor that portion of the cash bond, which the plaintiff says in his complaint is not in dispute, upon application of the lienor. The magistrate or judge shall direct appropriate disbursement of the disputed or undisbursed portion of the bond in the judgment of the court. In the event an action by the owner pursuant to this section is heard in district or superior court, the substantially prevailing party in such court may be awarded a reasonable attorney's fee in the discretion of the judge.

(b) Notice and Hearings. -

(1) If the property upon which the lien is claimed is a motor vehicle that is required to be registered, the lienor following the expiration of the relevant time period provided by subsection (a) shall give notice to the Division of Motor Vehicles that a lien is asserted and sale is proposed and shall remit to the Division a fee of ten dollars ($10.00). The Division of Motor Vehicles shall issue notice by certified mail, return receipt requested, to the person having legal title to the property, if reasonably ascertainable, to the person with whom the lienor dealt if different, and to each secured party and other person claiming an interest in the property who is actually known to the Division or who can be reasonably ascertained. The notice shall state that a lien has been asserted against specific property and shall identify the lienor, the date that the lien arose, the general nature of the services performed and materials used or sold for which the lien is asserted, the amount of the lien, and that the lienor intends to sell the property in satisfaction of the lien. The notice shall inform the recipient

that the recipient has the right to a judicial hearing at which time a determination will be made as to the validity of the lien prior to a sale taking place. The notice shall further state that the recipient has a period of 10 days from the date of receipt in which to notify the Division by certified mail, return receipt requested, that a hearing is desired and that if the recipient wishes to contest the sale of his property pursuant to such lien, the recipient should notify the Division that a hearing is desired. The notice shall state the required information in simplified terms and shall contain a form whereby the recipient may notify the Division that a hearing is desired by the return of such form to the Division. The Division shall notify the lienor whether such notice is timely received by the Division. In lieu of the notice by the lienor to the Division and the notices issued by the Division described above, the lienor may issue notice on a form approved by the Division pursuant to the notice requirements above. If notice is issued by the lienor, the recipient shall return the form requesting a hearing to the lienor, and not the Division, within 10 days from the date the recipient receives the notice if a judicial hearing is requested. If the certified mail notice has been returned as undeliverable and the notice of a right to a judicial hearing has been given to the owner of the motor vehicle in accordance with G.S. 20-28.4, no further notice is required. Failure of the recipient to notify the Division or lienor, as specified in the notice, within 10 days of the receipt of such notice that a hearing is desired shall be deemed a waiver of the right to a hearing prior to the sale of the property against which the lien is asserted, and the lienor may proceed to enforce the lien by public or private sale as provided in this section and the Division shall transfer title to the property pursuant to such sale. If the Division or lienor, as specified in the notice, is notified within the 10-day period provided above that a hearing is desired prior to sale, the lien may be enforced by sale as provided in this section and the Division will transfer title only pursuant to the order of a court of competent jurisdiction.

If the certified mail notice has been returned as undeliverable, or if the name of the person having legal title to the vehicle cannot reasonably be ascertained and the fair market value of the vehicle is less than eight hundred dollars ($800.00), the lienor may institute a special proceeding in the county where the vehicle is being held, for authorization to sell that vehicle. Market value shall be determined by the schedule of values adopted by the Commissioner under G.S. 105-187.3.

In such a proceeding a lienor may include more than one vehicle, but the proceeds of the sale of each shall be subject only to valid claims against that vehicle, and any excess proceeds of the sale shall be paid immediately to the Treasurer for disposition pursuant to Chapter 116B of the General Statutes.

The application to the clerk in such a special proceeding shall contain the notice of sale information set out in subsection (f) hereof. If the application is in proper form the clerk shall enter an order authorizing the sale on a date not less than 14 days therefrom, and the lienor shall cause the application and order to be sent immediately by first-class mail pursuant to G.S. 1A-1, Rule 5, to each person to whom notice was mailed pursuant to this subsection. Following the authorized sale the lienor shall file with the clerk a report in the form of an affidavit, stating that the lienor has complied with the public or private sale provisions of G.S. 44A-4, the name, address, and bid of the high bidder or person buying at a private sale, and a statement of the disposition of the sale proceeds. The clerk then shall enter an order directing the Division to transfer title accordingly.

If prior to the sale the owner or legal possessor contests the sale or lien in a writing filed with the clerk, the proceeding shall be handled in accordance with G.S. 1-301.2.

(2) If the property upon which the lien is claimed is other than a motor vehicle required to be registered, the lienor following the expiration of the 30-day period provided by subsection (a) shall issue notice to the person having legal title to the property, if reasonably ascertainable, and to the person with whom the lienor dealt if different by certified mail, return receipt requested. Such notice shall state that a lien has been asserted against specific property and shall identify the lienor, the date that the lien arose, the general nature of the services performed and materials used or sold for which the lien is asserted, the amount of the lien, and that the lienor intends to sell the property in satisfaction of the lien. The notice shall inform the recipient that the recipient has the right to a judicial hearing at which time a determination will be made as to the validity of the lien prior to a sale taking place. The notice shall further state that the recipient has a period of 10 days from the date of receipt in which to notify the lienor by certified mail, return receipt requested, that a hearing is desired and that if the recipient wishes to contest the sale of his property pursuant to such lien, the recipient should notify the lienor that a hearing is desired. The notice shall state the required information in simplified terms and shall contain a form whereby the recipient may notify the lienor that a hearing is desired by the return of such form to the lienor. Failure of the recipient to notify the lienor within 10 days of the receipt of such notice that a hearing is desired shall be deemed a waiver of the right to a hearing prior to sale of the property against which the lien is asserted and the lienor may proceed to enforce the lien by public or private sale as provided in this section. If the lienor is notified within the 10-day period

provided above that a hearing is desired prior to sale, the lien may be enforced by sale as provided in this section only pursuant to the order of a court of competent jurisdiction.

(c)   Private Sale. - Sale by private sale may be made in any manner that is commercially reasonable. If the property upon which the lien is claimed is a motor vehicle, the sale may not be made until notice is given to the Commissioner of Motor Vehicles pursuant to G.S. 20-114(c). Not less than 30 days prior to the date of the proposed private sale, the lienor shall cause notice to be mailed, as provided in subsection (f) hereof, to the person having legal title to the property, if reasonably ascertainable, to the person with whom the lienor dealt if different, and to each secured party or other person claiming an interest in the property who is actually known to the lienor or can be reasonably ascertained. Notices provided pursuant to subsection (b) hereof shall be sufficient for these purposes if such notices contain the information required by subsection (f) hereof. The lienor shall not purchase, directly or indirectly, the property at private sale and such a sale to the lienor shall be voidable.

(d)   Request for Public Sale. - If an owner, the person with whom the lienor dealt, any secured party, or other person claiming an interest in the property notifies the lienor prior to the date upon or after which the sale by private sale is proposed to be made, that public sale is requested, sale by private sale shall not be made. After request for public sale is received, notice of public sale must be given as if no notice of sale by private sale had been given.

(e)   Public Sale. -

(1)   Not less than 20 days prior to sale by public sale the lienor:

a.   Shall notify the Commissioner of Motor Vehicles as provided in G.S. 20-114(c) if the property upon which the lien is claimed is a motor vehicle; and

a1.   Shall cause notice to be mailed to the person having legal title to the property if reasonably ascertainable, to the person with whom the lienor dealt if different, and to each secured party or other person claiming an interest in the property who is actually known to the lienor or can be reasonably ascertained, provided that notices provided pursuant to subsection (b) hereof shall be sufficient for these purposes if such notices contain the information required by subsection (f) hereof; and

b.   Shall advertise the sale by posting a copy of the notice of sale at the courthouse door in the county where the sale is to be held;

and shall publish notice of sale once a week for two consecutive weeks in a newspaper of general circulation in the same county, the date of the last publication being not less than five days prior to the sale. The notice of sale need not be published if the vehicle has a market value of less than three thousand five hundred dollars ($3,500), as determined by the schedule of values adopted by the Commissioner under G.S. 105-187.3.

(2)   A public sale must be held on a day other than Sunday and between the hours of 10:00 A.M. and 4:00 P.M.:

a.   In any county where any part of the contract giving rise to the lien was performed, or

b.   In the county where the obligation secured by the lien was contracted for.

(3)   A lienor may purchase at public sale.

(f)   Notice of Sale. - The notice of sale shall include:

(1)   The name and address of the lienor;

(2)   The name of the person having legal title to the property if such person can be reasonably ascertained and the name of the person with whom the lienor dealt;

(3)   A description of the property;

(4)   The amount due for which the lien is claimed;

(5)   The place of the sale;

(6)   If a private sale the date upon or after which the sale is proposed to be made, or if a public sale the date and hour when the sale is to be held.

(g)   Damages for Noncompliance. - If the lienor fails to comply substantially with any of the provisions of this section, the lienor shall be liable to the person having legal title to the property or any other party injured by such noncompliance in the sum of one hundred dollars ($100.00), together with a reasonable attorney's fee as awarded by the court. Damages provided by this section shall be in addition to actual damages to which any party is otherwise entitled. (1967, c. 1029, s. 1; 1975, c. 438, s. 1; c. 716, s. 5; 1977, c. 74, s. 4; c. 793, s. 1; 1981, c. 690, s. 26; 1983, c. 44, ss. 1, 2; 1985, c. 655, ss. 4, 5; 1989, c. 770, s. 10; 1991, c. 344, s. 1; c. 731, s. 3; 1995 (Reg. Sess., 1996), c. 635, ss. 2-4; 1998-182, s. 15; 1999-216, s. 10; 1999-460, s. 7; 2004-128, s. 5; 2012-175, s. 12(a).)

§ 44A-5. Proceeds of sale.

The proceeds of the sale shall be applied as follows:

(1) Payment of reasonable expenses incurred in connection with the sale. Expenses of sale include but are not limited to reasonable storage and boarding expenses after giving notice of sale.

(2) Payment of the obligation secured by the lien.

(3) Any surplus shall be paid to the person entitled thereto; but when such person cannot be found, the surplus shall be paid to the clerk of superior court of the county in which the sale took place, to be held by the clerk for the person entitled thereto. (1967, c. 1029, s. 1; 1971, c. 544, s. 2.)

§ 44A-6. Title of purchaser.

A purchaser for value at a properly conducted sale, and a purchaser for value without constructive notice of a defect in the sale, whether or not the purchaser is the lienor or an agent of the lienor, acquires title to the property free of any interests over which the lienor was entitled to priority. (1967, c. 1029, s. 1; 1995, c. 480, s. 2.)

§ 44A-6.1. Action to regain possession of a motor vehicle or vessel.

(a) When the lienor involuntarily relinquishes possession of the property and the property upon which the lien is claimed is a motor vehicle or vessel, the lienor may institute an action to regain possession of the motor vehicle or vessel in small claims court any time following the lienor's involuntary loss of possession and following maturity of the obligation to pay charges. The lienor shall serve a copy of the summons and the complaint pursuant to G.S. 1A-1, Rule 4, on each secured party claiming an interest in the vehicle or vessel. For purposes of this section, involuntary relinquishment of possession includes only those situations where the owner or other party takes possession of the motor vehicle or vessel without the lienor's permission or without judicial process. If in the court action the owner or other party retains possession of the motor vehicle or vessel, the owner or other party shall pay the amount of the lien asserted as bond into the clerk of the court in which the action is pending.

If within three days after service of the summons and complaint, as the number of days is computed in G.S. 1A-1, Rule 6, neither the defendant nor a secured party claiming an interest in the vehicle or vessel files a contrary statement of the amount of the lien at the time of the filing of the complaint, the amount set forth in the complaint shall be deemed to be the amount of the asserted lien. The clerk may at any time disburse to the lienor that portion of the cash bond which is not in dispute, upon application of the lienor. The magistrate shall:

(1) Direct appropriate disbursement of the disputed or undisbursed portion of the bond; and

(2) Direct appropriate possession of the motor vehicle or vessel if, in the judgment of the court, the plaintiff has a valid right to a lien.

(b) Either party to an action pursuant to subsection (a) of this section may appeal to district court for a trial de novo. (1991, c. 344, s. 2, c. 731, s. 4.)

Article 2.

Statutory Liens on Real Property.

Part 1. Liens of Mechanics, Laborers, and Materialmen Dealing with Owner.

§ 44A-7. Definitions.

Unless the context otherwise requires, the following definitions apply in this Article:

(1)   Contractor. - A person who contracts with an owner to improve real property.

(2)   First tier subcontractor. - A person who contracts with a contractor to improve real property.

(3)   Improve. - To build, effect, alter, repair, or demolish any improvement upon, connected with, or on or beneath the surface of any real property, or to excavate, clear, grade, fill or landscape any real property, or to construct driveways and private roadways, or to furnish materials, including trees and shrubbery, for any of such purposes, or to perform any labor upon such improvements, and shall also mean and include any design or other professional or skilled services furnished by architects, engineers, land surveyors and landscape architects registered under Chapter 83A, 89A or 89C of the General Statutes, and rental of equipment directly utilized on the real property in making the improvement.

(4)   Improvement. - All or any part of any building, structure, erection, alteration, demolition, excavation, clearing, grading, filling, or landscaping, including trees and shrubbery, driveways, and private roadways, on real property.

(4a)   Inspection department. - Any city or county building inspection department authorized by Chapter 160A or Chapter 153A of the General Statutes.

(4b)   Lien agent. - A title insurance company or title insurance agency designated by an owner pursuant to G.S. 44A-11.1.

(5)   Obligor. - An owner, contractor, or subcontractor in any tier who owes money to another as a result of the other's partial or total performance of a contract to improve real property.

(6)   Owner. - A person who has an interest in the real property improved and for whom an improvement is made and who ordered the improvement to be

made. "Owner" includes successors in interest of the owner and agents of the owner acting within their authority.

(6a) Potential lien claimant. - Any person entitled to claim a lien for improvements to real property under this Article who is subject to G.S. 44A-11.1.

(7) Real property. - The real estate that is improved, including lands, leaseholds, tenements and hereditaments, and improvements placed thereon.

(8) Second tier subcontractor. - A person who contracts with a first tier subcontractor to improve real property.

(9) Third tier subcontractor. - A person who contracts with a second tier subcontractor to improve real property. (1969, c. 1112, s. 1; 1975, c. 715, s. 1; 1985, c. 689, s. 13; 1995 (Reg. Sess., 1996), c. 607, s. 1; 2012-158, s. 1; 2012-175, s. 1.)

§ 44A-8. Mechanics', laborers', and materialmen's lien; persons entitled to claim of lien on real property.

Any person who performs or furnishes labor or professional design or surveying services or furnishes materials or furnishes rental equipment pursuant to a contract, either express or implied, with the owner of real property for the making of an improvement thereon shall, upon complying with the provisions of this Article, have a right to file a claim of lien on real property on the real property to secure payment of all debts owing for labor done or professional design or surveying services or material furnished or equipment rented pursuant to the contract. (1969, c. 1112, s. 1; 1975, c. 715, s. 2; 1995 (Reg. Sess., 1996), c. 607, s. 2; 2005-229, s. 1.)

§ 44A-9. Extent of claim of lien on real property.

A claim of lien on real property authorized under this Article shall extend to the improvement and to the lot or tract on which the improvement is situated, to the extent of the interest of the owner. When the lot or tract on which a building is erected is not surrounded at the time of making the contract with the owner by an enclosure separating it from adjoining land of the same owner, the lot or tract to which any claim of lien on real property extends shall be the area that is reasonably necessary for the convenient use and occupation of the building, but in no case shall the area include a building, structure, or improvement not normally used or occupied or intended to be used or occupied with the building with respect to which the claim of lien on real property is claimed. (1969, c. 1112, s. 1; 2005-229, s. 1.)

§ 44A-10. Effective date of claim of lien on real property.

A claim of lien on real property granted by this Article shall relate to and take effect from the time of the first furnishing of labor or materials at the site of the improvement by the person claiming the claim of lien on real property. (1969, c. 1112, s. 1; 2005-229, s. 1.)

§ 44A-11. Perfecting claim of lien on real property.

(a)   Perfection. - A claim of lien on real property granted by this Article shall be perfected as of the time provided in G.S. 44A-10 upon the occurrence of all of the following:

(1)   Service of a copy of the claim of lien on real property upon the record owner of the real property claimed to be subject to the claim of lien and, if the claim of lien on real property is being asserted pursuant to G.S. 44A-23, also upon the contractor through which subrogation is being asserted.

(2)   Filing of the claim of lien on real property under G.S. 44A-12.

(b)   Method of Service. - Service of the claim of lien on real property pursuant to subsection (a) of this section shall not require proof of actual receipt by the listed recipient and shall be complete upon the occurrence of any of the following:

(1)   Personal delivery of a copy of the claim of lien on real property upon the recipient.

(2) Deposit of a copy of the claim of lien on real property in a postpaid, properly addressed wrapper in either of the following:

a. A post office or official depository under the exclusive care and custody of the United States Postal Service.

b. An authorized depository under the exclusive care and custody of a designated delivery service authorized pursuant to 26 U.S.C. § 7502(f)(2).

(c) Service Address. - For purposes of this section, a wrapper addressed to a party required to be served under subdivision (1) of subsection (a) of this section shall be conclusively deemed properly addressed if it uses any of the following addresses:

(1) The address for the party to be served listed on the permit issued for the improvement.

(2) The address for the party to be served listed with the tax rolls for any county in North Carolina.

(3) The address of the registered agent for the party to be served listed with the North Carolina Secretary of State's office. (1969, c. 1112, s. 1; 2005-229, s. 1; 2012-175, s. 2.)

§ 44A-11.1. Lien agent; designation and duties.

(a) With regard to any improvements to real property to which this Article is applicable for which the costs of the undertaking are thirty thousand dollars ($30,000) or more, either at the time that the original building permit is issued or, in cases in which no building permit is required, at the time the contract for the improvements is entered into with the owner, the owner shall designate a lien agent no later than the time the owner first contracts with any person to improve the real property. Provided, however, that the owner is not required to designate a lien agent for improvements to an existing single-family residential dwelling unit as defined in G.S. 87-15.5(7) that is occupied by the owner as a residence, or for the addition of an accessory building or accessory structure as defined in the North Carolina Uniform Residential Building Code, the use of which is incidental to that residence. The owner shall deliver written notice of designation to its designated lien agent by any method authorized in G.S. 44A-11.2(f), and shall include in its notice the street address, tax map lot and block number, reference to recorded instrument, or any other description that reasonably identifies the real property for the improvements to which the lien agent has been designated, and the owner's contact information. Designation of a lien agent pursuant to this section does not make the lien agent an agent of the owner for purposes of receiving a Claim of Lien on Real Property, a Notice of Claim of Lien upon Funds or for any purpose other than the receipt of notices to the lien agent required under G.S. 44A-11.2.

(b) The lien agent shall be chosen from among the list of registered lien agents maintained by the Department of Insurance pursuant to G.S. 58-26-45.

(c) Upon receipt of written notification of designation by an owner pursuant to subsection (a) of this section, the lien agent shall have the duties as set forth in G.S. 58-26-45(b).

(d) In the event that the lien agent resigns, is no longer licensed to serve as a lien agent, revokes its consent to serve as lien agent or is removed by the owner, or otherwise becomes unable or unwilling to serve before the completion of all improvements to the real property, the owner shall within three business days of notice of such event do all of the following:

(1) Designate a successor lien agent and provide written notice of designation to the successor lien agent pursuant to subsection (a) of this section.

(2) Provide the contact information for the successor lien agent to the inspection department that issued any required building permit and to any persons who requested information from the owner relating to the predecessor lien agent.

(3) Display the contact information for the successor lien agent on the building permit or attachment thereto posted on the improved property or, if no building permit was required, on a sign complying with G.S. 44A-11.2(e).

(e) Until such time as the owner has fully complied with subsection (d) of this section, notice transmitted to the predecessor lien agent shall be deemed effective notice, notwithstanding the fact that the lien agent may have resigned or otherwise become unable or unwilling to serve.

(f) Any attorney who, in connection with a transaction involving improved real property subject to this section for which the attorney is serving as the closing attorney, contacts the lien agent in writing and requests copies of the notices received by the lien agent relating to the real property not more than five business days prior to the date of recordation of a deed or deed of trust on the real property, shall be deemed to have fulfilled the attorney's professional obligation as closing attorney to check such notices to lien agent and shall have no further duty to request that the lien agent provide information pertaining to notices received subsequently by the lien agent. (2012-158, s. 2; 2013-16, s. 1; 2013-117, s. 1.)

§ 44A-11.2. Identification of lien agent; notice to lien agent; effect of notice.

(a) As used in this section, the term "contact information" shall mean the name, physical and mailing address, telephone number, facsimile number, and electronic mail address of the lien agent designated by the owner pursuant to G.S. 44A-11.1.

(b) Within seven days of receiving a written request by a potential lien claimant by any delivery method specified in subsection (f) of this section, the owner shall provide a notice to the potential lien claimant containing the contact information for the lien agent, by the same delivery method used by the potential lien claimant in making the request.

(b1) A potential lien claimant making a request pursuant to subsection (b) of this section who did not receive the lien agent contact information pursuant to subsection (c) of this section, and who has not furnished labor, materials, rental equipment, or professional design or surveying services at the site of the improvements, or who last furnished labor, materials, rental equipment, or professional design or surveying services at the site of the improvements prior to the posting of the contact information for the lien agent pursuant to subsection (d) or (e) of this section, shall have no obligation to give notice to the lien agent under this section until the potential lien claimant has received the contact information from the owner.

(c) A contractor or subcontractor for improvements to real property subject to G.S. 44A-11.1 shall, within three business days of contracting with a lower-tier subcontractor who is not required to furnish labor, materials, rental equipment, or professional design or surveying services at the site of the improvements, provide the lower-tier subcontractor with a written notice containing the contact information for the lien agent designated by the owner. This notice shall be given pursuant to subsection (f) of this section or may be given by including the lien agent contact information in a written subcontract entered into by, or a written purchase order issued to, the lower-tier subcontractor entitled to the notice required by this subsection. Any contractor or subcontractor who has previously received notice of the lien agent contact information, whether from the building permit, the inspections office, a notice from the owner, contractor, or subcontractor, or by any other means, and who fails to provide the lien agent contact information to the lower-tier subcontractor in the time required under this subsection, shall be liable to the lower-tier subcontractor for any actual damages incurred by the lower-tier subcontractor as a result of the failure to give notice.

(d) For any improvement to real property subject to G.S. 44A-11.1, any building permit issued pursuant to G.S. 160A-417(d) or G.S. 153A-357(e) shall be conspicuously and continuously posted on the property for which the permit is issued until the completion of all construction.

(e) For any improvement to real property subject to G.S. 44A-11.1, a sign disclosing the contact information for the lien agent shall be conspicuously and continuously posted on the property until the completion of all construction if the contact information for the lien agent is not contained in a building permit or attachment thereto posted on the property.

(f) In complying with any requirement for written notice pursuant to this section, the notice shall be addressed to the person required to be provided with the notice and shall be delivered by any of the following methods:

(1) Certified mail, return receipt requested.

(2) Signature confirmation as provided by the United States Postal Service.

(3) Physical delivery and obtaining a delivery receipt from the lien agent.

(4) Facsimile with a facsimile confirmation.

(5) Depositing with a designated delivery service authorized pursuant to 26 U.S.C. § 7502(f)(2).

(6) Electronic mail, with delivery receipt.

(7) Utilizing an Internet Web site approved for such use by the designated lien agent to transmit to the designated lien agent, with delivery receipt, all information required to notify the lien agent of its designation pursuant to G.S. 44A-11.1 or to provide a notice to the designated lien agent pursuant to this section.

As used in this subsection, "delivery receipt" includes an electronic or facsimile confirmation. A return receipt or other receipt showing delivery of the notice to the addressee or written evidence that such notice was delivered by the postal service or other carrier to but not accepted by the addressee shall be prima facie evidence of receipt.

(g) For purposes of this subsection, "custom contractor" means a contractor duly licensed as a general contractor pursuant to Article 1 of Chapter 87 of the General Statutes who has contracted with an owner who is not an affiliate, relative, or insider of the contractor to build a single-family residence on the owner's property to be occupied by the owner as a residence. A custom contractor will be deemed to have met the requirement of notice under subsections (l) and (m) of this section on the date of the lien agent's receipt of notice of its designation as lien agent delivered to it by the custom contractor in accordance with this section if, at the time of the lien agent's receipt of the notice, all of the following conditions are met:

(1) The owner has not previously designated a lien agent for the improvements to which the notice of designation of lien agent relates.

(2) The custom contractor is authorized to designate the lien agent on behalf of the owner under the written contract between the owner and custom contractor.

(3) In addition to the information required to be included pursuant to G.S. 44A-11.1(a), the notice of designation of lien agent contains the following information:

a. The custom contractor's name, mailing address, telephone number, fax number (if available), and electronic mailing address (if available).

b. The name of the owner with whom the custom contractor has contracted to improve the real property identified in the notice.

After receiving a notice of its designation from a custom contractor pursuant to this subsection, the designated lien agent shall include the custom contractor's name and contact information in responding to any request for information pursuant to G.S. 58-26-45(b)(7).

(h) When a lien agent is not identified in a contract for improvements to real property subject to G.S. 44A-11.1 entered into between an owner and a design professional, the design professional will be deemed to have met the requirement of notice under subsections (l) and (m) of this section on the date of the lien agent's receipt of the owner's designation of the lien agent. The owner shall provide written notice to the lien agent containing the information pertaining to the design professional required in a notice to lien agent pursuant to subdivisions (1) through (3) of subsection (i) of this section, by any method of delivery authorized in subsection (f) of this section. The lien agent shall include the design professional's name and address in its response to any persons requesting information relating to persons who have given notice to the lien agent pursuant to this section. For purposes of this subsection, the term "design professional" shall mean any architects, engineers, land surveyors, and landscape architects registered under Chapter 83A, 89A, or 89C of the General Statutes.

(i) The form of the notice to be given under this section shall be substantially as follows:

NOTICE TO LIEN AGENT

(1) Potential lien claimant's name, mailing address, telephone number, fax number (if available), and electronic mailing address (if available):

(2) Name of the party with whom the potential lien claimant has contracted to improve the real property described below:

(3) A description of the real property sufficient to identify the real property, such as the name of the project, if applicable, the physical address as shown on the building permit or notice received from the owner:

(4) I give notice of my right subsequently to pursue a claim of lien for improvements to the real property described in this notice.

Dated: _____

_____

Potential Lien Claimant

(j)   The service of the Notice to Lien Agent does not satisfy the service or filing requirements applicable to a Notice of Claim of Lien upon Funds under Part 2 of Article 2 of this Chapter or a Claim of Lien on Real Property under Part 1 or Part 2 of Article 2 of this Chapter.

(k)   The notice to lien agent shall not be filed with the clerk of superior court. An inaccuracy in the description of the improved real property provided in the notice shall not bar a person from claiming a lien under this Article or otherwise perfecting or enforcing a claim of lien as provided in this Article, if the improved real property can otherwise reasonably be identified from the information contained in the notice.

(l)   Except as otherwise provided in this section, for any improvement to real property subject to G.S. 44A-11.1, a potential lien claimant may perfect a claim of lien on real property only if at least one of the following conditions is met:

(1)   The lien agent identified in accordance with this section has received a Notice to Lien Agent from the potential lien claimant no later than 15 days after the first furnishing of labor or materials by the potential lien claimant.

(2)   Any of the following conditions is met:

a.   The lien agent identified in accordance with this section has received a Notice to Lien Agent from the potential lien claimant prior to the date of recordation of a conveyance of the property interest in the real property to a bona fide purchaser for value protected under G.S. 47-18 who is not an affiliate, relative, or insider of the owner.

b.   The potential lien claimant has perfected its claim of lien on real property pursuant to G.S. 44A-11 prior to the recordation of a conveyance of the property interest in the real property to a bona fide purchaser for value protected under G.S. 47-18 who is not an affiliate, relative, or insider of the owner.

As used in this subdivision, the terms "affiliate," "relative," and "insider" shall have the meanings as set forth in G.S. 39-23.1.

(m) Except as otherwise provided in this section, for any improvement to real property subject to G.S. 44A-11.1, the claim of lien on real property of a potential lien claimant that is not perfected pursuant to G.S. 44A-11 prior to the recordation of any mortgage or deed of trust for the benefit of one who is not an affiliate, relative, or insider of the owner shall be subordinate to the previously recorded mortgage or deed of trust unless at least one of the following conditions is met:

(1) The lien agent identified in accordance with this section has received a Notice to Lien Agent from the potential lien claimant no later than 15 days after the first furnishing of labor or materials by the potential lien claimant.

(2) The lien agent identified in accordance with this section has received a Notice to Lien Agent from the potential lien claimant prior to the date of recordation of the mortgage or deed of trust.

(n) For any improvement to real property subject to G.S. 44A-11.1, a potential lien claimant shall not be required to comply with this section if the lien agent contact information is neither contained in the building permit or attachment thereto or sign posted on the improved property pursuant to subsection (d) or (e) of this section at the time when the potential lien claimant was furnishing labor, materials, rental equipment, or professional design or surveying services at the site of the improvements, nor timely provided by the owner in response to a written request by the potential lien claimant made pursuant to subsection (b) of this section. The lien rights of a potential lien claimant who is given erroneous information by the owner regarding the identity of the lien agent will not be extinguished under subsection (l) of this section nor subordinated under subsection (m) of this section.

(o) Except as provided in subsections (l) and (m) of this section, nothing contained in this section shall affect a claim of lien upon funds pursuant to G.S. 44A-18.

(p) A potential lien claimant may provide the notice to lien agent required under this section regardless of whether the improvements for which the potential lien claimant is responsible are contracted, started, in process, or completed at the time of submitting the notice. (2012-158, s. 2; 2013-16, s. 2; 2013-117, s. 2.)

§ 44A-12. Filing claim of lien on real property.

(a) Place of Filing. - All claims of lien on real property must be filed in the office of the clerk of superior court in each county where the real property subject to the claim of lien on real property is located. The clerk of superior court shall note the claim of lien on real property on the judgment docket and index the same under the name of the record owner of the real property at the time the claim of lien on real property is filed. An additional copy of the claim of lien on real property may also be filed with any receiver, referee in bankruptcy or assignee for benefit of creditors who obtains legal authority over the real property.

(b) Time of Filing. - Claims of lien on real property may be filed at any time after the maturity of the obligation secured thereby but not later than 120 days after the last furnishing of labor or materials at the site of the improvement by the person claiming the lien.

(c) Contents of Claim of Lien on Real Property to Be Filed. - All claims of lien on real property must be filed using a form substantially as follows:

CLAIM OF LIEN ON REAL PROPERTY

(1) Name and address of the person claiming the claim of lien on real property:

(2) Name and address of the record owner of the real property claimed to be subject to the claim of lien on real property at the time the claim of lien on real property is filed and, if the claim of lien on real property is being asserted pursuant to G.S. 44A-23, the name of the contractor through which subrogation is being asserted:

(3) Description of the real property upon which the claim of lien on real property is claimed: (Street address, tax lot and block number, reference to recorded instrument, or any other description of real property is sufficient, whether or not it is specific, if it reasonably identifies what is described.)

(4) Name and address of the person with whom the claimant contracted for the furnishing of labor or materials:

(5) Date upon which labor or materials were first furnished upon said property by the claimant:

(5a) Date upon which labor or materials were last furnished upon said property by the claimant:

(6) General description of the labor performed or materials furnished and the amount claimed therefor:

I hereby certify that I have served the parties listed in (2) above in accordance with the requirements of G.S. 44A-11.

_____

                                                                       Lien Claimant

Filed this ____ day of ____, ____

_____

Clerk of Superior Court

A general description of the labor performed or materials furnished is sufficient. It is not necessary for lien claimant to file an itemized list of materials or a detailed statement of labor performed.

(d) No Amendment of Claim of Lien on Real Property. - A claim of lien on real property may not be amended. A claim of lien on real property may be cancelled by a claimant or the claimant's authorized agent or attorney and a new claim of lien on real property substituted therefor within the time herein provided for original filing.

(e) Notice of Assignment of Claim of Lien on Real Property. - When a claim of lien on real property has been filed, it may be assigned of record by the lien claimant in a writing filed with the clerk of superior court who shall note the assignment in the margin of the judgment docket containing the claim of lien on real property. Thereafter the assignee becomes the lien claimant of record.

(f) Waiver of Right to File, Serve, or Claim Liens as Consideration for Contract Against Public Policy. - An agreement to waive the right to file a claim of lien on real property granted under this Part, or an agreement to waive the right to serve a notice of claim of lien upon funds granted under Part 2 of this

Article, which agreement is in anticipation of and in consideration for the awarding of any contract, either expressed or implied, for the making of an improvement upon real property under this Article is against public policy and is unenforceable. This section does not prohibit subordination or release of a lien granted under this Part or Part 2 of this Article. (1969, c. 1112, s. 1; 1977, c. 369; 1983, c. 888; 1999-456, s. 59; 2005-229, s. 1; 2012-175, s. 3.)

§ 44A-12.1. No docketing of lien unless authorized by statute.

(a) The clerk of superior court shall not index, docket, or record a claim of lien on real property or other document purporting to claim or assert a lien on real property in such a way as to affect the title to any real property unless the document:

(1) Is offered for filing under this Article or another statute that provides for indexing and docketing of claims of lien on real property; and

(2) Appears on its face to contain all of the information required by the statute under which it is offered for filing.

(b) The clerk may accept, for filing only, any document that does not meet the criteria established for indexing, docketing, or recording under subsection (a) of this section. If the clerk does accept this document, the clerk shall inform the person offering the document that it will not be indexed, docketed, or recorded in any way as to affect the title to any real property.

(c) Any person who causes or attempts to cause a claim of lien on real property or other document to be filed, knowing that the filing is not authorized by statute, or with the intent that the filing is made for an improper purpose such as to hinder, harass, or otherwise wrongfully interfere with any person, shall be guilty of a Class I felony.

(d) A claim of lien on real property, a claim of lien on real property with a notice of claim of lien upon funds attached thereto, or other document purporting to claim or assert a lien on real property that is filed by an attorney licensed in the State of North Carolina and that otherwise complies with subsection (a) of this section shall not be rejected by the clerk of superior court for indexing, docketing, recording, or filing. (2001-495, s. 1; 2005-229, s. 1; 2012-150, s. 6.1.)

§ 44A-13. Action to enforce claim of lien on real property.

(a) Where and When Action Commenced. - An action to enforce a claim of lien on real property may be commenced in any county where venue is otherwise proper. No such action may be commenced later than 180 days after the last furnishing of labor or materials at the site of the improvement by the person claiming the claim of lien on real property. If the title to the real property against which the claim of lien on real property is asserted is by law vested in a receiver or is subject to the control of the bankruptcy court, the claim of lien on real property shall be enforced in accordance with the orders of the court having jurisdiction over said real property. The filing of a proof of claim with a receiver or in bankruptcy and the filing of a notice of lis pendens in each county where the real property subject to the claim of lien on real property is located within the time required by this section satisfies the requirement for the commencement of a civil action.

(b) Judgment. - A judgment enforcing a lien under this Article may be entered for the principal amount shown to be due, not exceeding the principal amount stated in the claim of lien enforced thereby. The judgment shall direct a sale of the real property subject to the lien thereby enforced.

(c) Notice of Action. - In order for the sale under G.S. 44A-14(a) to pass all title and interest of the owner to the purchaser good against all claims or interests recorded, filed or arising after the first furnishing of labor or materials at the site of the improvement by the person claiming the claim of lien on real property, a notice of lis pendens shall be filed in each county in which the real property subject to the claim of lien on real property is located except the county in which the action is commenced. The notice of lis pendens shall be filed within the time provided in subsection (a) of this section for the commencement of the action by the lien claimant. If neither an action nor a notice of lis pendens is filed in accordance with this section, the judgment entered in the action enforcing the claim of lien on real property shall not direct a sale of the real property subject to the claim of lien on real property enforced thereby nor be entitled to any priority under the provisions of G.S. 44A-14(a), but shall be entitled only to those priorities accorded by law to money judgments.

(d) Former Owner Not a Necessary Party to Action. - In an action brought under this section, a former owner of the improved property at the time the lien arose, who holds no ownership interest in the property at the time the action is commenced and against whom the plaintiff seeks no relief, is not a necessary party to the action.

(e) Subsequent Purchaser and Lender Not Necessary or Proper Parties to Action Filed After Claim of Lien Is Discharged. - If a claim of lien on real property filed under this Article is discharged pursuant to G.S. 44A-16(a)(5) or G.S. 44A-16(a)(6) prior to the filing of an action to enforce the claim of lien under this section, then neither a subsequent purchaser of the real property upon which the lien is claimed nor the subsequent purchaser's lender shall be a necessary or proper party to the action. However, nothing herein precludes the lien claimant from asserting any claims against any party that are separate and distinct from enforcement of the lien.

(f) Subsequent Purchaser and Lender No Longer Necessary or Proper Parties Upon Discharge of Claim of Lien After Action Is Filed. - If an action to enforce a lien under this section is commenced before the claim of lien is discharged pursuant to G.S. 44A-16(a)(5) or G.S. 44A-16(a)(6), a subsequent purchaser of the real property upon which the lien is claimed and the subsequent purchaser's lender shall cease to be a necessary or proper party to the action, and any claim for lien enforcement asserted against the subsequent purchaser of the real property upon which the lien is claimed or the subsequent purchaser's lender shall be dismissed upon motion of any party upon a showing that the claim of lien was discharged pursuant to G.S. 44A-16. However, nothing herein precludes the lien claimant from continuing to pursue any claims against any party that are separate and distinct from enforcement of the lien.

(g) Bonds Prohibited From Requiring Subsequent Purchaser or Lender to Remain Parties to Action After Discharge of Claim of Lien. - The fact that a subsequent purchaser of the real property upon which the lien is claimed or the subsequent purchaser's lender is not a party to an action to enforce a claim of lien on real property subsequent to discharge of that claim of lien by the contractor under G.S. 44A-16 shall not invalidate the claim of lien under this Chapter, nor shall it invalidate any bond filed under G.S. 44A-16 to discharge the claim of lien. Further, a bond filed under G.S. 44A-16(a)(6) shall not require that a subsequent purchaser of the real property upon which the lien is claimed or the subsequent purchaser's lender remain a party to an action to enforce a claim of lien after the claim of lien has been discharged pursuant to G.S. 44A-16.

(h) Definition of "Subsequent Purchaser." - For purposes of this section, a "subsequent purchaser" means a party whose record interest is protected under G.S. 47-18, including any beneficiary of a deed of trust or mortgagee of that party, the priority of whose interest is protected under the provisions of G.S. 47-20, and who was not the owner of the real property at the time of the improvements giving rise to the lien claim as defined in G.S. 44A-7(6). (1969, c. 1112, s. 1; 1977, c. 883; 2005-229, s. 1; 2012-175, s. 4.)

§ 44A-14. Sale of property in satisfaction of judgment enforcing claim of lien on real property or upon order prior to judgment; distribution of proceeds.

(a) Execution Sale; Effect of Sale. - Except as provided in subsection (b) of this section, sales under this Article and distribution of proceeds thereof shall be made in accordance with the execution sale provisions set out in G.S. 1-339.41 through 1-339.76. The sale of real property to satisfy a claim of lien on real property granted by this Article shall pass all title and interest of the owner to the purchaser, good against all claims or interests recorded, filed or arising after the first furnishing of labor or materials at the site of the improvement by the person claiming a lien.

(b) Sale of Property upon Order Prior to Judgment. - A resident judge of superior court in the district in which the action to enforce the claim of lien on real property is pending, a judge regularly holding the superior courts of the said district, any judge holding a session of superior court, either civil or criminal, in the said district, a special judge of superior court residing in the said district, or the chief judge of the district court in which the action to enforce the claim of lien on real property is pending, may, upon notice to all interested parties and after a hearing thereupon and upon a finding that a sale prior to judgment is necessary to prevent substantial waste, destruction, depreciation or other damage to said real property prior to the final determination of said action, order any real property against which a claim of lien on real property under this Article is asserted, sold in any manner determined by said judge to be commercially reasonable. The rights of all parties shall be transferred to the proceeds of the sale. Application for such order and further proceedings thereon may be heard in or out of session. (1969, c. 1112, s. 1; 2005-229, s. 1.)

§ 44A-15. Attachment available to lien claimant.

In addition to other grounds for attachment, in all cases where the owner removes or attempts or threatens to remove an improvement from real property subject to a claim of lien on real property under this Article, without the written permission of the lien claimant or with the intent to deprive the lien claimant of his or her claim of lien on real property, the remedy of attachment of the property subject to the claim of lien on real property shall be available to the lien claimant or any other person. (1969, c. 1112, s. 1; 2005-229, s. 1.)

§ 44A-16. Discharge of record claim of lien on real property.

(a) Any claim of lien on real property filed under this Article may be discharged by any of the following methods:

(1) The lien claimant of record, the claimant's agent or attorney, in the presence of the clerk of superior court may acknowledge the satisfaction of the claim of lien on real property indebtedness, whereupon the clerk of superior court shall forthwith make upon the record of such claim of lien on real property an entry of such acknowledgment of satisfaction, which shall be signed by the lien claimant of record, the claimant's agent or attorney, and witnessed by the clerk of superior court.

(2) The owner may exhibit an instrument of satisfaction signed and acknowledged by the lien claimant of record which instrument states that the claim of lien on real property indebtedness has been paid or satisfied, whereupon the clerk of superior court shall cancel the claim of lien on real property by entry of satisfaction on the record of such claim of lien on real property.

(3) By failure to enforce the claim of lien on real property within the time prescribed in this Article.

(4) By filing in the office of the clerk of superior court the original or certified copy of a judgment or decree of a court of competent jurisdiction showing that the action by the claimant to enforce the claim of lien on real property has been dismissed or finally determined adversely to the claimant.

(5) Whenever a sum equal to the amount of the claim or claims of lien on real property claimed is deposited with the clerk of court, to be applied to the

payment finally determined to be due, whereupon the clerk of superior court shall cancel the claim or claims of lien on real property or claims of lien on real property of record.

(6) Whenever a corporate surety bond, in a sum equal to one and one-fourth times the amount of the claim or claims of lien on real property claimed and conditioned upon the payment of the amount finally determined to be due in satisfaction of said claim or claims of lien on real property, is deposited with the clerk of court, whereupon the clerk of superior court shall cancel the claim or claims of lien on real property of record.

(b) The clerk may release funds held or a corporate surety bond upon receipt of one of the following:

(1) Written agreement of the parties.

(2) A final judgment of a court of competent jurisdiction.

(3) A consent order.

(c) For improvements performed in conjunction with a development contract under G.S. 143-128.1C, a claim of lien on real property or a claim of lien on funds served on a private developer may also be discharged by the private developer and the surety on a payment bond issued under G.S. 143-128.1C(g)(1) in accordance with this subsection. The claim of lien may be discharged by the private developer and surety jointly filing with the clerk of superior court of the county where the project is located a copy of the payment bond together with an affidavit executed by the surety stating that, as of the date of the filing of the payment bond with the clerk of superior court, the amount of the penal sum of the payment bond minus any amounts paid in good faith to other claimants on the project and minus the amount of all other claims of lien on real property filed against the property improved by the project exceeds the amount claimed by the lien claim being discharged by at least one hundred twenty-five percent (125%). Notwithstanding any other contractual provision or law, where a claimant's lien claim has been discharged under this subsection, the claimant shall have no less than one year from the date of being served with the payment bond and affidavit to file suit on the payment bond. (1969, c. 1112, s. 1; 1971, c. 766; 2005-229, s. 1; 2011-411, s. 3; 2013-401, s. 6.)

Part 2. Liens of Mechanics, Laborers, and Materialmen Dealing with One Other Than Owner.

§ 44A-17: Repealed by Session Laws 2012-175, s. 5, effective January 1, 2013.

§ 44A-18. Grant of lien upon funds; subrogation; perfection.

(a) A first tier subcontractor who furnished labor, materials, or rental equipment at the site of the improvement shall have a lien upon funds that are owed to the contractor with whom the first tier subcontractor dealt and that arise out of the improvement on which the first tier subcontractor worked or furnished materials.

(b) A second tier subcontractor who furnished labor, materials, or rental equipment at the site of the improvement shall have a lien upon funds that are owed to the first tier subcontractor with whom the second tier subcontractor dealt and that arise out of the improvement on which the second tier subcontractor worked or furnished materials. A second tier subcontractor, to the extent of the second tier subcontractor's lien provided in this subdivision, shall also be subrogated to the lien upon funds of the first tier subcontractor with whom the second tier contractor dealt provided for in subdivision (1) of this section and shall perfect it by service of the notice of claim of lien upon funds to the extent of the claim.

(c) A third tier subcontractor who furnished labor, materials, or rental equipment at the site of the improvement shall have a lien upon funds that are owed to the second tier subcontractor with whom the third tier subcontractor dealt and that arise out of the improvement on which the third tier subcontractor worked or furnished materials. A third tier subcontractor, to the extent of the third tier subcontractor's lien upon funds provided in this subdivision, shall also be subrogated to the lien upon funds of the second tier subcontractor with whom the third tier contractor dealt and to the lien upon funds of the first tier subcontractor with whom the second tier subcontractor dealt to the extent that the second tier subcontractor is subrogated thereto, and in either case shall perfect it by service of the notice of claim of lien upon funds to the extent of the claim.

(d)   Subcontractors more remote than the third tier who furnished labor, materials, or rental equipment at the site of the improvement shall have a lien upon funds that are owed to the person with whom they dealt and that arise out of the improvement on which they furnished labor, materials, or rental equipment, but such remote tier subcontractor shall not be entitled to subrogation to the rights of other persons.

(e)   The liens upon funds granted under this section shall secure amounts earned by the lien claimant as a result of having furnished labor, materials, or rental equipment at the site of the improvement under the contract to improve real property, including interest at the legal rate provided in G.S. 24-5, whether or not such amounts are due and whether or not performance or delivery is complete. In the event insufficient funds are retained to satisfy all lien claimants, subcontractor lien claimants may recover the interest due under this subdivision on a pro rata basis, but in no event shall interest due under this subdivision increase the liability of the obligor under G.S. 44A-20.

(f)   A lien upon funds granted under this section arises, attaches, and is effective immediately upon the first furnishing of labor, materials, or rental equipment at the site of the improvement by a subcontractor. Any lien upon funds granted under this section is perfected upon the giving of notice of claim of lien upon funds in writing to the obligor as provided in G.S. 44A-19.

(g)   Until a lien claimant gives notice of a claim of lien upon funds in writing to the obligor as provided in G.S. 44A-19, any owner, contractor, or subcontractor against whose interest the lien upon funds is claimed may make, receive, use, or collect payments thereon and may use such proceeds in the ordinary course of its business. (1971, c. 880, s. 1; 1985, c. 702, s. 3; 1995 (Reg. Sess., 1996), c. 607, s. 3; 2005-229, s. 1; 2012-175, s. 6.)

§ 44A-19. Notice of claim of lien upon funds.

(a)   Notice of a claim of lien upon funds shall set forth all of the following information:

(1)   The name and address of the person claiming the lien upon funds.

(2)   A general description of the real property improved.

(3)   The name and address of the person with whom the lien claimant contracted to improve real property.

(4)   The name and address of each person against or through whom subrogation rights are claimed.

(5)   A general description of the contract and the person against whose interest the lien upon funds is claimed.

(6)   The amount of the lien upon funds claimed by the lien claimant under the contract.

(b)   All notices of claims of liens upon funds by first, second, or third tier subcontractors must be given using a form substantially as follows:

NOTICE OF CLAIM OF LIEN UPON FUNDS BY

FIRST, SECOND, OR THIRD TIER SUBCONTRACTOR

To:

1. _____, owner of property involved.

(Name and address)

2. _____, contractor.

(Name and address)

3. _____, first tier subcontractor against or through

(Name and address)   whom subrogation is claimed, if any.

4. _____, second tier subcontractor against or through

(Name and address)   whom subrogation is claimed, if any.

General description of real property on which labor performed or material furnished:

_____
_____

_____
_____
_____

_____
_____
_____

General description of undersigned lien claimant's contract including the names of the parties thereto:

_____
_____
_____

_____
_____
_____

The amount of lien upon funds claimed pursuant to the above described contract:

$ _____

The undersigned lien claimant gives this notice of claim of lien upon funds pursuant to North Carolina law and claims all rights of subrogation to which he is entitled under Part 2 of Article 2 of Chapter 44A of the General Statutes of North Carolina.

Dated _____

_____, Lien Claimant

_____

(Address)

(c)   All notices of claims of liens upon funds by subcontractors more remote than the third tier must be given using a form substantially as follows:

NOTICE OF CLAIM OF LIEN UPON FUNDS BY SUBCONTRACTOR

MORE REMOTE THAN THE THIRD TIER

To:

_____, person holding funds against which lien upon funds is claimed.

(Name and Address)

General description of real property on which labor performed or material furnished:

_____

_____

_____

_____

_____

_____

General description of undersigned lien claimant's contract including the names of the parties thereto:

_____

_____

_____

_____

The amount of lien upon funds claimed pursuant to the above described contract:

$ _____

The undersigned lien claimant gives this notice of claim of lien upon funds pursuant to North Carolina law and claims all rights to which he or she is entitled under Part 2 of Article 2 of Chapter 44A of the General Statutes of North Carolina.

Dated: _____

_____, Lien Claimant

_____

(Address)

(d)   Notices of claims of lien upon funds under this section shall be served upon the obligor by personal delivery or in any manner authorized by Rule 4 of the North Carolina Rules of Civil Procedure. A copy of the notice of claim of lien upon funds shall be attached to any claim of lien on real property filed pursuant to G.S. 44A-20(d).

(e)   Notices of claims of lien upon funds shall not be filed with the clerk of superior court and shall not be indexed, docketed, or recorded in any way as to affect title to any real property, except a notice of a claim of lien upon funds may be filed with the clerk of superior court under either of the following circumstances:

(1)   When the notice of claim of lien upon funds is attached to a claim of lien on real property filed pursuant to G.S. 44A-20(d).

(2)   When the notice of claim of lien upon funds or a copy thereof is filed by the obligor for the purpose of discharging the claim of lien upon funds in accordance with G.S. 44A-20(e).

(f)   Filing a notice of claim of lien upon funds pursuant to subsection (e) of this section is not a violation of G.S. 44A-12.1. (1971, c. 880, s. 1; 1985, c. 702, s. 1; 2005-229, s. 1; 2012-175, s. 7; 2013-16, s. 3.)

§ 44A-20. Duties and liability of obligor.

(a)   Upon receipt of the notice of claim of lien upon funds provided for in this Article, the obligor shall be under a duty to retain any funds subject to the lien or liens upon funds under this Article up to the total amount of such liens upon funds as to which notices of claims of lien upon funds have been received.

(b)	If, after the receipt of the notice of claim of lien upon funds to the obligor, the obligor makes further payments to a contractor or subcontractor against whose interest the lien or liens upon funds are claimed, the lien upon funds shall continue upon the funds in the hands of the contractor or subcontractor who received the payment, and in addition the obligor shall be personally liable to the person or persons entitled to liens upon funds up to the amount of such wrongful payments, not exceeding the total claims with respect to which the notice of claim of lien upon funds was received prior to payment.

(c)	If an obligor makes a payment after receipt of notice of claim of lien on funds and incurs personal liability under subsection (b) of this section, the obligor shall be entitled to reimbursement and indemnification from the party receiving such payment.

(d)	If the obligor is an owner of the property being improved, the lien claimant shall be entitled to a claim of lien upon real property upon the interest of the obligor in the real property to the extent of the owner's personal liability under subsection (b) of this section, which claim of lien on real property shall be enforced only in the manner set forth in G.S. 44A-7 through G.S. 44A-16 and which claim of lien on real property shall be entitled to the same priorities and subject to the same filing requirements and periods of limitation applicable to the contractor. The claim of lien on real property is perfected as of the time set forth in G.S. 44A-10 upon satisfaction of those requirements set forth in G.S. 44A-11. A lien waiver signed by the contractor prior to a subcontractor's perfecting its claim of lien on real property in accordance with G.S. 44A-11 waives the subcontractor's right to enforce the contractor's claim of lien on real property, but does not affect the subcontractor's right to a claim of lien on funds or the subcontractor's right to a claim of lien on real property allowed under this subsection. The claim of lien on real property as provided under this subsection shall be in the form set out in G.S. 44A-12(c) and shall contain, in addition, a copy of the notice of claim of lien upon funds given pursuant to G.S. 44A-19 as an exhibit together with proof of service thereof by affidavit, and shall state the grounds the lien claimant has to believe that the obligor is personally liable for the debt under subsection (b) of this section.

(e)	A notice of claim of lien upon funds under G.S. 44A-19 may be filed by the obligor with the clerk of superior court in each county where the real property upon which the filed notice of claim of lien upon funds is located for the purpose of discharging the notice of claim of lien upon funds by any of the methods described in G.S. 44A-16.

(f)   A bond deposited under this section to discharge a filed notice of claim of lien upon funds shall be effective to discharge any claim of lien on real property filed by the same lien claimant pursuant to subsection (d) of this section or G.S. 44A-23 and shall further be effective to discharge any notices of claims of lien upon funds served by lower tier subcontractors or any claims of lien on real property filed by lower tier subcontractors pursuant to subsection (d) of this section or G.S. 44A-23 claiming through or against the contractor or higher tier subcontractors up to the amount of the bond. (1971, c. 880, s. 1; 1985, c. 702, s. 2; 2005-229, s. 1; 2012-175, s. 8; 2013-16, s. 4.)

§ 44A-21. Pro rata payments.

(a)   Where the obligor is a contractor or subcontractor and the funds in the hands of the obligor and the obligor's personal liability, if any, under G.S. 44A-20 are less than the amount of valid liens upon funds that have been received by the obligor under this Article, the parties entitled to liens upon funds shall share the funds on a pro rata basis.

(b)   Where the obligor is an owner and the funds in the hands of the obligor and the obligor's personal liability, if any, under G.S. 44A-20 are less than the sum of the amount of valid claims of liens upon funds that have been received by the obligor under this Article and the amount of the valid claims of liens on real property upon the owner's property filed by the subcontractors with the clerk of superior court under G.S. 44A-23, the parties entitled to liens upon funds and the parties entitled to subrogation claims of liens on real property upon the owner's property shall share the funds on a pro rata basis. (1971, c. 880, s. 1; 1998-217, s. 4(d); 2005-229, s. 1.)

§ 44A-22. Priority of liens upon funds.

Liens upon funds perfected under this Article have priority over all other interests or claims theretofore or thereafter created or suffered in the funds by the person against whose interest the lien upon funds is asserted, including, but not limited to, liens arising from garnishment, attachment, levy, judgment, assignments, security interests, and any other type of transfer, whether voluntary or involuntary. Any person who receives payment from an obligor in bad faith with knowledge of a lien upon funds shall take such payment subject to the lien upon funds. (1971, c. 880, s. 1; 2005-229, s. 1.)

§ 44A-23. Contractor's claim of lien on real property; perfection of subrogation rights of subcontractor.

(a) First tier subcontractor. - A first tier subcontractor may, to the extent of its claim, enforce the claim of lien on real property of the contractor created by Part 1 of this Article. The manner of such enforcement shall be as provided by G.S. 44A-7 through 44A-16. The claim of lien on real property is perfected as of the time set forth in G.S. 44A-10 upon satisfaction of those requirements set forth in G.S. 44A-11.

(a1) No action of the contractor shall be effective to prejudice the rights of a first tier subcontractor without its written consent once the first tier subcontractor has perfected its claim of lien on real property in accordance with G.S. 44A-11.

(b) Second or third tier subcontractor. -

(1) A second or third tier subcontractor may, to the extent of his claim, enforce the claim of lien on real property of the contractor created by Part 1 of Article 2 of the Chapter except when:

a. The owner or contractor, within 30 days following the date the permit is issued for the improvement of the real property involved or within 30 days following the date the contractor is awarded the contract for the improvement of the real property involved, whichever is later, posts on the property in a visible location adjacent to the posted permit, if a permit is required, and files in the office of the clerk of superior court in each county wherein the real property to be improved is located, a completed and signed notice of contract form and the second or third tier subcontractor fails to serve upon the contractor a completed and signed notice of subcontract form by the same means of service as described in G.S. 44A-19(d); or

b. After the posting and filing of a signed notice of contract and the service upon the contractor of a signed notice of subcontract, the contractor serves upon the second or third tier subcontractor, within five days following each subsequent payment, by the same means of service as described in G.S. 44A-19(d), the written notice of payment setting forth the date of payment and the period for which payment is made as requested in the notice of subcontract form set forth herein.

(2) The form of the notice of contract to be so utilized under this section shall be substantially as follows and the fee for filing the same with the clerk of superior court shall be the same as charged for filing a claim of lien on real property:

"NOTICE OF CONTRACT

"(1) Name and address of the Contractor:

"(2) Name and address of the owner of the real property at the time this Notice of Contract is recorded:

"(3) General description of the real property to be improved (street address, tax map lot and block number, reference to recorded instrument, or any other description that reasonably identifies the real property):

"(4) Name and address of the person, firm or corporation filing this Notice of Contract:

"Dated: _____

_____

"Contractor

"Filed this the ____ day of _____, ____.

_____

Clerk of Superior Court"

(3) The form of the notice of subcontract to be so utilized under this section shall be substantially as follows:

"NOTICE OF SUBCONTRACT

"(1) Name and address of the subcontractor:

"(2) General description of the real property on which the labor was performed or the material was furnished (street address, tax map lot and block number, reference to recorded instrument, or any description that reasonably identifies the real property):

"(3)

"(i) General description of the subcontractor's contract, including the names of the parties thereto:

"(ii) General description of the labor and material performed and furnished thereunder:

"(4) Request is hereby made by the undersigned subcontractor that he be notified in writing by the contractor of, and within five days following, each subsequent payment by the contractor to the first tier subcontractor for labor performed or material furnished at the improved real property within the above descriptions of such in paragraph (2) and subparagraph (3)(ii), respectively, the date payment was made and the period for which payment is made.

"Dated: _____

_____

Subcontractor"

(4) The manner of such enforcement shall be as provided by G.S. 44A-7 through G.S. 44A-16. The lien is perfected as of the time set forth in G.S. 44A-10 upon the filing of a claim of lien on real property pursuant to G.S. 44A-12.

(5) No action of the contractor shall be effective to prejudice the rights of the second or third tier subcontractor without its written consent once the second or third tier subcontractor has perfected its claim of lien on real property in accordance with G.S. 44A-11.

(c) A lien waiver signed by the contractor before the occurrence of all of the actions specified in subsection (a1) and subdivision (5) of subsection (b) of this section waives the subcontractor's right to enforce the contractor's claim of lien on real property, but does not affect the subcontractor's right to a claim of lien on funds or the subcontractor's right to a claim of lien on real property allowed under G.S. 44A-20(d).

(d)   When completing the claim of lien on real property form to perfect the contractor's claim of lien on real property, a first, second, or third tier subcontractor may use as the date upon which labor or materials were first or last furnished on the real property either any date on or after the date of the first furnishing of labor or materials on the real property, or any date on or before the date of the last furnishing of labor or materials on the real property by the subcontractor making the claim, or any date on or after the date of the first furnishing of labor or materials on the real property, or any date on or before the date of the last furnishing of labor or materials on the real property by the contractor through which the claim of lien on real property is being asserted. (1971, c. 880, s. 1; 1985, c. 702, s. 4; 1991 (Reg. Sess., 1992), c. 1010, s. 1; 1993, c. 553, s. 13; 1997-456, s. 27; 1999-456, s. 59; 2005-229, s. 1; 2012-158, s. 6.1; 2012-175, s. 9; 2012-194, s. 65(a), (b); 2013-16, s. 5.)

Part 3. Criminal Sanctions for Furnishing a False Statement in Connection with Improvement to Real Property.

§ 44A-24. False statement a misdemeanor and grounds for disciplinary action against a licensed contractor or qualifying party.

If any contractor or other person receiving payment from an obligor for an improvement to real property or from a purchaser for a conveyance of real property with improvements subject to this Article or to Article 3 of this Chapter shall knowingly furnish to such obligor, purchaser, or to a lender who obtains a security interest in said real property, or to a title insurance company insuring title to such real property, a false written statement of the sums due or claimed to be due for labor or material furnished at the site of improvements to such real property, then such contractor, subcontractor or other person shall be guilty of a Class 1 misdemeanor. Upon conviction and in the event the court shall grant any defendant a suspended sentence, the court may in its discretion include as a condition of such suspension a provision that the defendant shall reimburse the party who suffered loss on such conditions as the court shall determine are proper.

The elements of the offense herein stated are the furnishing of the false written statement with knowledge that it is false and the subsequent or simultaneous receipt of payment from an obligor or purchaser by the person signing the document, a person directing another to sign the document, or any person or entity for whom the document was signed. In any criminal prosecution hereunder it shall not be necessary for the State to prove that the obligor, purchaser, lender or title insurance company relied upon the false statement or that any person was injured thereby.

In addition to the criminal sanctions created by this section, conduct constituting the offense herein stated and causing actual harm to any person by any licensed contractor or qualifying party, as that term is used in Chapter 87 of the General Statutes, shall constitute deceit and misconduct subject to disciplinary action under Chapter 87 of the General Statutes, including revocation, suspension, or restriction of a license or the ability to act as a qualifying party for a license. (1971, c. 880, s. 1.1; 1973, c. 991; 1993, c. 539, s. 406; 1994, Ex. Sess., c. 24, s. 14(c); 2012-175, s. 10.)

Part 4. Commercial Real Estate Broker Lien Act.

§ 44A-24.1. Short title.

This Part shall be known and may be cited as the "Commercial Real Estate Broker Lien Act." (2011-165, s. 1.)

§ 44A-24.2. Definitions.

The following definitions apply in this Part:

(1) Broker. - A real estate broker licensed pursuant to Chapter 93A of the General Statutes.

(2) Broker services. - Services for which a license issued by the North Carolina Real Estate Commission is required pursuant to Chapter 93A of the General Statutes.

(3) Commercial real estate. - Any real property or interest therein, whether freehold or nonfreehold, which at the time the property or interest is made the subject of an agreement for broker services:

a. Is lawfully used primarily for sales, office, research, institutional, warehouse, manufacturing, industrial, or mining purposes or for multifamily residential purposes involving five or more dwelling units;

b. May lawfully be used for any of the purposes listed in sub-subdivision (3)a. of this section by a zoning ordinance adopted pursuant to the provisions of Article 18 of Chapter 153A or Article 19 of Chapter 160A of the General Statutes or which is the subject of an official application or petition to amend the applicable zoning ordinance to permit any of the uses listed in sub-subdivision (3)a. of this section which is under consideration by the government agency with authority to approve the amendment; or

c. Is in good faith intended to be immediately used for any of the purposes listed in sub-subdivision (3)a. of this section by the parties to any contract, lease, option, or offer to make any contract, lease, or option.

(4) Commission. - Any compensation which is due a broker for performance of broker services.

(5) Lien claimant. - A broker claiming a lien pursuant to this Part.

(6) Owner. - The owner of record of any interest in commercial real estate. (2011-165, s. 1; 2012-194, s. 15.)

§ 44A-24.3. Commercial real estate lien.

(a) A broker shall have a lien upon commercial real estate in the amount that the broker is due under a written agreement for broker services signed by the owner or signed by the owner's duly authorized agent, if:

(1) The broker has performed under the provisions of the agreement;

(2) The written agreement for broker services clearly sets forth the broker's duties to the owner; and

(3) The written agreement for broker services sets forth the conditions upon which the compensation shall be earned and the amount of such compensation.

(b) The lien under this section shall be available only to the broker named in the instrument signed by the owner or the owner's duly authorized agent. A lien under this section shall be available only against the commercial real estate which is the subject of the written agreement for broker services.

(c) When payment of commission to a broker is due in installments, a portion of which is due only after the conveyance or transfer of the commercial real estate, any notice of lien for those payments due after the transfer or conveyance may be recorded at any time subsequent to the transfer or conveyance of the commercial real estate and within 90 days of the date on which the payment is due. The notice of lien shall be effective as a lien against the owner's interest in the commercial real estate only to the extent funds are owed to the owner by the transferee, but the lien shall be effective as a lien against the transferee's interest in the commercial real estate. A single claim for lien filed prior to transfer or conveyance of the commercial real estate claiming all commissions due in installments shall also be valid and enforceable as it pertains to payments due after the transfer or conveyance; provided, however, that as payments or partial payments of commission are received, the broker shall provide partial releases for those payments, thereby reducing the amount due the broker under the broker's lien. (2011-165, s. 1.)

§ 44A-24.4. When lien attaches to commercial real estate.

A lien authorized by this Part attaches to the commercial real estate only when the lien claimant files a timely notice of the lien conforming to the requirements of G.S. 44A-24.5 and this section in the office of the clerk of superior court. A notice of lien is timely if it is filed after the claimant's performance under the written agreement for broker services and before the conveyance or transfer of the commercial real estate which is the subject of the lien, except that in the case of a lease or transfer of a nonfreehold interest, the notice of a lien shall be filed no later than 90 days following the tenant's possession of the commercial real estate or no later than 60 days following any date or dates set out in the written agreement for broker services for subsequent payment or payments. When a notice of a lien is filed more than 30 days preceding the date for settlement or possession set out in an offer to purchase, sales contract, or lease, which establishes the broker's claim of performance, the lien shall be available only upon grounds of the owner's breach of the written agreement for broker services. (2011-165, s. 1.)

§ 44A-24.5. Lien notice; content.

(a)   A lien notice under this Part shall be signed by the lien claimant and shall contain an attestation by the lien claimant that the information contained in the notice is true and accurate to the best of the lien claimant's knowledge and belief.

(b)   The lien notice shall include all of the following information:

(1)   The name of the lien claimant.

(2)   The name of the owner.

(3)   A description of the commercial real estate upon which the lien is being claimed.

(4)   The amount for which the lien is claimed and whether the amount is due in installments.

(5)   The claimant's grounds for the lien, including a reference to the written agreement for broker services that is the basis for the lien. (2011-165, s. 1.)

§ 44A-24.6. When lien claim release or satisfaction to be filed.

If a claim for a lien has been filed with the clerk of superior court and a condition occurs that would preclude the lien claimant from receiving compensation under the terms of the written agreement for broker services on which the lien is based, the lien claimant shall file and serve the owner of record a written release or satisfaction of the lien promptly, and in no event more than 30 days after the demand. (2011-165, s. 1.)

§ 44A-24.7. Lien claimant to mail copy of notice of lien to owner by certified mail.

Any lien claimant who files a lien on commercial real estate pursuant to the provisions of this Part shall mail a copy of the notice of the lien to the owner of the commercial real estate by certified mail, return receipt requested, or shall serve a copy of the notice of the lien in accordance with any of the provisions for service of process set forth in G.S. 1A-1, Rule 4. The lien claimant shall file proof of service with the clerk of the superior court. The lien is void if the lien claimant does not file and serve the lien as provided in this Part. (2011-165, s. 1.)

§ 44A-24.8. Enforcing lien.

A lien claimant may bring suit to enforce a lien which attaches pursuant to the provisions of this Part in any court of competent jurisdiction in the county where the commercial real estate is located. The lien claimant shall commence proceedings within 18 months after filing the lien, and failure to commence proceedings within the 18 months shall extinguish the lien. If a claim is based upon an option to purchase the commercial real estate, the lien claimant shall commence proceedings within one year of the option to purchase being exercised. A claim for the same lien extinguished pursuant to this section and G.S. 44A-24.10 may not be asserted in any subsequent proceeding. A lender shall not be made a party to any suit to enforce a lien under this Part unless the lender has willfully caused the nonpayment of the commission giving rise to the lien. (2011-165, s. 1.)

§ 44A-24.9. Complaint; content; parties' foreclosure action; procedure.

(a) A complaint filed pursuant to the provisions of this section and G.S. 44A-24.8 shall contain all of the following:

(1) A statement of the terms of the written agreement for broker services on which the lien is based or a copy of the written contract or agreement.

(2) The date when the written agreement for broker services was made.

(3) A description of the services performed.

(4) The amount due and unpaid.

(5) A description of the property that is subject to the lien.

(6) Any other facts necessary for a full understanding of the rights of the parties.

(b) The plaintiff shall file the action against all parties that have an interest of record in the commercial real estate; provided that a lender shall not be made a party to any suit to enforce a lien under this Part unless the lender has willfully caused the nonpayment of the commission giving rise to the lien: a foreclosure action for a lien claimed pursuant to this Part shall be brought pursuant to the provisions of this Article.

(c) Valid prior recorded liens or mortgages shall have priority over a lien under this Part. (2011-165, s. 1.)

§ 44A-24.10. Lien extinguished for lien claimant failing to file suit or answer in pending suit within 30 days after service on owner.

If a lien claimant fails to file a suit to enforce the lien or fails to file an answer in a pending suit to enforce a lien within 30 days after a properly served written demand of the owner, lienee, or other authorized agent, the lien shall be extinguished. Service of the demand shall be by certified mail, return receipt requested, or by personal service. The claimant shall file proof of properly served written demand with the clerk of the superior court. The provisions of this section shall not extend to any other deadline provided by law for the filing of any pleadings or for the foreclosure of any lien governed by this Part. (2011-165, s. 1; 2012-175, s. 12(b).)

§ 44A-24.11. Satisfaction or release of lien.

If a claim for a lien has been filed pursuant to the provisions of this Part with the clerk of superior court and the claim has been paid in full, or if the lien claimant fails to institute a suit to enforce the lien within the time as provided by law, the lien claimant shall acknowledge satisfaction or release of the lien in writing upon written demand of the owner promptly, and in no event more than 30 days after the demand. (2011-165, s. 1.)

§ 44A-24.12. Cost of proceeding to be paid by nonprevailing party.

The costs of any proceeding brought to enforce a lien filed pursuant to this Part, including reasonable attorneys' fees and prejudgment interest due to the prevailing party, shall be paid by the nonprevailing party or parties. If more than one party is responsible for costs, fees, and prejudgment interest, the costs, fees, and prejudgment interest shall be equitably apportioned by the court among the responsible parties. (2011-165, s. 1.)

§ 44A-24.13. Discharge of lien.

(a)   Unless an alternative procedure is available and is acceptable to the transferee in a real estate transaction, any claim of lien on commercial real estate filed under this Article may be discharged by any of the following methods:

(1)   The lien claimant of record, the claimant's agent, or attorney, in the presence of the clerk of superior court, may acknowledge the satisfaction of the claim of lien on the commercial real estate indebtedness, whereupon the clerk of superior court shall enter on the record of the claim of lien on the commercial real estate the acknowledgment of satisfaction, which shall be signed by the lien claimant of record, the claimant's agent, or attorney, and witnessed by the clerk of superior court.

(2)   The owner may exhibit an instrument of satisfaction signed and acknowledged by the lien claimant of record, which instrument states that the claim of lien on the commercial real estate indebtedness has been paid or satisfied, whereupon the clerk of superior court shall cancel the claim of lien on the commercial real estate by entry of satisfaction on the record of the claim of lien on the commercial real estate.

(3)   By failure to enforce the claim of lien on the commercial real estate within the time prescribed in this Article.

(4)   By filing in the office of the clerk of superior court the original or certified copy of a judgment or decree of a court of competent jurisdiction showing that

the action by the claimant to enforce the claim of lien on the commercial real estate has been dismissed or finally determined adversely to the claimant.

(5) Whenever funds in an amount equal to one hundred twenty-five percent (125%) of the amount of the claim of lien on the commercial real estate is deposited with the clerk of superior court to be applied to the payment finally determined to be due, whereupon the clerk of superior court shall cancel the claim of lien on the commercial real estate.

(6) Whenever a corporate surety bond, in an amount equal to one hundred twenty-five percent (125%) of the amount of the claim of lien on the commercial real estate and conditioned upon the payment of the amount finally determined to be due in satisfaction of the claim of lien on the commercial real estate is deposited with the clerk of superior court, whereupon the clerk of superior court shall cancel the claim of lien on the commercial real estate.

(7) By failure to file documentation if required pursuant to G.S. 44A-24.6 or G.S. 44A-24.10.

(b) If funds in an amount equal to one hundred twenty-five percent (125%) of the amount that is sufficient to release the claim of lien have been deposited with the clerk of superior court, or a bond in an equal amount has been secured, the lien claimant shall release the claim for the lien on the commercial real estate, and the lien claimant shall have a lien on the funds deposited with the clerk of superior court. (2011-165, s. 1.)

§ 44A-24.14. Priority of lien under this Part.

Any claim of lien on real property or claim of lien on funds allowed under Part 1 or Part 2 of this Article shall be deemed superior in all respects to any lien asserted under this Part, regardless of the effective date of the competing liens and shall survive notwithstanding any judgment awarding a lien under this Part. No lien claimant filing a lien pursuant to this Part shall be entitled to participate in any pro rata distributions to claimants proceeding under G.S. 44A-21. (2011-165, s. 1.)

Article 3.

Model Payment and Performance Bond.

§ 44A-25. Definitions.

Unless the context otherwise requires in this Article:

(1) "Claimant" includes any individual, firm, partnership, association or corporation entitled to maintain an action on a bond described in this Article and shall include the "contracting body" in a suit to enforce the performance bond.

(2) "Construction contract" means any contract for the construction, reconstruction, alteration or repair of any public building or other public work or public improvement, including highways.

(3) "Contracting body" means any department, agency, or political subdivision of the State of North Carolina which has authority to enter into construction contracts.

(4) "Contractor" means any person who has entered into a construction contract with a contracting body.

(5) "Labor or materials" shall include all materials furnished or labor performed in the prosecution of the work called for by the construction contract regardless of whether or not the labor or materials enter into or become a component part of the public improvement, and further shall include gas, power, light, heat, oil, gasoline, telephone services and rental of equipment or the reasonable value of the use of equipment directly utilized in the performance of the work called for in the construction contract.

(6) "Subcontractor" means any person who has contracted to furnish labor or materials to, or who has performed labor for, a contractor or another subcontractor in connection with a construction contract. (1973, c. 1194, s. 1.)

§ 44A-26. Bonds required.

(a) When the total amount of construction contracts awarded for any one project exceeds three hundred thousand dollars ($300,000), a performance and payment bond as set forth in (1) and (2) is required by the contracting body from any contractor or construction manager at risk with a contract more than fifty thousand dollars ($50,000); provided that, for State departments, State agencies, and The University of North Carolina and its constituent institutions, a performance and payment bond is required in accordance with this subsection if the total amount of construction contracts awarded for any one project exceeds five hundred thousand dollars ($500,000). In the discretion of the contracting body, a performance and payment bond may be required on any construction contract as follows:

(1) A performance bond in the amount of one hundred percent (100%) of the construction contract amount, conditioned upon the faithful performance of the contract in accordance with the plans, specifications and conditions of the contract. Such bond shall be solely for the protection of the contracting body that is constructing the project.

(2) A payment bond in the amount of one hundred percent (100%) of the construction contract amount, conditioned upon the prompt payment for all labor or materials for which a contractor or subcontractor is liable. The payment bond shall be solely for the protection of the persons furnishing materials or performing labor for which a contractor, subcontractor, or construction manager at risk is liable.

(b) The performance bond and the payment bond shall be executed by one or more surety companies legally authorized to do business in the State of North Carolina and shall become effective upon the awarding of the construction contract. (1973, c. 1194, s. 1; 1983, c. 818; 1987 (Reg. Sess., 1988), c. 1108, s. 10; 1995, c. 367, s. 3; 2001-496, s. 7; 2010-148, s. 1.)

§ 44A-27. Actions on payment bonds; service of notice.

(a) Subject to the provision of subsection (b) hereof, any claimant who has performed labor or furnished materials in the prosecution of the work required by any contract for which a payment bond has been given pursuant to the provisions of this Article, and who has not been paid in full therefor before the expiration of 90 days after the day on which the claimant performed the last such labor or furnished the last such materials for which he claims payment, may bring an action on such payment bond in his own name, to recover any amount due him for such labor or materials and may prosecute such action to final judgment and have execution on the judgment.

(b) Any claimant who has a direct contractual relationship with any subcontractor but has no contractual relationship, express or implied, with the contractor may bring an action on the payment bond only if he has given written notice of claim on payment bond to the contractor within 120 days from the date on which the claimant performed the last of the labor or furnished the last of the materials for which he claims payment, stating with substantial accuracy the amount claimed and the name of the person for whom the work was performed or to whom the material was furnished. The contractor shall, in response to a written request served by any claimant in accordance with the provisions of subsection (c) of this section, send a copy of the payment bond required by this Article to the claimant making the request within seven calendar days after receipt of such request. Subject to the exception set forth in subsection (e) of this section, unless the contractor has failed to satisfy its obligation to timely furnish a copy of the payment bond to a claimant upon proper request by the claimant, the claim of such a claimant shall not include labor or materials provided more than 75 days prior to the claimant's service, in accordance with subsections (c) and (d) of this section, of its written notice of public subcontract to the contractor.

(c) The notices required by and any requests for copy of payment bond referenced by subsection (b) of this section, shall be served by certified mail, or by signature confirmation as provided by the United States Postal Service, postage prepaid, in an envelope addressed to such contractor at any place where his office is regularly maintained for the transaction of business or to such agent identified in the contractor's project statement referenced in subdivision (1) of subsection (f) of this section or served in any manner provided by law for the service of summons.

(d) The form of the notice of public subcontract to be served pursuant to subsection (b) of this section shall be substantially as follows:

"NOTICE OF PUBLIC SUBCONTRACT

(1) Name and address of the subcontractor giving notice of public subcontract:

(2)   General description of the real property on which the labor was or is to be performed or the material was or is to be furnished (street address, tax map lot and block number, reference to recorded instrument, or any description that reasonably identifies the real property):

(3)   General description of the subcontractor's contract, including the names and addresses of the parties thereto:

(4)   General description of the labor and material performed and furnished thereunder:

Dated: _____

_____

Subcontractor"

(e)   Notwithstanding subsections (b), (c), and (d) of this section, the obligation to provide a notice of public subcontract shall not apply to claims of twenty thousand dollars ($20,000) or less and, for any claim exceeding twenty thousand dollars ($20,000), shall apply only to that portion of the claim in excess of twenty thousand dollars ($20,000).

(f)   In connection with any construction contract for which a bond is required by G.S. 44A-26(a), all of the following shall apply:

(1)   The contractor shall provide to each subcontractor that it engages to perform labor or furnish materials in the performance of the construction contract a contractor's project statement containing all of the following information:

a.   The name of the project.

b.   The physical address of the project.

c.   The name of the contracting body.

d.   The name of the contractor.

e.   The name, phone number, and mailing address of an agent authorized by the contractor to accept service of the requests for payment bond, the notice of public subcontract, and the notice of claim on payment bond referenced in subsection (b) of this section.

f. The name and address of the principal place of business of the surety issuing the payment bond required by G.S. 44A-26(a) for the construction contract.

(2) Each subcontractor shall provide each subcontractor that it engages to perform labor or furnish materials in the performance of the construction contract a copy of the contractor's project statement.

(3) No agreement entered into between a contractor and a subcontractor or between a subcontractor and its subcontractor shall be enforceable against the lower tier party until the contractor's project statement has been provided to the lower tier party. (1973, c. 1194, s. 1; 1987, c. 569; 2001-177, s. 1; 2001-487, s. 100; 2012-175, s. 11; 2013-16, s. 6.)

§ 44A-28. Actions on payment bonds; venue and limitations.

(a) Every action on a payment bond as provided in G.S. 44A-27 shall be brought in a court of appropriate jurisdiction in a county where the construction contract or any part thereof is to be or has been performed.

(b) No action on a payment bond shall be commenced after the expiration of the longer period of one year from the day on which the last of the labor was performed or material was furnished by the claimant, or one year from the day on which final settlement was made with the contractor. (1973, c. 1194, s. 1.)

§ 44A-29. Limitation of liability of a surety.

No surety shall be liable under a payment bond for a total amount greater than the face amount of the payment bond. A judgment against any surety may be reduced or set aside upon motion by the surety and a showing that the total amount of claims paid and judgments previously rendered under such payment bond, together with the amount of the judgment to be reduced or set aside, exceeds the face amount of the bond. (1973, c. 1194, s. 1.)

§ 44A-30. Variance of liability; contents of bond.

(a)   No act of or agreement between a contracting body, a contractor or a surety shall reduce the period of time for giving notice under G.S. 44A-27(b) or commencing action under G.S. 44A-28(b) or otherwise reduce or limit the liability of the contractor or surety as prescribed in this Article.

(b)   Every bond given by a contractor to a contracting body pursuant to this Article shall be conclusively presumed to have been given in accordance herewith, whether or not such bond be so drawn as to conform to this Article. This Article shall be conclusively presumed to have been written into every bond given pursuant thereto. (1973, c. 1194, s. 1.)

§ 44A-31. Certified copy of bond and contract.

(a)   Any person entitled to bring an action or any defendant in an action on a payment bond shall have a right to require the contracting body to certify and furnish a copy of the payment bond and of the construction contract covered by the bond. It shall be the duty of such contracting body to give any such person a certified copy of the payment bond and the construction contract upon not less than 10 days' notice and request. The contracting body may require a reasonable payment for the actual cost of furnishing the certified copy.

(b)   A copy of any payment bond and of the construction contract covered by the bond certified by the contracting body shall constitute prima facie evidence of the contents, execution and delivery of such bond and construction contract. (1973, c. 1194, s. 1.)

§ 44A-32. Designation of official; violation a misdemeanor.

Each contracting body shall designate an official thereof to require the bonds described by this Article. If the official so designated shall fail to require said bond, he shall be guilty of a Class 1 misdemeanor. (1973, c. 1194, s. 1; 1993, c. 539, s. 407; 1994, Ex. Sess., c. 24, s. 14(c).)

§ 44A-33. Form.

(a)   A performance bond form containing the following provisions shall comply with this Article: the date the bond is executed; the name of the principal; the name of the surety; the name of the contracting body; the amount of the bond; the contract number; and the following conditions:

"KNOW ALL MEN BY THESE PRESENTS, That we, the PRINCIPAL AND SURETY above named, are held and firmly bound unto the above named Contracting Body, hereinafter called the Contracting Body, in the penal sum of the amount stated above for the payment of which sum well and truly to be made, we bind ourselves, our heirs, executors, administrators, and successors, jointly and severally, firmly by these presents.

"THE CONDITION OF THIS OBLIGATION IS SUCH, that whereas the Principal entered into a certain contract with the Contracting Body, numbered as shown above and hereto attached:

"NOW THEREFORE, if the Principal shall well and truly perform and fulfill all the undertakings, covenants, terms, conditions, and agreements of said contract during the original term of said contract and any extensions thereof that may be granted by the Contracting Body, with or without notice to the Surety, and during the life of any guaranty required under the contract, and shall also well and truly perform and fulfill all the undertakings, covenants, terms, conditions, and agreements of any and all duly authorized modifications of said contract that may hereafter be made, notice of which modifications to the Surety being hereby waived, then, this obligation to be void; otherwise to remain in full force and virtue.

"IN WITNESS WHEREOF, the above-bounden parties have executed this instrument under their several seals on the date indicated above, the name and corporate seal of each corporate party being hereto affixed and these presents duly signed by its undersigned representative, pursuant to authority of its governing body."

Appropriate places for execution by the surety and principal shall be provided.

(b)   A payment bond form containing the following provisions shall comply with this Article: the date the bond is executed; the name of the principal; the name of the surety; the name of the contracting body; the contract number; and the following conditions:

"KNOW ALL MEN BY THESE PRESENTS, That we, the PRINCIPAL and SURETY above named, are held and firmly bound unto the above named Contracting Body, hereinafter called the Contracting Body, in the penal sum of the amount stated above, for the payment of which sum well and truly to be made, we bind ourselves, our heirs, executors, administrators, and successors, jointly and severally, firmly by these presents.

"THE CONDITION OF THIS OBLIGATION IS SUCH, that whereas the Principal entered into a certain contract with the Contracting Body, numbered as shown above and hereto attached;

"NOW THEREFORE, if the Principal shall promptly make payment to all persons supplying labor and material in the prosecution of the work provided for in said contract, and any and all duly authorized modifications of said contract that may hereafter be made, notice of which modifications to the Surety being hereby waived, then this obligation to be void; otherwise to remain in full force and virtue.

"IN WITNESS WHEREOF, the above-bounden parties have executed this instrument under their several seals on the date indicated above, the name and corporate seal of each corporate party being hereto affixed and these presents duly signed by its undersigned representative, pursuant to authority of its governing body."

Appropriate places for execution by the surety and principal shall be provided. (1973, c. 1194, s. 1.)

§ 44A-34. Construction of Article.

The addition of this Article shall not be construed as making the provisions of Articles 1 and 2 of Chapter 44A of the General Statutes apply to public bodies or public buildings. (1973, c. 1194, s. 3.)

§ 44A-35. Attorneys' fees.

In any suit brought or defended under the provisions of Article 2 or Article 3 of this Chapter, the presiding judge may allow a reasonable attorneys' fee to the attorney representing the prevailing party. This attorneys' fee is to be taxed as part of the court costs and be payable by the losing party upon a finding that there was an unreasonable refusal by the losing party to fully resolve the matter which constituted the basis of the suit or the basis of the defense. For purposes of this section, "prevailing party" is a party plaintiff or third party plaintiff who obtains a judgment of at least fifty percent (50%) of the monetary amount sought in a claim or is a party defendant or third party defendant against whom a claim is asserted which results in a judgment of less than fifty percent (50%) of the amount sought in the claim defended. Notwithstanding the foregoing, in the event an offer of judgment is served in accordance with G.S. 1A-1, Rule 68, a "prevailing party" is an offeree who obtains judgment in an amount more favorable than the last offer or is an offeror against whom judgment is rendered in an amount less favorable than the last offer. (1991 (Reg. Sess., 1992), c. 1010, s. 3; 1993 (Reg. Sess., 1994), c. 763, s. 1.)

§§ 44A-36 through 44A-39. Reserved for future codification purposes.

Article 4.

Self-Service Storage Facilities.

§ 44A-40. Definitions.

As used in this Article, unless the context clearly requires otherwise:

(1) "E-mail" or "electronic mail" means an electronic message or an executable program or computer file that contains an image of a message that is transmitted between two or more computers or electronic terminals. The term includes electronic messages that are transmitted within or between computer networks.

(1a) "Independent bidder" means a person who is not related to the lienor, within the meaning of G.S. 25-9-102(62), in the case of a lienor who is an individual, or G.S. 25-9-102(63), in the case of a lienor that is an organization.

(1b) "Last known address" means that mailing address or e-mail address provided by the occupant in the latest rental agreement or the address provided by the occupant in a subsequent written notice of a change of address.

(2) "Lienor" means any person entitled to a lien under this Article.

(3) "Occupant" means a person, his sublessee, successor, or assign, entitled to the use of the storage space at a self-service storage facility under a rental agreement, to the exclusion of others.

(4) "Owner" means the owner, operator, lessor, or sublessor of a self-service storage facility, his agent, or any other person authorized by him to manage the facility or to receive rent from an occupant under a rental agreement.

(5) "Personal property" means movable property not affixed to land and includes, but is not limited to, goods, merchandise, household items, and watercraft.

(6) "Rental agreement" means any agreement or lease, written or oral, that establishes or modifies the terms, conditions, rules or any other provisions concerning the use and occupancy of a self-service storage facility.

(7) "Self-service storage facility" means any real property designed and used for the purpose of renting or leasing individual storage space to occupants who are to have access to such for the purpose of storing and removing personal property. No occupant shall use a self-service storage facility for residential purposes. A self-service storage facility is not subject to the provisions of Article 7 of General Statutes Chapter 25. Provided, however, if an owner issues any warehouse receipt, bill of lading, or other document of title for the personal property stored, the owner and the occupant are subject to the provisions of Article 7 of General Statutes Chapter 25 and the provisions of this Article do not apply.

(8) "Verified electronic mail" means electronic mail that is transmitted to an e-mail address that the sender has verified by any reasonable means as being a

working electronic mail address. (1981 (Reg. Sess., 1982), c. 1275, s. 1; 2013-239, s. 1.)

§ 44A-41. Self-service storage facility owner entitled to lien.

The owner of a self-service storage facility has a lien upon all personal property stored at the facility for rent, expenses necessary for the preservation of the personal property, and expenses reasonably incurred in the sale or other disposition of the personal property pursuant to this Article. This lien shall not have priority over any security interest which is perfected at the time the occupant stores the property at the self-service storage facility. For purposes of this Article, to identify an existing security interest in stored property, the owner shall conduct an online search for Uniform Commercial Code financing statements filed with the Office of the Secretary of State in the name of the occupant. (1981 (Reg. Sess., 1982), c. 1275, s. 1; 2009-201, s. 1.)

§ 44A-42. When self-service storage facility lien arises and terminates.

The lien conferred under this Article arises only when the owner acquires possession of the property stored in the self-service storage facility; and it shall terminate when the owner relinquishes possession of the property upon which the lien might be claimed, or when the occupant or any other person having a security or other interest in the property tenders prior to sale the amount of the rent, plus the expenses incurred by the owner for the preservation of the property. The reacquisition of possession of the property stored in the self-service storage facility, which was relinquished, shall not reinstate the lien. (1981 (Reg. Sess., 1982), c. 1275, s. 1.)

§ 44A-43. Enforcement of self-service storage facility lien.

(a) If the rent and other charges for which the lien is claimed under this Article remain unpaid or unsatisfied for 15 days following the maturity of the obligation to pay rent, the owner may enforce the lien by a public sale or other disposition of the property as provided in this section. The owner may bring an action to collect rent and other charges in any court of competent jurisdiction at any time following the maturity of the obligation to pay the rent.

The occupant or any other person having a security or other interest in the property stored in the self-service storage facility may bring an action to request the immediate possession of the property, at any time following the assertion of the lien by the owner. Before such possession is granted, the occupant or the person with a security or other interest in the property shall pay the amount of the lien asserted to the clerk of court in which the action is pending, or post a bond for double the amount. The clerk shall then issue an order to the owner to relinquish possession of the property to the occupant or other party.

(b)   Notice and Hearing:

(1)   If the property upon which the lien is claimed is a motor vehicle, the lienor, following the expiration of the 15-day period provided by subsection (a), shall give notice to the Division of Motor Vehicles that a lien is asserted and that a sale is proposed. The lienor shall remit to the Division a fee of two dollars ($2.00); and shall also furnish the Division with the last known address of the occupant. The Division of Motor Vehicles shall issue notice by certified mail, return receipt requested to the person having legal title to the vehicle, if reasonably ascertainable, and to the occupant, if different, at his last known address. The notice shall:

a.   State: (i) that a lien is being asserted against the specific vehicle by the lienor or owner of the self-service storage facility, (ii) that the lien is being asserted for rental charges at the self-service storage facility, (iii) the amount of the lien, and (iv) that the lienor intends to sell or otherwise dispose of the vehicle in satisfaction of the lien;

b.   Inform the person having legal title and the occupant of their right to a judicial hearing at which a determination will be made as to the validity of the lien prior to a sale taking place; and

c.   State that the legal title holder and the occupant have a period of 10 days from the date of receipt of the notice in which to notify the Division of Motor Vehicles by certified mail, return receipt requested, that a hearing is desired to contest the sale of the vehicle pursuant to the lien.

The person with legal title or the occupant must, within 10 days of receipt of the notice from the Division of Motor Vehicles, notify the Division of his desire to contest the sale of the vehicle pursuant to the lien, and that the Division should so notify lienor.

Failure of the person with legal title or the occupant to notify the Division that a hearing is desired shall be deemed a waiver of the right to a hearing prior to sale of the vehicle against which the lien is asserted. Upon such failure, the Division shall so notify the lienor; the lienor may proceed to enforce the lien by a public sale as provided by this section; and the Division shall transfer title to the property pursuant to such sale.

If the Division is notified within the 10-day period provided in this section that a hearing is desired prior to the sale, the lien may be enforced by a public sale as provided in this section and the Division will transfer title only pursuant to the order of a court of competent jurisdiction.

(1a) If the property upon which the lien is claimed is a motor vehicle, watercraft, or trailer, and rent and other charges related to the property remain unpaid or unsatisfied for 60 days following the maturity of the obligation to pay rent, the lienor may have the property towed. If a motor vehicle is towed as authorized in this subdivision, the lienor shall not be liable for the motor vehicle or any damages to the motor vehicle once the tower takes possession of the property.

(2) If the property upon which the lien is claimed is other than a motor vehicle, watercraft, or trailer, the lienor following the expiration of the 15-day period provided by subsection (a) shall issue notice to the person having a security or other interest in the property, if reasonably ascertainable, and to the occupant, if different, at his last known address. Notice given pursuant to this subdivision shall be presumed delivered when it is properly addressed, first-class postage prepaid, and deposited with the United States Postal Service, or when it is sent by verified electronic mail to the occupant's last known address, if the occupant has made an election in the rental agreement to receive notice by electronic mail.

The notice shall:

a. State: (i) that a lien is being asserted against the specific property by the lienor, (ii) that the lien is being asserted for rental charges at the self-service storage facility, (iii) the amount of the lien, and (iv) that the lienor intends to sell or otherwise dispose of the property in satisfaction of the lien;

b. Provide a brief and general description of the personal property subject to the lien. The description shall be reasonably adequate to permit the person notified to identify it, except that any container including, but not limited to, a trunk, valise, or box that is locked, fastened, sealed, or tied in a manner which deters immediate access to its contents may be described as such without describing its contents;

c. Inform the person with a security or other interest in the property and occupant, if different, of their right to a judicial hearing at which a determination will be made as to the validity of the lien prior to a sale taking place;

d. State that the person with a security or other interest in the property or the occupant, if different, has a period of 10 days from the date of the mailing of the notice to notify the lienor by registered, or certified mail, return receipt requested, that a hearing is desired, and that if the legal title holder or occupant wishes to contest the sale of his property pursuant to the lien he should notify the lienor that a hearing is desired.

The person with a security or other interest in the property or the occupant must, within 10 days from the date of the mailing of the notice from the lienor, notify the lienor of his desire for a hearing, and state whether or not he wishes to contest the sale of the property pursuant to the lien.

Failure of the person with a security or other interest in the property, or the occupant to notify the lienor that a hearing is desired shall be deemed a waiver of the right to a hearing prior to the sale of the property against which the lien is asserted. Upon such failure the lienor may proceed to enforce the lien by a public sale as provided by this section. Upon the expiration of the 10-day notice, the occupant's tenancy shall be terminated, and the lienor may move the occupant's property to another place of safekeeping.

If the lienor is notified, within the 10-day period as provided by this section, that a hearing is desired prior to the sale, the lien may be enforced by a public sale as provided in this section only pursuant to the order of a court of competent jurisdiction.

(c) Public Sale. -

(1) Not less than 20 days prior to sale by public sale the lienor:

a. Shall cause notice to be delivered by certified mail to the person having a security interest in the property if reasonably ascertainable, and to the occupant at the occupant's last known address by certified mail or by verified electronic mail if the occupant has made an election in the rental agreement to receive notice by electronic mail. Notice given by certified mail pursuant to this subdivision shall be presumed delivered when it is properly addressed, first-class postage prepaid, and deposited with the United States Postal Service. Notice given by verified electronic mail pursuant to this subdivision shall be presumed delivered when it is transmitted.

b. Repealed by Session Laws 2009-201, s. 1, effective October 1, 2009.

(1a) Not less than five days prior to sale by public sale, the lienor shall publish notice of sale either (i) in a newspaper of general circulation in the county where the sale is to be held or (ii) in any other commercially reasonable manner. The manner of advertisement shall be deemed commercially reasonable if at least three independent bidders attend the sale at the time and place advertised and the sale is otherwise consistent with the definition set out in G.S. 25-9-627.

(2) Repealed by Session Laws 2013-239, s. 2, effective October 1, 2013.

(2a) The sale shall be conducted in a commercially reasonable manner, as defined in G.S. 25-9-627, including offering property to an audience of bidders through an online, publicly accessible auction Web site. If the sale is a live auction conducted at the facility, the nearest suitable place where the property is held or stored, or in the county where the obligation secured by the lien was contracted for, the sale must be held on a day other than Sunday and between the hours of 9:00 A.M. and 4:00 P.M. A lienor may purchase at public sale.

(3) Repealed by Session Laws 2013-239, s. 2, effective October 1, 2013.

(d) Repealed by Session Laws 2013-239, s. 2, effective October 1, 2013. (1981 (Reg. Sess., 1982), c. 1275, s. 1; 2006-264, s. 38.5; 2009-201, s. 1; 2012-175, s. 12(c); 2013-239, s. 2.)

§ 44A-44. Right of redemption; good faith purchaser's right; disposition of proceeds; lienor's liability.

(a) Before the sale authorized by G.S. 44A-43, or other disposition of the property, the occupant may pay the amount necessary to satisfy the lien plus the reasonable expenses incurred by the owner for the preservation of the property and thereby redeem the property. Upon receipt of such payment, the owner shall return the personal property to the occupant; and thereafter shall have no further claim against such personal property on account of the lien which was asserted. The partial payment of rent or other charges shall not satisfy the lien or stop or delay the owner's right to sell the occupant's property unless the owner agrees to satisfaction or a stop or delay in a writing signed by the owner.

(b) A purchaser in good faith, and without knowledge of any defect in the sale of the personal property sold to satisfy a lien provided for in this Article takes the property free of any rights of persons against whom the lien was valid.

(c) Proceeds of a sale under this section shall be applied as follows:

(1) Payment of reasonable expenses incurred in connection with the sale;

(2) Payment of the obligation secured by any security interest that was perfected at the time the occupant stored the property at the self-service storage facility;

(3) Payment of the obligation secured by the self-service storage facility lien;

(4) Any balance shall be paid to the occupant or other person lawfully entitled thereto; but if such person cannot be found, the balance shall be paid to the clerk of superior court of the county in which the sale took place, to be held by the clerk for the person entitled thereto.

(d) If the lienor fails to comply substantially with any of the provisions of this section, he shall be liable to the occupant or any other party injured by such noncompliance in the sum of one hundred dollars ($100.00), together with reasonable attorney's fees as awarded by the court. Damages provided by this section shall be in addition to actual damages to which any party is otherwise entitled. (1981 (Reg. Sess., 1982), c. 1275, s. 1; 2009-201, s. 1.)

§ 44A-44.1. Possession vested in occupant.

Unless the rental agreement specifically provides otherwise, the exclusive care, custody, and control of all personal property stored in a storage space at a self-service storage facility shall remain vested in the occupant until the property is sold as provided in this Article or otherwise disposed of. The owner of a self-service storage facility is a commercial landlord who rents space. Unless the rental agreement specifically provides otherwise, while the personal property remains on the owner's premises, the owner is liable for damage caused by the intentional acts or negligence of the owner or the owner's employees. (2009-201, s. 1.)

§ 44A-45. Article is supplemental to lien created by contract.

Nothing in this Article shall be construed as in any manner impairing or affecting the right of parties to create liens by contract or agreement. (1981 (Reg. Sess., 1982), c. 1275, s. 1.)

§ 44A-46. Application.

All rental agreements entered into before September 1, 1982, and not extended or renewed after that date, and the rights and duties and interests flowing from them, shall remain valid, and may be enforced or terminated in accordance with their terms or as permitted by any other law of this State. (1981 (Reg. Sess., 1982), c. 1275, s. 1.)

§ 44A-47: Reserved for future codification purposes.

§ 44A-48: Reserved for future codification purposes.

§ 44A-49: Reserved for future codification purposes.

Article 5.

Aircraft Labor and Storage Liens.

§ 44A-50. Definitions.

As used in this Article, the following terms mean:

(1) Aircraft. - As the term is defined in G.S. 63-1(3), or any engine, part, component, or accessory, whether affixed to or separate from the aircraft.

(2) Lienor. - A person entitled to a lien under this Article.

(3) Owner. - As the term is defined in G.S. 44A-1(3) for an aircraft, or any person authorized by an owner, as defined in G.S. 44A-1(3), to perform, contract, or arrange for the provision of labor, skill, materials, or storage with respect to any aircraft.

(4) Person. - Any individual, corporation, association, partnership, whether limited or general, limited liability company, or other entity. (2006-222, s. 1.1.)

§ 44A-55. Persons entitled to a lien on an aircraft.

Any person who has expended labor, skill, or materials on an aircraft or has furnished storage for an aircraft at the request of its owner has a perfected lien on the aircraft beginning on the date the expenditure of labor, skill, or materials or the storage commenced, for the contract price for the expenditure of labor, skill, or materials or for the storage, or, in the absence of a contract price, for the reasonable worth of the expenditure of labor, skill, or materials, or of the storage. The lien under this section survives even if the possession of the aircraft is surrendered by the lienor. (2006-222, s. 1.1.)

§ 44A-60. Notice of lien on an aircraft.

(a) The lien under G.S. 44A-55 expires 120 days after the date the lienor voluntarily surrenders possession of the aircraft, unless the lienor, prior to the expiration of the 120-day period, files a notice of lien in the office of the clerk of court of the county in which the labor, skill, or materials were expended on the aircraft, or the storage was furnished for the aircraft.

(b) The notice of lien shall state all of the following:

(1) The name of the lienor.

(2) The name of the registered owner of the aircraft, if known.

(3) The name of the person with whom the lienor entered into a contract for labor, skill, or materials on the aircraft, or storage of the aircraft.

(4) A description of the aircraft sufficient for identification.

(5) The amount for which the lien is claimed.

(6) The dates upon which the expenditure of labor, skill, materials, or storage was commenced and completed, or, if not completed, the date through which the claimed amount is calculated.

(c) The notice of lien shall be sworn to or affirmed, and subscribed by the lienor, or by someone on the lienor's behalf having personal knowledge of the facts.

(d) The notice of lien shall be in substantially the following form:

"NOTICE OF LIEN ON AIRCRAFT

[Lienor] Lienor, v. [Owner] Owner

Notice is hereby given that [Lienor](name) claims a lien upon _____ [aircraft](describe the aircraft) for labor, skill, or materials expended on, and for storage furnished for, this aircraft; that the name of the registered owner or reputed owner, if the aircraft is not registered or the registered owner is not known, is [Owner](name), that the labor, skill, or materials were expended on the aircraft commencing the ____ day of _____, and storage was furnished on the aircraft commencing the ____ day of _____, and the labor, skill, materials, and storage furnished by the lienor [was completed] [is ongoing] on the ____ day of _____; that 120 days have not elapsed since the aircraft was released by the lienor; that the amount the lienor demands for the labor, skill, materials, and storage furnished, as of the date hereof is $_____ (amount); that no part thereof has been paid except $_____ (amount); and that there is now due and remaining unpaid, after deducting all credits and offsets, the sum of $_____ (amount), in which amount [Lienor](name) claims a lien upon the aircraft.

(Signed) _____ (Lienor)

Address of Lienor _____

State of North Carolina

County of _____

Sworn to (or affirmed) and subscribed before me this day by [name of principal].

Date:_____ [Official Signature of Notary]

_____ [Notary's printed or typed name], Notary Public

_____ My Commission Expires:[Date]

[Official Seal]" (2006-222, s. 1.1.)

§ 44A-65. Notice of lien filed by the clerk of court.

Upon presentation of a notice of lien pursuant to this Article, the clerk of court shall file the notice of lien and shall index the notice of lien in a record maintained by the clerk for that purpose. (2006-222, s. 1.1.)

§ 44A-70. Priority of a lien on an aircraft.

The lien under this Article shall have priority over perfected and unperfected security interests. (2006-222, s. 1.1.)

§ 44A-75. Termination of a lien on an aircraft.

(a) Termination by Payment of Amount Owed. - Any lien under this Article shall be terminated upon receipt by the lienor of the full amount owed for the labor, skill, or materials on the aircraft, and for storage of the aircraft, which amount shall not be limited to any amount shown on the notice of lien filed under G.S. 44A-60, if a notice of lien has been filed by the lienor. Upon receipt of the amount owed, the lienor or the lienor's agent shall release the aircraft to the owner, if the aircraft is in the possession of the lienor, and shall, within 20 days following a request in writing by the aircraft owner, file with the clerk of court a notice of satisfaction of lien, if a notice of lien has been filed by the lienor. A notice of satisfaction of lien shall state that the amount owed for the lienor's expenditure of labor, skill, or materials on the aircraft, and for the storage of the aircraft, has been paid and the lien against the aircraft has been terminated. The notice of satisfaction of lien shall be sworn to or affirmed, and subscribed by the lienor or by someone on the lienor's behalf having personal knowledge of the facts. Upon the filing of a notice of satisfaction of lien, the clerk of court shall make an entry of acknowledgment of satisfaction in the index.

(b) Termination by Deposit of Surety Bond. - Any lien under this Article shall be terminated by the clerk of court whenever a surety bond in a sum equal to one and one-fourth times the amount of the lien claimed against the aircraft and conditioned upon the payment of the amount finally determined to be due in satisfaction of the lien is deposited with the clerk of court. When a deposit that satisfies this subsection is made, the lienor or the lienor's agent shall release the aircraft to the owner, if the aircraft is in the possession of the lienor. (2006-222, s. 1.1; 2013-17, s. 1.)

§ 44A-80. Fees.

The clerk of court shall collect fees for filing, copying, and certifying any document under this Article as set forth in G.S. 7A-308. (2006-222, s. 1.1.)

§ 44A-85. Enforcement of lien by sale.

A lien filed under this Article may be enforced in accordance with G.S. 44A-4, and the proceeds of sale shall be applied as set forth in G.S. 44A-5, except that the three-day time period set forth in G.S. 44A-4(a) for the lienor to file a contrary statement of the amount of the lien at the time of the filing of a complaint by the owner shall be extended to 30 days. An owner may seek immediate possession of an aircraft in accordance with G.S. 44A-4. (2006-222, s. 1.1.)

§ 44A-90. Title of purchaser.

(a)   A purchaser for value at a properly conducted sale under this Article, and a purchaser for value without constructive notice of a defect in the sale, whether or not the purchaser is the lienor or an agent of the lienor, acquires title to the property free of any interests over which the lienor was entitled to priority.

(b)   Upon the completion of a sale conducted under this Article, the lienor or a person acting on behalf of the lienor, who conducted the sale shall furnish to the purchaser for value a bill of sale for the aircraft signed by the person who conducted the sale that includes a statement that the sale was conducted in accordance with this Article. (2006-222, s. 1.1.)

Chapter 45.

Mortgages and Deeds of Trust.

Article 1.

Chattel Securities.

§§ 45-1 through 45-3.1: Repealed by Sessions Laws 1967, c. 562, s. 2.

Article 2.

Right to Foreclose or Sell under Power.

§ 45-4. Representative succeeds on death of mortgagee or trustee in deeds of trust; parties to action.

When the mortgagee in a mortgage, or the trustee in a deed in trust, executed for the purpose of securing a debt, containing a power of sale, dies before the payment of the debt secured in such mortgage or deed in trust, all the title, rights, powers and duties of such mortgagee or trustee pass to and devolve upon the executor or administrator or collector of such mortgagee or trustee, including the right to bring an action of foreclosure in any of the courts of this State as prescribed for trustees or mortgagees, and in such action it is unnecessary to make the heirs at law of such deceased mortgagee or trustee parties thereto. (1887, c. 147; 1895, c. 431; 1901, c. 186; 1905, c. 425; Rev., s. 1031; C.S., s. 2578; 1933, c. 199.)

§ 45-5. Foreclosures by representatives validated.

In all actions which were brought or prosecuted prior to the fourth day of March, 1905, for the foreclosure of any mortgage or deed in trust by any executor or administrator of any deceased mortgagee or trustee where the heirs of the mortgagee were duly made parties and regular and orderly decrees of foreclosure entered by the court and sale had by a commissioner appointed by the court for that purpose and deed made after confirmation, the title so conveyed to purchaser at such judicial sale shall be deemed and held to be vested in such purchaser, whether the heir of such deceased mortgagee or trustee was a party to such foreclosure proceeding or not, and such heir of any deceased mortgagee is estopped to bring or prosecute any further action against such purchaser for the recovery of such property or foreclosure of such mortgage or deed in trust. (1905, c. 425, s. 2; Rev., s. 1032; C.S., s. 2579.)

§ 45-6. Renunciation by representative; clerk appoints trustee.

The executor or administrator of any deceased mortgagee or trustee in any mortgage or deed of trust heretofore or hereafter executed may renounce in writing, before the clerk of the superior court before whom he qualifies, the trust under the mortgage or deed of trust at the time he qualifies as executor or administrator, or at any time thereafter before he intermeddles with or exercises any of the duties under said mortgage or deed of trust, except to preserve the property until a trustee can be appointed. In every such case of renunciation the clerk of the superior court of any county wherein the said mortgage or deed of trust is registered has power and authority, upon proper proceedings instituted before him, as in other cases of special proceedings, to appoint some person to act as trustee and execute said mortgage or deed of trust. The clerk, in addition to recording his proceedings in his book of orders and decrees, shall record a separate instrument, as required by G.S. 161-14.1, containing the name of the substituted trustee or mortgagee, with the register of deeds of said county. (1905, c. 128; Rev., s. 1038; C.S., s. 2580; 1991, c. 114, s. 5; 2011-246, s. 1.)

§ 45-7. Agent to sell under power may be appointed by parol.

All sales of real property, under a power of sale contained in any mortgage or deed of trust to secure the payment of money, by any mortgagee or trustee, through an agent or attorney for that purpose, appointed orally or in writing by such mortgagee or trustee, whether such writing has been or shall be registered or not, shall be valid, whether or not such mortgagee or trustee was or shall be present at such sale. (1895, c. 117; Rev., s. 1035; C.S., s. 2581; 1967, c. 562, s. 2.)

§ 45-8. Survivorship among donees of power of sale.

In all mortgages and deeds of trust of real property wherein two or more persons, as trustees or otherwise, are given power to sell the property therein conveyed or embraced, and one or more of such persons dies, any one of the persons surviving having such power may make sale of such property in the manner directed in such deed, and execute such assurances of title as are proper and lawful under the power so given; and the act of such person, in pursuance of said power, shall be as valid and binding as if the same had been done by all the persons on whom the power was conferred. (1885, c. 327, s. 2; Rev., s. 1033; C.S., s. 2582; 1967, c. 562, s. 2.)

§ 45-9. Clerk appoints successor to incompetent trustee.

When the sole or last surviving trustee named in a will or deed of trust dies, removes from the county where the will was probated or deed executed and/or recorded and from the State, or in any way becomes incompetent to execute the said trust, or is a nonresident of this State, or has disappeared from the community of his residence and his whereabouts remains unknown in such community for a period of three months and cannot, after diligent inquiry be ascertained, the clerk of the superior court of the county wherein the will was probated or deed of trust was executed and/or recorded is authorized and empowered, in proceedings to which all persons interested shall be made parties, to appoint some discreet and competent person to act as trustee and execute the trust according to its true intent and meaning, and as fully as if originally appointed: Provided, that in all actions or proceedings had under this section prior to January 1, 1900, before the clerks of the superior court in which any trustee was appointed to execute a deed of trust where any trustee of a deed of trust has died, removed from the county where the deed was executed and from the State, or in any way become incompetent to execute the said trust, whether such appointment of such trustee by order or decree, or otherwise, was made upon the application or petition of any person or persons ex parte, or whether made in proceedings where all the proper parties were made, are in all things confirmed and made valid so far as regards the parties to said actions and proceedings to the same extent as if all proper parties had originally been made in such actions or proceedings. (1869-70, c. 188; 1873-4, c. 126; Code, s. 1276; 1901, c. 576; Rev., s. 1037; C.S., s. 2583; 1933, c. 493.)

§ 45-10. Substitution of trustees in mortgages and deeds of trust.

(a) In addition to the rights and remedies now provided by law, the holders or owners of a majority in amount of the indebtedness, notes, bonds, or other instruments evidencing a promise or promises to pay money and secured by mortgages, deeds of trust, or other instruments conveying real property, or creating a lien thereon, may, in their discretion, substitute a trustee whether the trustee then named in the instrument is the original or a substituted trustee or a holder or owner of any or all of the obligations secured thereby, by the execution of a written document properly recorded pursuant to Chapter 47 of the North Carolina General Statutes.

(b)   If the name of a trustee is omitted from an instrument that appears on its face to be intended to be a deed of trust, the instrument shall be deemed to be a deed of trust, the owner or owners executing the deed of trust and granting an interest in the real property shall be deemed to be the constructive trustee or trustees of record for the secured party or parties named in the instrument, and a substitution of trustee may be undertaken under subsection (a) of this section. However, no such constructive trustee shall have the authority or power to take any of the following actions without the consent and joinder of the holders or owners of a majority in amount of the obligations secured by the deed of trust: (i) effect a substitution of trustee, (ii) effect the satisfaction of the deed of trust, (iii) release any property or any interest therein from the lien of the deed of trust, or (iv) modify or amend the terms of the deed of trust. Any substitute trustee named under the authority of subsection (a) of this section shall succeed to all the rights, titles, authority, and duties of the trustee under the terms of the deed of trust without regard to the limitations imposed by this subsection on the authority of a constructive trustee.

(c)   If the trustee named in a deed of trust is also the beneficiary named in that deed of trust, the instrument shall be deemed to be a deed of trust, and any substitute trustee named under the authority of subsection (a) of this section shall succeed to all the rights, titles, authority, and duties of the trustee under the terms of the deed of trust. (1931, c. 78, ss. 1, 2; 1935, c. 227; 1943, c. 543; 1967, c. 562, s. 2; 1975, c. 66; 1985, c. 320; c. 689, s. 14; 2009-176, s. 1; 2011-312, s. 2.)

§ 45-11. Appointment of substitute trustee upon application of subsequent or prior lienholders; effect of substitution.

When any person, firm, corporation, county, city or town holding a lien on real property upon which there is a subsequent or prior lien created by a mortgage, deed of trust or other instrument, the mortgagee or trustee therein named being dead or having otherwise become incompetent to act, files a written application with the clerk of the superior court of the county in which said property is located, setting forth the facts showing that said mortgagee or trustee is then dead or has become incompetent to act, the said clerk of the superior court, upon a proper finding of fact that said mortgagee or trustee is dead or has become incompetent to act, shall enter an order appointing some suitable and competent person, firm or corporation as substitute trustee upon whom service of process may be made, and said substitute trustee shall thereupon be vested with full power and authority to defend any action instituted to foreclose said property as fully as if he had been the original mortgagee or trustee named; but the substitute trustee shall have no power to cancel said mortgage or deed of trust without the joinder of the holder of the notes secured thereby. Said application shall not be made prior to the expiration of 30 days from the date the original mortgagee or trustee becomes incompetent to act. (1941, c. 115, s. 1; 1967, c. 562, s. 2.)

§ 45-12. Repealed by Session Laws 1973, c. 1208.

§ 45-13. Repealed by Session Laws 1981, c. 599, s. 12.

§ 45-14. Acts of trustee prior to removal not invalidated.

If any such trustee who has been substituted as provided in G.S. 45-10 or in G.S. 45-11 shall have performed any functions as such trustee and shall thereafter be removed as provided in G.S. 45-10 to 45-17, such removal shall not invalidate or affect the validity of such acts insofar as any purchaser or third person shall be affected or interested, and any conveyances made by such trustee before removal if otherwise valid, shall be and remain valid and effectual to all intents and purposes, but if any trustee upon such hearing is declared to have been wrongfully removed, he shall have his right of action against the substituted trustee for any compensation that he would have received in case he had not been wrongfully removed from such trust. (1931, c. 78, s. 5; 1941, c. 115, s. 3.)

§ 45-15. Registration of substitution constructive notice.

The registration of such paper-writing designating a new trustee under G.S. 45-10 or under G.S. 45-11 shall be from and after registration, constructive notice to all persons, and no appeal or other proceedings shall be instituted to contest the same after one year from and after such registration. (1931, c. 78, s. 6; 1941, c. 115, s. 4.)

§ 45-16: Repealed by Session Laws 2012-18, s. 1.2, effective July 1, 2012.

§ 45-17. Substitution made as often as justifiable.

The powers set out in G.S. 45-10 and in G.S. 45-11 may be exercised as often and as many times as the right to make such substitution may arise under the terms of such section, and all the privileges and requirements and rights to contest the same as set out in G.S. 45-10 to 45-17 shall apply to each deed of trust or mortgage and to each substitution. (1931, c. 78, s. 8; 1941, c. 115, s. 5.)

§ 45-18. Validation of certain acts of substituted trustees.

Whenever before January 1, 1979, a trustee has been substituted in a deed of trust in the manner provided by G.S. 45-10 to 45-17, but the instrument executed by the holder and/or owners of all or a majority in amount of the indebtedness, notes, bonds, or other instruments secured by said deed of trust, has not been registered as provided by said sections until after the substitute trustee has exercised some or all of the powers conferred by said deed of trust upon the trustee therein, including the advertising of the property conveyed by said deed of trust for sale, the sale thereof, and the execution of a deed by such substituted trustee to the purchaser at such sale, all such acts of said substituted trustee shall be deemed valid and effective in the same manner and to the same extent as if said instrument substituting said trustee, had been registered prior to the performance by said substituted trustee of any one or more of said acts, or other acts authorized by such deed of trust. (1939, c. 13; 1963, c. 241; 1967, c. 945; 1969, c. 477; 1971, c. 57; 1973, c. 20; 1979, c. 580.)

§ 45-19. Mortgage to guardian; powers pass to succeeding guardian.

When a guardian to whom a mortgage has been executed dies or is removed or resigns before the payment of the debt secured in such mortgage, all the rights, powers and duties of such mortgagee shall devolve upon the succeeding guardian. (1905, c. 433; Rev., s. 1034; C.S., s. 2584.)

§ 45-20. Sales by mortgagees and trustees confirmed.

All sales of real property made prior to February 10, 1905, by mortgagees and trustees under powers of sale contained in any mortgage or deed of trust in compliance with the powers, terms, conditions and advertisement set forth and required in any such mortgage or deed of trust, are hereby in all respects ratified and confirmed. (Ex. Sess. 1920, c. 27; C.S., s. 2584(a).)

§ 45-20.1. Validation of trustees' deeds where seals omitted.

All deeds executed prior to January 1, 1991, by any trustee or substitute trustee in the exercise of the power of sale vested in him under any deed, deed of trust, mortgage, will, or other instrument in which the trustee or substitute trustee has omitted to affix his seal after his signature are validated. (1943, c. 71; 1981, c. 183, s. 1; 1983, c. 398, s. 1; 1985, c. 70, s. 1; 1987, c. 277, s. 1; 1989, c. 390, s. 1; 1991, c. 489, s. 1.)

§ 45-20.2. Repealed by Session Laws 1981, c. 183, s. 2.

§ 45-20.3. Validation of deeds where seal omitted on power of attorney.

All deeds and other conveyances executed prior to January 1, 1991, by any attorney-in-fact in the exercise of a power of attorney are valid even though the signature of the principal was not affixed under seal on the instrument creating the power of attorney. (1991, c. 489, s. 1.1.)

§ 45-21. Validation of appointment of and conveyances to corporations as trustees.

In all deeds of trust made prior to March 15, 1941, wherein property has been conveyed to corporations as trustees to secure indebtedness, the appointment of said corporations as trustees, the conveyances to said corporate trustees, and the action taken under the powers of such deeds of trust by said corporate trustees are hereby confirmed and validated to the same extent as if such corporate trustees had been individual trustees. (1941, c. 245, s. 1.)

Article 2A.

Sales under Power of Sale.

Part 1. General Provisions.

§ 45-21.1. Definitions; construction.

(a) The following definitions apply in this Article:

(1) "Resale" means a resale of real property or a resale of any leasehold interest created by a lease of real property held pursuant to G.S. 45-21.30.

(2) "Sale" means a sale of real property or a sale of any leasehold interest created by a lease of real property pursuant to (i) an express power of sale contained in a mortgage, deed of trust, leasehold mortgage, or leasehold deed of trust or (ii) a "power of sale", under this Article, authorized by other statutory provisions.

(b) The following constructions apply in this Article:

(1) The terms "mortgage" or "deed of trust" include leasehold mortgages or leasehold deeds of trust.

(2) The terms "mortgagee" or "trustee" include any person or entity exercising a power of sale pursuant to this Article.

(3) The terms "real property" or "property" include any leasehold interest created by a lease of real property. (1949, c. 720, s. 1; 1967, c. 562, s. 2; 1991, c. 255; 1993, c. 305, s. 1.)

§ 45-21.2. Article not applicable to foreclosure by court action.

This Article does not affect any right to foreclosure by action in court, and is not applicable to any such action. (1949, c. 720, s. 1.)

§ 45-21.3. Repealed by Session Laws 1993, c. 305, s. 2.

§ 45-21.4. Place of sale of real property.

(a) Every sale of real property shall be held in the county where the property is situated unless the property consists of a single tract situated in two or more counties.

(b) A sale of a single tract of real property situated in two or more counties may be held in any one of the counties in which any part of the tract is situated. As used in this section, a "single tract" means any tract which has a continuous boundary, regardless of whether parts thereof may have been acquired at different times or from different persons, or whether it may have been subdivided into other units or lots, or whether it is sold as a whole or in parts.

(c) When a mortgage or deed of trust with power of sale of real property designates the place of sale within the county, the sale shall be held at the place so designated.

(d) When a mortgage or deed of trust with power of sale of real property confers upon the mortgagee or trustee the right to designate the place of sale, the sale shall be held at the place designated by the notice of sale, which place shall be either on the premises to be sold or as follows:

(1) Property situated wholly within a single county shall be sold at the courthouse door of the county in which the land is situated.

(2) A single tract of property situated in two or more counties may be sold at the courthouse door of any one of the counties in which some part of the real property is situated.

(e) When a mortgage or deed of trust with power of sale of real property does not designate, or confer upon the mortgagee or trustee the right to designate, the place of sale, or when it designates as the place of sale some county in which no part of the property is situated, such real property shall be sold as follows:

(1) Property situated wholly within a single county shall be sold at the courthouse door of the county in which the land is situated.

(2) A single tract of property situated in two or more counties may be sold at the courthouse door of any one of the counties in which some part of the real property is situated. (1949, c. 720, s. 1; 1975, c. 57, s. 1.)

§§ 45-21.5 through 45-21.6. Repealed by Session Laws 1967, c. 562, s. 2.

§ 45-21.7. Sale of separate tracts in different counties.

(a) When the property to be sold consists of separate tracts of real property situated in different counties, there shall be a separate advertisement, sale and report of sale of the property in each county. The report of sale for the property in any one county shall be filed with the clerk of the superior court of the county in which such property is situated. The sale of each such tract shall be subject to separate upset bids. The clerk of the superior court of the county where the property is situated has jurisdiction with respect to upset bids of property situated within his county. To the extent the clerk deems necessary, the sale of each separate tract within his county, with respect to which an upset bid is received, shall be treated as a separate sale for the purpose of determining the procedure applicable thereto.

(b) The exercise of the power of sale with respect to a separate tract of property in one county does not extinguish or otherwise affect the right to exercise the power of sale with respect to tracts of property in another county to satisfy the obligation secured by the mortgage or deed of trust. (1949, c. 720, s. 1; 1993, c. 305, s. 3.)

§ 45-21.8. Sale as a whole or in parts.

(a) When the instrument pursuant to which a sale is to be held contains provisions with respect to whether the property therein described is to be sold as a whole or in parts, the terms of the instrument shall be complied with.

(b) When the instrument contains no provisions with respect to whether the property therein described is to be sold as a whole or in parts, the person exercising the power of sale may, in his discretion, subject to the provisions of G.S. 45-21.9, sell the property as a whole or in such parts or parcels thereof as are separately described in the instrument, or he may offer the property for sale by each method and sell the property by the method which produces the highest price.

(b1) When real property is sold in parts, the sale of any such part is subject to a separate upset bid; and, to the extent the clerk of superior court having jurisdiction deems advisable, the sale of each such part shall thereafter be treated as a separate sale for the purpose of determining the procedure applicable thereto.

(c) This section does not affect the equitable principle of marshaling assets. (1949, c. 720, s. 1; 1993, c. 305, s. 4.)

§ 45-21.9. Amount to be sold when property sold in parts; sale of remainder if necessary.

(a) When a person exercising a power of sale sells property in parts pursuant to G.S. 45-21.8 he shall sell as many of such separately described units and parcels as in his judgment seems necessary to satisfy the obligation secured by the instrument pursuant to which the sale is being made, and the costs and expenses of the sale.

(b) If the proceeds of a sale of only a part of the property are insufficient to satisfy the obligation secured by the instrument pursuant to which the sale is made and the costs and expenses of the sale, the person authorized to exercise the power of sale may readvertise the unsold property and may sell as many additional units or parcels thereof as in his judgment seems necessary to satisfy the remainder of the secured obligation and the costs and expenses of the sale. As to any such sale, it shall not be necessary to comply with the provisions of G.S. 45-21.16 but the requirements of G.S. 45-21.17 relating to notices of sale shall be complied with.

(c) When the entire obligation has been satisfied by a sale of only a part of the property with respect to which a power of sale exists, the lien on the part of the property not so sold is discharged.

(d) The fact that more property is sold than is necessary to satisfy the obligation secured by the instrument pursuant to which the power of sale is exercised does not affect the validity of the title of any purchaser of property at any such sale. (1949, c. 720, s. 1; 1975, c. 492, s. 15.)

§ 45-21.9A. Simultaneous foreclosure of two or more instruments.

When two or more mortgages or deeds of trust held by the same person are secured in whole or in part by the same property, and there are no intervening liens, except for ad valorem taxes, between such mortgages or deeds of trust, the obligations secured by such mortgages or deeds of trust may be combined and the property sold once to satisfy the combined obligations if (i) powers of sale are provided in all such instruments; (ii) there is no provision in any such instrument which would not permit such a procedure; (iii) all the terms of all such instruments requiring compliance by the lender in connection with foreclosure sales are complied with; and (iv) all requirements of this Chapter governing power of sale foreclosures are met with respect to all such instruments. The proceeds of any sale shall be applied as provided in this Chapter. As between the combined obligations being foreclosed, proceeds shall be applied in the order of priority of the instruments securing them, and any deficiencies shall be determined accordingly. (1985, c. 515, s. 1; 1993, c. 305, s. 5.)

§ 45-21.10. Requirement of cash deposit at sale.

(a) If a mortgage or deed of trust contains provisions with respect to a cash deposit at the sale, the terms of the instrument shall be complied with.

(b) If the instrument contains no provision with respect to a cash deposit at the sale, the mortgagee or trustee may require the highest bidder immediately to make a cash deposit not to exceed the greater of five percent (5%) of the amount of the bid or seven hundred fifty dollars ($750.00).

(c) If the highest bidder fails to make the required deposit, the person holding the sale may at the same time and place immediately reoffer the property for sale. (1949, c. 720, s. 1; 1993, c. 305, s. 6.)

§ 45-21.11. Application of statute of limitations to serial notes.

When a series of notes maturing at different times is secured by a mortgage or deed of trust and the exercise of the power of sale for the satisfaction of one or more of the notes is barred by the statute of limitations, that fact does not bar the exercise of the power of sale for the satisfaction of indebtedness represented by other notes of the series not so barred. (1949, c. 720, s. 1; 1967, c. 562, s. 2.)

§ 45-21.12. Power of sale barred when foreclosure barred.

(a) Except as provided in subsection (b), no person shall exercise any power of sale contained in any mortgage or deed of trust, or provided by statute, when an action to foreclose the mortgage or deed of trust, is barred by the statute of limitations.

(b) If a sale pursuant to a power of sale contained in a mortgage or deed of trust, or provided by statute, is commenced within the time allowed by the statute of limitations to foreclose such mortgage or deed of trust, the sale may be completed although such completion is effected after the time when commencement of an action to foreclose would be barred by the statute. For the purpose of this section, a sale is commenced when the notice of hearing or the notice of sale is first filed, given, served, posted, or published, whichever occurs first, as provided by this Article or by the terms of the instrument pursuant to which the power of sale is being exercised. (1949, c. 720, s. 1; 1967, c. 562, s. 2; 1969, c. 984, s. 1; 1977, c. 359, s. 1.)

§ 45-21.12A. Power of sale barred during periods of military service.

(a) Power of Sale Barred. - A mortgagee, trustee, or other creditor shall not exercise a power of sale contained in a mortgage or deed of trust, or provided by statute, during, or within 90 days after, a mortgagor's, trustor's, or debtor's period of military service. The clerk of court shall not conduct a hearing pursuant to G.S. 45-21.16(d) unless the mortgagee, trustee or other creditor seeking to exercise a power of sale under a mortgage or deed of trust, or provided by statute, files with the clerk a certification that the hearing will take place at a time that is not during, or within 90 days after, a period of military service for the mortgagor, trustor or debtor. This subsection applies only to mortgages and deeds of trust that originated before the mortgagor's or trustor's period of military service.

(b) Waiver. - This section shall not apply if the mortgagor, trustor, or debtor waives his or her rights under this section pursuant to a written agreement of the parties executed during or after the mortgagor's, trustor's, or debtor's period of military service, as an instrument separate from the obligation or liability to which the waiver applies. Any waiver in writing of a right or protection provided by this section must be in at least 12 point type and shall specify the legal instrument creating the obligation or liability to which the waiver applies.

(c) Purpose. - The purpose of this section is to supplement and complement the provisions of the Servicemembers Civil Relief Act, 50 U.S.C. App. § 501, et seq., and to afford greater peace and security for persons in federal active duty.

(d) Definitions. - The following definitions apply in this section:

(1) Military service. -

a. In the case of a member of the United States Army, Navy, Air Force, Marine Corps, or Coast Guard:

1. Active duty, as defined in 10 U.S.C. § 101(d)(1), and

2. In the case of a member of the National Guard, includes service under a call to active service authorized by the President or the Secretary of Defense for a period of more than 30 consecutive days under 32 U.S.C. § 502(f), for purposes of responding to a national emergency declared by the President and supported by federal funds.

b. In the case of a servicemember who is a commissioned officer of the Public Health Service or the National Oceanic and Atmospheric Administration, active service, and

c. Any period during which a servicemember is absent from duty on account of sickness, wounds, leave, or other lawful cause.

(2) Period of military service. - The period beginning on the date on which a servicemember enters military service and ending on the date on which the servicemember is released from military service or dies while in military service.

(3) Servicemember. - A member of the United States Army, Navy, Air Force, Marine Corps, Coast Guard, the commissioned corps of the National Oceanic and Atmospheric Administration, or the commissioned corps of the Public Health Service. (2010-190, s. 1; 2011-183, s. 127(b).)

§ 45-21.13. Repealed by Session Laws 1967, c. 562, s. 2.

§ 45-21.14. Clerk's authority to compel report or accounting; contempt proceeding.

Whenever any person fails to file any report or account, as provided by this Article, or files an incorrect or incomplete report or account, the clerk of the superior court having jurisdiction on his own motion or the motion of any interested party, may issue an order directing such person to file a correct and complete report or account within 20 days after service of the order on him. If such person fails to comply with the order, the clerk may issue an attachment against him for contempt, and may commit him to jail until he files such correct and complete report or account. (1949, c. 720, s. 1.)

§ 45-21.15. Trustee's fees.

(a) When a sale has been held, the trustee is entitled to such compensation, if any, as is stipulated in the instrument.

(b) When no sale has actually been held, compensation for a trustee's services is determined as follows:

(1) If no compensation for the trustee's services in holding a sale is provided for in the instrument, the trustee is not entitled to any compensation;

(2) If compensation is specifically provided for the trustee's services when no sale is actually held, the trustee is entitled to such compensation;

(3) If the instrument provides for compensation for the trustee's services in actually holding a sale, but does not provide compensation for the trustee's services when no sale is actually held, the trustee is entitled to compensation as follows: (i) one-fourth of the completed sale compensation before the trustee files the notice of hearing; (ii) one-half after the filing of the notice of hearing; and (iii) three-fourths after the hearing.

(4) Repealed by Session Laws 1993, c. 305, s. 7. (1949, c. 720, s. 1; 1993, c. 305, s. 7.)

Part 2. Procedure for Sale.

§ 45-21.16. Notice and hearing.

(a) The mortgagee or trustee granted a power of sale under a mortgage or deed of trust who seeks to exercise such power of sale shall file with the clerk of court a notice of hearing in accordance with the terms of this section. After the notice of hearing is filed, the notice of hearing shall be served upon each party entitled to notice under this section. The notice shall specify a time and place for the hearing before the clerk of court and shall be served not less than 10 days prior to the date of such hearing. The notice shall be served and proof of service shall be made in any manner provided by the Rules of Civil Procedure for service of summons, including service by registered mail or certified mail, return receipt requested. However, in those instances that publication would be authorized, service may be made by posting a notice in a conspicuous place and manner upon the property not less than 20 days prior to the date of the hearing, and if service upon a party cannot be effected after a reasonable and diligent effort in a manner authorized above, notice to such party may be given by posting the notice in a conspicuous place and manner upon the property not less than 20 days prior to the date of hearing. Service by posting may run concurrently with any other effort to effect service. The notice shall be posted by the sheriff. In the event that the service is obtained by posting, an affidavit shall be filed with the clerk of court showing the circumstances warranting the use of service by posting.

If any party is not served or is not timely served prior to the date of the hearing, the clerk shall order the hearing continued to a date and time certain, not less than 10 days from the date scheduled for the original hearing. All notices already timely served remain effective. The mortgagee or trustee shall satisfy the notice requirement of this section with respect to those parties not served or not timely served with respect to the original hearing. Any party timely served, who has not received actual notice of the date to which the hearing has been continued, shall be sent the order of continuance by first-class mail at his last known address.

(b)   Notice of hearing shall be served in a manner authorized in subsection (a) upon:

(1)   Any person to whom the security interest instrument itself directs notice to be sent in case of default.

(2)   Any person obligated to repay the indebtedness against whom the holder thereof intends to assert liability therefor, and any such person not notified shall not be liable for any deficiency remaining after the sale.

(3)   Every record owner of the real estate whose interest is of record in the county where the real property is located at the time the notice of hearing is filed in that county. The term "record owner" means any person owning a present or future interest in the real property, which interest is of record at the time that the notice of hearing is filed and would be affected by the foreclosure proceeding, but does not mean or include the trustee in a deed of trust or the owner or holder of a mortgage, deed of trust, judgment, mechanic's or materialman's lien, or other lien or security interest in the real property. Tenants in possession under unrecorded leases or rental agreements shall not be considered record owners.

(c) Notice shall be in writing and shall state in a manner reasonably calculated to make the party entitled to notice aware of the following:

(1) The particular real estate security interest being foreclosed, with such a description as is necessary to identify the real property, including the date, original amount, original holder, and book and page of the security instrument.

(2) The name and address of the holder of the security instrument at the time that the notice of hearing is filed.

(3) The nature of the default claimed.

(4) The fact, if such be the case, that the secured creditor has accelerated the maturity of the debt.

(5) Any right of the debtor to pay the indebtedness or cure the default if such is permitted.

(5a) The holder has confirmed in writing to the person giving the notice, or if the holder is giving the notice, the holder shall confirm in the notice, that, within 30 days of the date of the notice, the debtor was sent by first-class mail at the debtor's last known address a detailed written statement of the amount of principal, interest, and any other fees, expenses, and disbursements that the holder in good faith is claiming to be due as of the date of the written statement, together with a daily interest charge based on the contract rate as of the date of the written statement. Nothing herein is intended to authorize any fees, charges, or methods of charging interest which is not otherwise permitted under contract between the parties and other applicable law.

(5b) To the knowledge of the holder, or the servicer acting on the holder's behalf, whether in the two years preceding the date of the statement any requests for information have been made by the borrower to the servicer pursuant to G.S. 45-93 and, if so, whether such requests have been complied with. If the time limits set forth in G.S. 45-93 for complying with any such requests for information have not yet expired as of the date of the notice, the notice shall so state. If the holder is not giving the notice, the holder shall confirm in writing to the person giving the notice the information required by this subsection to be stated in the notice.

(6) Repealed by Session Laws 1977, c. 359, s. 7.

(7) The right of the debtor (or other party served) to appear before the clerk of court at a time and on a date specified, at which appearance he shall be afforded the opportunity to show cause as to why the foreclosure should not be allowed to be held. The notice shall contain all of the following:

a. A statement that if the debtor does not intend to contest the creditor's allegations of default, the debtor does not have to appear at the hearing and that the debtor's failure to attend the hearing will not affect the debtor's right to pay the indebtedness and thereby prevent the proposed sale, or to attend the actual sale, should the debtor elect to do so.

b. A statement that the trustee, or substitute trustee, is a neutral party and, while holding that position in the foreclosure proceeding, may not advocate for the secured creditor or for the debtor in the foreclosure proceeding.

c. A statement that the debtor has the right to apply to a judge of the superior court pursuant to G.S. 45-21.34 to enjoin the sale, upon any legal or equitable ground that the court may deem sufficient prior to the time that the rights of the parties to the sale or resale become fixed, provided that the debtor complies with the requirements of G.S. 45-21.34.

d. A statement that the debtor has the right to appear at the hearing and contest the evidence that the clerk is to consider under G.S. 45-21.16(d), and that to authorize the foreclosure the clerk must find the existence of: (i) valid debt of which the party seeking to foreclose is the holder, (ii) default, (iii) right to foreclose under the instrument, and (iv) notice to those entitled to notice.

e. A statement that if the debtor fails to appear at the hearing, the trustee will ask the clerk for an order to sell the real property being foreclosed.

f. A statement that the debtor has the right to seek the advice of an attorney and that free legal services may be available to the debtor by contacting Legal Aid of North Carolina or other legal services organizations.

(8) That if the foreclosure sale is consummated, the purchaser will be entitled to possession of the real estate as of the date of delivery of his deed, and that the debtor, if still in possession, can then be evicted.

(8a) The name, address, and telephone number of the trustee or mortgagee.

(9)   That the debtor should keep the trustee or mortgagee notified in writing of his address so that he can be mailed copies of the notice of foreclosure setting forth the terms under which the sale will be held, and notice of any postponements or resales.

(10)   If the notice of hearing is intended to serve also as a notice of sale, such additional information as is set forth in G.S. 45-21.16A.

(11)   That the hearing may be held on a date later than that stated in the notice and that the party will be notified of any change in the hearing date.

(12)   That if the debtor is currently on military duty the foreclosure may be prohibited by G.S. 45-21.12A.

(c1)   The person giving the notice of hearing, if other than the holder, may rely on the written confirmation received from the holder under subdivisions (c)(5a) and (c)(5b) of this section and is not liable for inaccuracies in the written confirmation.

(c2)   In any foreclosure filed on or after November 1, 2010, where the underlying mortgage debt is a home loan as defined in G.S. 45-101(1b), the notice required by subsection (b) of this section shall contain a certification by the filing party that the pre-foreclosure notice and information required by G.S. 45-102 and G.S. 45-103 were provided in all material respects and that the periods of time established by Article 11 of this Chapter have elapsed.

(d)   The hearing provided by this section shall be held before the clerk of court in the county where the land, or any portion thereof, is situated. In the event that the property to be sold consists of separate tracts situated in different counties or a single tract in more than one county, only one hearing shall be necessary. However, prior to that hearing, the mortgagee or trustee shall file the notice of hearing in any other county where any portion of the property to be sold is located. Upon such hearing, the clerk shall consider the evidence of the parties and may consider, in addition to other forms of evidence required or permitted by law, affidavits and certified copies of documents. If the clerk finds the existence of (i) valid debt of which the party seeking to foreclose is the holder, (ii) default, (iii) right to foreclose under the instrument, (iv) notice to those entitled to such under subsection (b), (v) that the underlying mortgage debt is not a home loan as defined in G.S. 45-101(1b), or if the loan is a home loan under G.S. 45-101(1b), that the pre-foreclosure notice under G.S. 45-102 was provided in all material respects, and that the periods of time established by

Article 11 of this Chapter have elapsed, and (vi) that the sale is not barred by G.S. 45-21.12A, then the clerk shall authorize the mortgagee or trustee to proceed under the instrument, and the mortgagee or trustee can give notice of and conduct a sale pursuant to the provisions of this Article. A certified copy of any authorization or order by the clerk shall be filed in any other county where any portion of the property to be sold is located before the mortgagee or trustee may proceed to advertise and sell any property located in that county. In the event that sales are to be held in more than one county, the provisions of G.S. 45-21.7 apply.

(d1) The act of the clerk in so finding or refusing to so find is a judicial act and may be appealed to the judge of the district or superior court having jurisdiction at any time within 10 days after said act. Appeals from said act of the clerk shall be heard de novo. If an appeal is taken from the clerk's findings, the appealing party shall post a bond with sufficient surety as the clerk deems adequate to protect the opposing party from any probable loss by reason of appeal; and upon posting of the bond the clerk shall stay the foreclosure pending appeal. If the appealing party owns and occupies the property to be sold as his or her principal residence, the clerk shall require a bond in the amount of one percent (1%) of the principal balance due on the note or debt instrument, provided that the clerk, in the clerk's discretion, may require a lesser amount in cases of undue hardship or for other good cause shown; and further provided that the clerk, in the clerk's discretion, may require a higher bond if there is a likelihood of waste or damage to the property during the pendency of the appeal or for other good cause shown.

(e) In the event of an appeal, either party may demand that the matter be heard at the next succeeding term of the court to which the appeal is taken which convenes 10 or more days after the hearing before the clerk, and such hearing shall take precedence over the trial of other cases except cases of exceptions to homesteads and appeals in summary ejectment actions, provided the presiding judge may in his discretion postpone such hearing if the rights of the parties or the public in any other pending case require that such case be heard first. In those counties where no session of court is scheduled within 30 days from the date of hearing before the clerk, either party may petition any regular or special superior court judge resident in a district or assigned to hold courts in a district where any part of the real estate is located, or the chief district judge of a district where any part of the real estate is located, who shall be authorized to hear the appeal. A certified copy of any order entered as a result of the appeal shall be filed in all counties where the notice of hearing has been filed.

(f)   Waiver of the right to notice and hearing provided herein shall not be permitted except as set forth herein. In any case in which the original principal amount of indebtedness secured was one hundred thousand dollars ($100,000), or more, any person entitled to notice and hearing may waive after default the right to notice and hearing by written instrument signed and duly acknowledged by such party. In all other cases, at any time subsequent to service of the notice of hearing provided above, the clerk, upon the request of the mortgagee or trustee, shall mail to all other parties entitled to notice of such hearing a form by which such parties may waive their rights to the hearing. Upon the return of the forms to the clerk bearing the signatures of each such party and that of a witness to each such party's signature (which witness shall not be an agent or employee of the mortgagee or trustee), the clerk in his discretion may dispense with the necessity of a hearing and proceed to issue the order authorizing sale as set forth above.

(g)   Any notice, order, or other papers required by this Article to be filed in the office of the clerk of superior court shall be filed in the same manner as a special proceeding. (1975, c. 492, s. 2; 1977, c. 359, ss. 2-10; 1983, c. 335, s. 1; 1983 (Reg. Sess., 1984), c. 1108, ss. 1, 2; 1993, c. 305, s. 8; 1995, c. 509, s. 135.1(g); 1999-137, ss. 1, 2; 2007-351, s. 4; 2008-226, ss. 2, 3; 2009-573, s. 2; 2010-168, ss. 2, 3, 9; 2010-190, ss. 2, 3; 2012-79, s. 2.17(g).)

§ 45-21.16A. Contents of notice of sale.

(a)   Except as provided in subsection (b) of this section, the notice of sale shall include all of the following:

(1)   Describe the instrument pursuant to which the sale is held, by identifying the original mortgagors and recording data. If the record owner is different from the original mortgagors, the notice shall also list the record owner of the property, as reflected on the records of the register of deeds not more than 10 days prior to posting the notice. The notice may also reflect the owner not reflected on the records if known.

(2)   Designate the date, hour and place of sale consistent with the provisions of the instrument and this Article.

(3) Describe the real property to be sold in a manner that is reasonably calculated to inform the public as to what is being sold. The description may be in general terms and may incorporate by reference the description used in the instrument containing the power of sale. Any property described in the instrument containing the power of sale which is not being offered for sale should also be described in a manner to enable prospective purchasers to determine what is and what is not being offered for sale.

(4) Repealed by Session Laws 1967, c. 562, s. 2.

(5) State the terms of the sale provided for by the instrument pursuant to which the sale is held, including the amount of the cash deposit, if any, to be made by the highest bidder at the sale.

(6) Include any other provisions required by the instrument to be included.

(7) State that the property will be sold subject to taxes and special assessments if it is to be so sold.

(8) State whether the property is being sold subject to or together with any subordinate rights or interests provided those rights and interests are sufficiently identified.

(b) In addition to the requirements contained in subsection (a) of this section, the notice of sale of residential real property with less than 15 rental units shall also state all of the following:

(1) That an order for possession of the property may be issued pursuant to G.S. 45-21.29 in favor of the purchaser and against the party or parties in possession by the clerk of superior court of the county in which the property is sold.

(2) Any person who occupies the property pursuant to a rental agreement entered into or renewed on or after October 1, 2007, may, after receiving the notice of sale, terminate the rental agreement upon 10 days' written notice to the landlord. The notice shall also state that upon termination of a rental agreement, the tenant is liable for rent due under the rental agreement prorated to the effective date of the termination. (1949, c. 720, s. 1; 1951, c. 252, s. 1; 1967, c. 562, s. 2; 1975, c. 492, s. 1; 1987, c. 493; 1993, c. 305, s. 9; 2007-353, s. 1.)

§ 45-21.16B: Repealed by Session Laws 2013-412, s. 7, effective August 23, 2013.

§ 45-21.16C. Opportunity for parties to resolve foreclosure of owner-occupied residential property.

(a) At the commencement of the hearing, the clerk shall inquire as to whether the debtor occupies the real property at issue as his or her principal residence. If it appears that the debtor does currently occupy the property as a principal residence, the clerk shall further inquire as to the efforts the mortgagee, trustee, or loan servicer has made to communicate with the debtor and to attempt to resolve the matter voluntarily before the foreclosure proceeding. The clerk's inquiry shall not be required if the mortgagee or trustee has submitted, at or before the hearing, an affidavit briefly describing any efforts that have been made to resolve the default with the debtor and the results of any such efforts.

(b) The clerk shall order the hearing continued if the clerk finds that there is good cause to believe that additional time or additional measures have a reasonable likelihood of resolving the delinquency without foreclosure. In determining whether to continue the hearing, the clerk may consider (i) whether the mortgagee, trustee, or loan servicer has offered the debtor an opportunity to resolve the foreclosure through forbearance, loan modification, or other commonly accepted resolution plan appropriate under the circumstances, (ii) whether the mortgagee, trustee, or loan servicer has engaged in actual responsive communication with the debtor, including telephone conferences or in-person meetings with the debtor or other actual two-party communications, (iii) whether the debtor has indicated that he or she has the intent and ability to resolve the delinquency by making future payments under a foreclosure resolution plan, and (iv) whether the initiation or continuance of good faith voluntary resolution efforts between the parties may resolve the matter without a foreclosure sale. Where good cause exists to continue the hearing, the clerk shall order the hearing continued to a date and time certain not more than 60 days from the date scheduled for the original hearing. Nothing in this part shall limit the authority of the clerk to continue a hearing for other good cause shown. (2009-573, s. 3.)

§ 45-21.17. Posting and publishing notice of sale of real property.

In addition to complying with such provisions with respect to posting or publishing notice of sale as are contained in the security instrument,

(1) Notice of sale of real property shall

a. Be posted, in the area designated by the clerk of superior court for posting public notices in the county in which the property is situated, at least 20 days immediately preceding the sale.

b. And in addition thereto,

1. The notice shall be published once a week for at least two successive weeks in a newspaper published and qualified for legal advertising in the county in which the property is situated.

2. If no such newspaper is published in the county, then notice shall be published once a week for at least two successive weeks in a newspaper having a general circulation in the county.

3. In addition to the required newspaper advertisement, the clerk may in his discretion, on application of any interested party, authorize such additional advertisement as in the opinion of the clerk will serve the interest of the parties, and permit the charges for such further advertisement to be taxed as a part of the costs of the foreclosure.

(2) When the notice of sale is published in a newspaper,

a. The period from the date of the first publication to the date of the last publication, both dates inclusive, shall not be less than seven days, including Sundays, and

b. The date of the last publication shall be not more than 10 days preceding the date of the sale.

(3) When the real property to be sold is situated in more than one county, the provisions of subdivisions (1) and (2) shall be complied with in each county in which any part of the property is situated.

(4) The notice of sale shall be mailed by first-class mail at least 20 days prior to the date of sale to each party entitled to notice of the hearing provided by G.S. 45-21.16 whose address is known to the trustee or mortgagee and in addition shall also be mailed by first-class mail to any party desiring a copy of the notice of sale who has complied with G.S. 45-21.17A. If the property is residential and contains less than 15 rental units, the notice of sale shall also be mailed to any person who occupies the property pursuant to a residential rental agreement by name, if known, at the address of the property to be sold. If the name of the person who occupies the property is not known, the notice shall be sent to "occupant" at the address of the property to be sold. Notice of the hearing required by G.S. 45-21.16 shall be sufficient to satisfy the requirement of notice under this section provided such notice contains the information required by G.S. 45-21.16A.

(5) Repealed by Session Laws 1993, c. 305, s. 10.

(6) Any time periods relating to notice of hearing or notice of sale that are provided in the security instrument may commence with and run concurrently with the time periods provided in G.S. 45-21.16, 45-21.17, or 45-21.17A. (1949, c. 720, s. 1; 1965, c. 41; 1967, c. 979, s. 3; 1975, c. 492, s. 3; 1977, c. 359, ss. 11-14; 1985, c. 567, s. 1; 1993, c. 305, s. 10; 2007-353, s. 2.)

§ 45-21.17A. Requests for copies of notice.

(a) Any person desiring a copy of any notice of sale may, at any time subsequent to the recordation of the security instrument and prior to the filing of notice of hearing provided for in G.S. 45-21.16, cause to be filed for record in the office of the register of deeds of each county where all or any part of the real property is situated, a duly acknowledged request for a copy of such notice of sale. This request shall be a separate instrument entitled "Request for Notice" and shall be signed and acknowledged by the party making the request, shall specify the name and address of the party to whom the notice is to be mailed, shall identify the deed of trust or mortgage by stating the names of the parties thereto, the date of recordation, and the book and page where the same is recorded, and shall be in substantially the following form:

"REQUEST FOR NOTICE"

In accordance with the provisions of G.S. 45-21.17A, request is hereby made that a copy of any notice of sale under the deed of trust (mortgage) recorded on _____, _____, in Book ____, page ____, records of _____ County, North Carolina, executed by _____ as trustor (mortgagor), in which _____ is named as beneficiary (mortgagee), and _____ as trustee, be mailed to _____ at the following address: _____.

Signature:_____

[Acknowledgement]

(b)   Register of Deeds' Duties. - Upon the filing for record of such request, the register of deeds shall index in the general index of grantors the names of the trustors (mortgagors) recited therein, and the names of the persons requesting copies, with a reference in the index of the book and page of the recorded security instrument to which the request refers.

(c)   Mailing Notice. - The mortgagee, trustee, or other person authorized to conduct the sale shall at least 20 days prior to the date of the sale cause to be deposited in the United States mail an envelope with postage prepaid containing a copy of the notice of sale, addressed to each person whose name and address are set forth in the Request for Notice, and directed to the address designated in such request.

(d)   Effect of Request on Title. - No request for a copy of any notice filed pursuant to this section nor any statement or allegation in any such request nor any record thereof shall affect the title to real property, or be deemed notice to any person that the person requesting copies of notice has any claim or any right, title or interest in, or lien or charge upon, the property described in the deed of trust or mortgage referred to therein.

(e)   Evidence of Compliance. - The affidavit of the mortgagee, trustee, or other person authorized to conduct the sale that copies of the notice of sale have been mailed to all parties filing requests for the same hereunder shall be deemed prima facie true. If on hearing it is proven that a party seeking to have the foreclosure sale set aside or seeking damages resulting from the foreclosure sale was mailed notice in accordance with this section or had actual notice of the sale before it was held (or if a resale was involved, prior to the date of the last resale), then the party shall not prevail. Costs, expenses, and reasonable attorneys' fees incurred by the prevailing party in any action to set aside the foreclosure sale or for damages resulting from the foreclosure sale shall be allowed as of course to the prevailing party.

(f) Action to Set Foreclosure Sale Aside for Failure to Comply. - A person entitled to notice of sale by virtue of this section shall not bring any action to set the sale aside on grounds that he was not mailed the notice of sale unless such action is brought prior to the filing of the final report and account as provided in G.S. 45-21.33, if the property was purchased by someone other than the secured party; or if brought by the secured party, unless such action is brought within six months of the date of such filing and prior to the time the secured party sells the property to a bona fide purchaser for value, if the property was purchased by the secured party. In either event, the party bringing such an action shall also tender an amount exceeding the reported sale price or the amount of the secured party's interest in the property, including all expenses and accrued interest, whichever is greater. Such tender shall be irrevocable pending final adjudication of the action.

(g) Action for Damages from Foreclosure Sale for Failure to Comply. - A person entitled to notice of sale by virtue of this section shall not bring any action for damages resulting from the sale on grounds that he was not mailed the notice unless such action is brought within six months of the date of the filing of the final report and account as provided in G.S. 45-21.33. The party bringing such an action shall also deposit with the clerk a cash or surety bond approved by the clerk and in such amount as the clerk deems adequate to secure the party defending the action for such costs, expenses, and reasonable attorneys' fees to be incurred in the action. (1993, c. 305, s. 11; 1999-456, s. 59; 2011-246, s. 2; 2012-18, s. 1.3.)

§§ 45-21.18 through 45-21.19. Repealed by Session Laws 1967, c. 562, s. 2.

§ 45-21.20. Satisfaction of debt after publishing or posting notice, but before completion of sale.

A power of sale is terminated if, prior to the time fixed for a sale, or prior to the expiration of the time for submitting any upset bid after a sale or resale has been held, payment is made or tendered of -

(1) The obligation secured by the mortgage or deed of trust, and

(2) The expenses incurred with respect to the sale or proposed sale, which in the case of a deed of trust also include compensation for the trustee's services under the conditions set forth in G.S. 45-21.15. (1949, c. 720, s. 1; 1967, c. 562, s. 2.)

§ 45-21.21. Postponement of sale.

(a) Any person exercising a power of sale may postpone the sale to a day certain not later than 90 days, exclusive of Sunday, after the original date for the sale -

(1) When there are no bidders, or

(2) When, in his judgment, the number of prospective bidders at the sale is substantially decreased by inclement weather or by any casualty, or

(3) When there are so many other sales advertised to be held at the same time and place as to make it inexpedient and impracticable, in his judgment, to hold the sale on that day, or

(4) When he is unable to hold the sale because of illness or for other good reason, or

(5) When other good cause exists.

The person exercising a power of sale may postpone the sale more than once whenever any of the above conditions are met, so long as the sale is held not later than 90 days after the original date for the sale.

(b) Upon postponement of a sale, the person exercising the power of sale shall personally, or through his agent or attorney -

(1) At the time and place advertised for the sale, publicly announce the postponement thereof;

(2)   On the same day, attach to or enter on the original notice of sale or a copy thereof, posted at the courthouse door, as provided by G.S. 45-21.17, a notice of the postponement; and

(3)   Give written or oral notice of postponement to each party entitled to notice of sale under G.S. 45-21.17.

(c)   The posted notice of postponement shall -

(1)   State that the sale is postponed,

(2)   State the hour and date to which the sale is postponed,

(3)   State the reason for the postponement, and

(4)   Be signed by the person authorized to hold the sale, or by his agent or attorney.

(d)   If a sale is not held at the time fixed therefor and is not postponed as provided by this section, or if a postponed sale is not held at the time fixed therefor or within 90 days of the date originally fixed for the sale, then prior to such sale taking place the provisions of G.S. 45-21.16 need not be complied with but the provisions of G.S. 45-21.16A, 45-21.17, and 45-21.17A shall be again complied with, or if on appeal, the appellate court orders the sale to be held, as to such sale so authorized the provisions of G.S. 45-21.16 need not be complied with again but those of G.S. 45-21.16A, 45-21.17, and 45-21.17A shall be.

(e)   A sale may be postponed more than once provided the final postponed sale date is not later than 90 days, exclusive of Sunday and legal holidays when the courthouse is closed for transactions, after the original date for the sale. (1949, c. 720, s. 1; 1967, c. 562, s. 2; 1975, c. 492, ss. 4-6; 1983, c. 335, s. 2; 1989, c. 257; 1991 (Reg. Sess., 1992), c. 777, s. 1; 1993, c. 305, s. 12; 1995, c. 509, s. 25; 2003-337, s. 3.)

§ 45-21.22. Procedure upon dissolution of order restraining or enjoining sale, or upon debtor's bankruptcy before completion of sale.

(a) When, before the date fixed for a sale, a judge dissolves an order restraining or enjoining the sale, he may, if the required notice of sale has been given, provide by order that the sale shall be held without additional notice at the time and place originally fixed therefor, or he may, in his discretion, make an order with respect thereto as provided in subsection (b).

(b) When, after the date fixed for a sale, a judge dissolves an order restraining or enjoining the sale, he shall by order fix the time and place for the sale to be held upon notice to be given in such manner and for such length of time as he deems advisable.

(c) When, after the entry of any authorization or order by the clerk of superior court pursuant to G.S. 45-21.16 and before the expiration of the 10-day upset bid period, the foreclosure sale is stayed pursuant to 11 U.S.C. § 105 or 362, and thereafter the stay is lifted, terminated, or dissolved, the trustee or mortgagee shall not be required to comply with the provisions of G.S. 45-21.16, but shall advertise and hold the sale in accordance with the provisions of G.S. 45-21.16A, 45-21.17, and 45-21.17A.

(d) In the event that completion of the foreclosure sale is stayed pursuant to 11 U.S.C. § 105 or 362, before the expiration of the 10-day upset bid period:

(1) The clerk of superior court who received a deposit from an upset bidder shall release any deposits held on behalf of the upset bidder to the upset bidder upon receipt of a certified copy of an order or notice from the bankruptcy court indicating that the debtor has filed a bankruptcy petition; or

(2) The trustee or mortgagee who received a cash deposit from the high bidder at the foreclosure sale, upon notification of the bankruptcy stay, shall release any deposits held on behalf of the high bidder to the high bidder. (1949, c. 720, s. 1; 1993, c. 305, s. 13; 2011-204, s. 1.)

§ 45-21.23. Time of sale.

A sale shall begin at the time designated in the notice of sale or as soon thereafter as practicable, but not later than one hour after the time fixed therefor unless it is delayed by other sales held at the same place. The sale shall be held between the hours of 10:00 A.M. and 4:00 P.M. on any day other than

Sunday or a legal holiday when the courthouse is closed for transactions. (1949, c. 720, s. 1; 1993, c. 305, s. 14; 2003-337, s. 4.)

§ 45-21.24. Continuance of uncompleted sale.

A sale commenced but not completed within the time allowed by G.S. 45-21.23 shall be continued by the person holding the sale to a designated time between 10:00 o'clock A.M. and 4:00 o'clock P.M. the next following day, other than Sunday or a legal holiday when the courthouse is closed for transactions. In case such continuance becomes necessary, the person holding the sale shall publicly announce the time to which the sale is continued. (1949, c. 720, s. 1; 1993, c. 305, s. 15; 2003-337, s. 5.)

§ 45-21.25. Repealed by Session Laws 1967, c. 562, s. 2.

§ 45-21.26. Preliminary report of sale of real property.

(a) The person exercising a power of sale of real property, shall, within five days after the date of the sale, file a report thereof with the clerk of the superior court of the county in which the sale was had.

(b) The report shall be signed by the person authorized to hold the sale, or by his agent or attorney, and shall show -

(1) The authority under which the person making the sale acted;

(2) The name of the mortgagor or grantor;

(3) The name of the mortgagee or trustee;

(4) The date, time and place of the sale;

(5) A reference to the book and page in the office of the register of deeds, where the instrument is recorded or, if not recorded, a description of the

property sold, sufficient to identify it, and, if sold in parts, a description of each part so sold;

(6)　The name or names of the person or persons to whom the property was sold;

(7)　The price at which the property, or each part thereof, was sold, and that such price was the highest bid therefor;

(8)　The name of the person making the report; and

(9)　The date of the report. (1949, c. 720, s. 1; 1951, c. 252, s. 2.)

§ 45-21.27. Upset bid on real property; compliance bonds.

(a)　An upset bid is an advanced, increased, or raised bid whereby any person offers to purchase real property theretofore sold, for an amount exceeding the reported sale price or last upset bid by a minimum of five percent (5%) thereof, but in any event with a minimum increase of seven hundred fifty dollars ($750.00). Subject to the provisions of subsection (b) of this section, an upset bid shall be made by delivering to the clerk of superior court, with whom the report of sale or last notice of upset bid was filed, a deposit in cash or by certified check or cashier's check satisfactory to the clerk in an amount greater than or equal to five percent (5%) of the amount of the upset bid but in no event less than seven hundred fifty dollars ($750.00). The deposit required by this section shall be filed with the clerk of the superior court, with whom the report of the sale or the last notice of upset bid was filed by the close of normal business hours on the tenth day after the filing of the report of the sale or the last notice of upset bid, and if the tenth day shall fall upon a Sunday or legal holiday when the courthouse is closed for transactions, or upon a day in which the office of the clerk is not open for the regular dispatch of its business, the deposit may be made and the notice of upset bid filed on the day following when said office is open for the regular dispatch of its business. Subject to the provisions of G.S. 45-21.30, there shall be no resales; rather, there may be successive upset bids each of which shall be followed by a period of 10 days for a further upset bid. When an upset bid is not filed following a sale, resale, or prior upset bid within the time specified, the rights of the parties to the sale or resale become fixed.

(b)   The clerk of the superior court may require an upset bidder or the highest bidder at a resale held pursuant to G.S. 45-21.30 also to deposit with the clerk a cash bond, or, in lieu thereof at the option of the bidder, a surety bond, approved by the clerk. The compliance bond shall be in such amount as the clerk deems adequate, but in no case greater than the amount of the bid of the person being required to furnish the bond, less the amount of any required deposit. The compliance bond shall be payable to the State of North Carolina for the use of the parties in interest and shall be conditioned on the principal obligor's compliance with the bid.

(c),   (d) Repealed by Session Laws 1993, c. 305, s. 16.

(e)   At the same time that an upset bid on real property is submitted to the court as provided for in subsection (a) above, together with a compliance bond if one is required, the upset bidder shall simultaneously file with the clerk a notice of upset bid. The notice of upset bid shall:

(1)   State the name, address, and telephone number of the upset bidder;

(2)   Specify the amount of the upset bid;

(3)   Provide that the sale shall remain open for a period of 10 days after the date on which the notice of upset bid is filed for the filing of additional upset bids as permitted by law; and

(4)   Be signed by the upset bidder or the attorney or the agent of the upset bidder.

(e1)   When an upset bid is made as provided in this section, the clerk shall notify the trustee or mortgagee who shall thereafter mail a written notice of upset bid by first-class mail to the last known address of the last prior bidder and the current record owner(s) of the property.

(f)   When an upset bid is made as provided in this section, the last prior bidder, regardless of how the bid was made, shall be released from any further obligation on account of the bid and any deposit or bond provided by him shall be released.

(g)   Any person offering to purchase real property by upset bid as permitted in this Article shall be subject to and bound by the terms of the original notice of sale except as modified by court order or the provisions of this Article.

(h) The clerk of superior court shall make all such orders as may be just and necessary to safeguard the interests of all parties, and shall have the authority to fix and determine all necessary procedural details with respect to upset bids in all instances in which this Article fails to make definite provisions as to that procedure. (1949, c. 720, s. 1; 1963, c. 377; 1967, c. 979, s. 3; 1993, c. 305, s. 16; 2003-337, s. 6.)

§ 45-21.28: Repealed by Session Laws 1993, c. 305, s. 17.

§ 45-21.29. Orders for possession.

(a)-(j) Repealed by Session Laws 1993, c. 305, s. 18.

(k) Orders for possession of real property sold pursuant to this Article, in favor of the purchaser and against any party or parties in possession at the time of application therefor, may be issued by the clerk of the superior court of the county in which the property is sold if all of the following apply:

(1) The property has been sold in the exercise of the power of sale contained in any mortgage, deed of trust, leasehold mortgage, leasehold deed of trust, or a power of sale authorized by any other statutory provisions.

(2) Repealed by Session Laws 1993, c. 305, s. 18.

(2a) The provisions of this Article have been complied with.

(3) The sale has been consummated, and the purchase price has been paid.

(4) The purchaser has acquired title to and is entitled to possession of the real property sold.

(5) Ten days' notice has been given to the party or parties who remain in possession at the time application is made, or, in the case of residential property containing 15 or more rental units, 30 days' notice has been given to the party or parties who remain in possession at the time the application is made.

(6) Application is made by petition to the clerk by the mortgagee, the trustee, the purchaser of the property, or any authorized representative of the mortgagee, trustee, or purchaser of the property.

(l) An order for possession issued pursuant to G.S. 45-21.29(k) shall be directed to the sheriff and shall authorize the sheriff to remove all occupants and their personal property from the premises and to put the purchaser in possession, and shall be executed in accordance with the procedure for executing a writ or order for possession in a summary ejectment proceeding under G.S. 42-36.2. The purchaser shall have the same rights and remedies in connection with the execution of an order for possession and the disposition of personal property following execution as are provided to a landlord under North Carolina law, including Chapters 42 and 44A of the General Statutes.

(m) When the real property sold is situated in more than one county, the provisions of subsection (l) of this section shall be complied with in each county in which any part of the property is situated. (1949, c. 720, s. 1; 1951, c. 252, s. 3; 1965, c. 299; 1967, c. 979, s. 3; 1975, c. 492, ss. 7-9; 1987, c. 627, s. 3; 1993, c. 305, s. 18; 2007-353, s. 4.)

§ 45-21.29A. No necessity for confirmation of sale.

No confirmation of sales or resales of real property made pursuant to this Article shall be required. If an upset bid is not filed following a sale, resale, or prior upset bid within the period specified in this Article, the rights of the parties to the sale or resale become fixed. (1967, c. 979, s. 3; 1993, c. 305, s. 19.)

§ 45-21.30. Failure of bidder to make cash deposit or to comply with bid; resale.

(a) If the terms of a sale of real property require the highest bidder to make a cash deposit at the sale, and he fails to make such required deposit, the person holding the sale shall at the same time and place again offer the property for sale.

(b) Repealed by Session Laws 1967, c. 562, s. 2.

(c) When the highest bidder at a sale or resale or any upset bidder fails to comply with his bid upon tender to him of a deed for the real property or after a bona fide attempt to tender such a deed, the clerk of superior court may, upon motion, enter an order authorizing a resale of the real property. The procedure for such resale shall be the same in every respect as is provided by this Article in the case of an original sale of real property except that the provisions of G.S. 45-21.16 are not applicable to the resale.

(d) A defaulting bidder at any sale or resale or any defaulting upset bidder is liable on his bid, and in case a resale is had because of such default, he shall remain liable to the extent that the final sale price is less than his bid plus all the costs of the resale. Any deposit or compliance bond made by the defaulting bidder shall secure payment of the amount, if any, for which the defaulting bidder remains liable under this section.

(e) Nothing in this section deprives any person of any other remedy against the defaulting bidder. (1949, c. 720, s. 1; 1967, c. 562, s. 2; 1975, c. 492, s. 10; 1977, c. 359, s, 15; 1993, c. 305, s. 20.)

§ 45-21.31. Disposition of proceeds of sale; payment of surplus to clerk.

(a) The proceeds of any sale shall be applied by the person making the sale, in the following order, to the payment of -

(1) Costs and expenses of the sale, including the trustee's commission, if any, and a reasonable auctioneer's fee if such expense has been incurred, and reasonable counsel fees for an attorney serving as a trustee if allowed pursuant to subsection (a1) of this section;

(2) Taxes due and unpaid on the property sold, as provided by G.S. 105-385, unless the notice of sale provided that the property be sold subject to taxes thereon and the property was so sold;

(3) Special assessments, or any installments thereof, against the property sold, which are due and unpaid, as provided by G.S. 105-385, unless the notice of sale provided that the property be sold subject to special assessments thereon and the property was so sold;

(4)   The obligation secured by the mortgage, deed of trust or conditional sale contract.

(a1)   The clerk of the superior court of the county where the sale was had may exercise discretion to allow reasonable counsel fees to an attorney serving as a trustee (in addition to the compensation allowed to the attorney as a trustee) where the attorney, on behalf of the trustee, renders professional services as an attorney that are different from the services normally performed by a trustee and of a type which would reasonably justify the retention of legal counsel by a trustee who is not licensed to practice law. Counsel fees are presumed reasonable if in compliance with G.S. 6-21.2(1) and (2). Nothing in this section, however, shall preclude the clerk of superior court from deeming a higher fee reasonable.

(b)   Any surplus remaining after the application of the proceeds of the sale as set out in subsection (a) shall be paid to the person or persons entitled thereto, if the person who made the sale knows who is entitled thereto. Otherwise, the surplus shall be paid to the clerk of the superior court of the county where the sale was had -

(1)   In all cases when the owner of the property sold is dead and there is no qualified and acting personal representative of his estate, and

(2)   In all cases when he is unable to locate the persons entitled thereto, and

(3)   In all cases when the mortgagee, trustee or vendor is, for any cause, in doubt as to who is entitled to such surplus money, and

(4)   In all cases when adverse claims thereto are asserted.

(c)   Such payment to the clerk discharges the mortgagee, trustee or vendor from liability to the extent of the amount so paid.

(d)   The clerk shall receive such money from the mortgagee, trustee or vendor and shall execute a receipt therefor.

(e)   The clerk is liable on his official bond for the safekeeping of money so received until it is paid to the party or parties entitled thereto, or until it is paid out under the order of a court of competent jurisdiction. (1949, c. 720, s. 1; 1951, c. 252, s. 1; 1967, c. 562, s. 2; 1981, c. 682, s. 10; 2013-104, s. 1.)

§ 45-21.32. Special proceeding to determine ownership of surplus.

(a)   A special proceeding may be instituted before the clerk of the superior court by any person claiming any money, or part thereof, paid into the clerk's office under G.S. 45-21.31, to determine who is entitled thereto.

(b)   All other persons who have filed with the clerk notice of their claim to the money or any part thereof, or who, as far as the petitioner or petitioners know, assert any claim to the money or any part thereof, shall be made defendants in the proceeding.

(c)   If any answer is filed raising issues of fact as to the ownership of the money, the proceeding shall be transferred to the civil issue docket of the superior court for trial. When a proceeding is so transferred, the clerk may require any party to the proceeding who asserts a claim to the fund by petition or answer to furnish a bond for costs in the amount of two hundred dollars ($200.00) or otherwise comply with the provisions of G.S. 1-109.

(d)   The court may, in its discretion, allow a reasonable attorney's fee for any attorney appearing in behalf of the party or parties who prevail, to be paid out of the funds in controversy, and shall tax all costs against the losing party or parties who asserted a claim to the fund by petition or answer. (1949, c. 720, s. 1.)

§ 45-21.33. Final report of sale of real property.

(a)   A person who holds a sale of real property pursuant to a power of sale shall file with the clerk of the superior court of the county where the sale is held a final report and account of his receipts and disbursements within 30 days after the receipt of the proceeds of such sale. Such report shall show whether the property was sold as a whole or in parts and whether all of the property was sold. The report shall also show whether all or only a part of the obligation was satisfied with respect to which the power of sale of property was exercised.

(b)   The clerk shall audit the account and record it.

(c)   The person who holds the sale shall also file with the clerk -

(1)   A copy of the notices of sale and resale, if any, which were posted, and

(2)   A copy of the notices of sale and resale, if any, which were published in a newspaper, together with an affidavit of publication thereof, if the notices were so published;

(3)   Proof as required by the clerk, which may be by affidavit, that notices of hearing, sale and resale were served upon all parties entitled thereto under G.S. 45-21.16, 45-21.17, 45-21.17A, and 45-21.30. In the absence of an affidavit to the contrary filed with the clerk, an affidavit by the person holding the sale that the notice of sale was posted in the area designated by the clerk of superior court for posting public notices in the county or counties in which the property is situated 20 days prior to the sale shall be proof of compliance with the requirements of G.S. 45-21.17(1)a.

(d)   The clerk's fee for auditing and recording the final account is a part of the expenses of the sale, and the person holding the sale shall pay the clerk's fee as part of such expenses. (1949, c. 720, s. 1; 1975, c. 492, s. 11; 1983, c. 799; 1993, c. 305, s. 21; 1995, c. 509, s. 26.)

Article 2B.

Injunctions; Deficiency Judgments.

§ 45-21.34. Enjoining mortgage sales on equitable grounds.

Any owner of real estate, or other person, firm or corporation having a legal or equitable interest therein, may apply to a judge of the superior court, prior to the time that the rights of the parties to the sale or resale becoming fixed pursuant to G.S. 45-21.29A to enjoin such sale, upon the ground that the amount bid or price offered therefor is inadequate and inequitable and will result in irreparable damage to the owner or other interested person, or upon any other legal or equitable ground which the court may deem sufficient: Provided, that the court or judge enjoining such sale, whether by a temporary restraining order or injunction to the hearing, shall, as a condition precedent, require of the plaintiff or applicant such bond or deposit as may be necessary to indemnify and save harmless the mortgagee, trustee, cestui que trust, or other person enjoined and affected thereby against costs, depreciation, interest and other damages, if any, which may result from the granting of such order or injunction: Provided further, that in other respects the procedure shall be as is now prescribed by law in cases of injunction and receivership, with the right of appeal to the appellate division from any such order or injunction. (1933, c. 275, s. 1; 1949, c. 720, s. 3; 1969, c. 44, s. 50; 1993, c. 305, s. 22.)

§ 45-21.35. Ordering resales; receivers for property; tax payments.

The court or judge granting such order or injunction, or before whom the same is returnable, shall have the right before, but not after, the rights of the parties to the sale or resale becoming fixed pursuant to G.S. 45-21.29A to order a resale by the mortgagee, trustee, commissioner, or other person authorized to make the same in such manner and upon such terms as may be just and equitable: Provided, the rights of all parties in interest, or who may be affected thereby, shall be preserved and protected by bond or indemnity in such form and amount as the court may require, and the court or judge may also appoint a receiver of the property or the rents and proceeds thereof, pending any sale or resale, and may make such order for the payment of taxes or other prior lien as may be necessary, subject to the right of appeal to the appellate division in all cases. (1933, c. 275, s. 2; 1949, c. 720, s. 3; 1969, c. 44, s. 51; 1993, c. 305, s. 23.)

§ 45-21.36. Right of mortgagor to prove in deficiency suits reasonable value of property by way of defense.

When any sale of real estate has been made by a mortgagee, trustee, or other person authorized to make the same, at which the mortgagee, payee or other holder of the obligation thereby secured becomes the purchaser and takes title either directly or indirectly, and thereafter such mortgagee, payee or other holder of the secured obligation, as aforesaid, shall sue for and undertake to recover a deficiency judgment against the mortgagor, trustor or other maker of any such obligation whose property has been so purchased, it shall be competent and lawful for the defendant against whom such deficiency judgment is sought to allege and show as matter of defense and offset, but not by way of counterclaim, that the property sold was fairly worth the amount of the debt secured by it at the time and place of sale or that the amount bid was substantially less than its true value, and, upon such showing, to defeat or offset any deficiency judgment against him, either in whole or in part: Provided, this section shall not affect nor apply to the rights of other purchasers or of innocent third parties, nor shall it be held to affect or defeat the negotiability of any note, bond or other obligation secured by such mortgage, deed of trust or other instrument: Provided, further, this section shall not apply to foreclosure sales made pursuant to an order or decree of court nor to any judgment sought or rendered in any foreclosure suit nor to any sale made and confirmed prior to April 18, 1933. (1933, c. 275, s. 3; 1949, c. 720, s. 3; 1967, c. 562, s. 2.)

§ 45-21.37. Certain sections not applicable to tax suits.

Sections 45-21.34 through 45-21.36 do not apply to tax foreclosure suits or tax sales. (1933, c. 275, s. 4; 1949, c. 720, s. 3.)

§ 45-21.38. Deficiency judgments abolished where mortgage represents part of purchase price.

In all sales of real property by mortgagees and/or trustees under powers of sale contained in any mortgage or deed of trust executed after February 6, 1933, or where judgment or decree is given for the foreclosure of any mortgage executed after February 6, 1933, to secure to the seller the payment of the balance of the purchase price of real property, the mortgagee or trustee or holder of the notes secured by such mortgage or deed of trust shall not be entitled to a deficiency judgment on account of such mortgage, deed of trust or obligation secured by the same: Provided, said evidence of indebtedness shows upon the face that it is for balance of purchase money for real estate: Provided, further, that when said note or notes are prepared under the direction and supervision of the seller or sellers, he, it, or they shall cause a provision to be inserted in said note disclosing that it is for purchase money of real estate; in default of which the seller or sellers shall be liable to purchaser for any loss which he might sustain by reason of the failure to insert said provisions as herein set out. (1933, c. 36; 1949, c. 720, s. 3; c. 856; 1961, c. 604; 1967, c. 562, s. 2.)

§ 45-21.38A. Deficiency judgments abolished where mortgage secured by primary residence.

(a) As used in this section, the term "nontraditional mortgage loan" means a loan in which all of the following apply:

(1) The borrower is a natural person.

(2) The debt is incurred by the borrower primarily for personal, family, or household purposes.

(3) The principal amount of the loan does not exceed the conforming loan size for a single family dwelling as established from time to time by Fannie Mae.

(4) The loan is secured by: (i) a security interest in a manufactured home, as defined in G.S. 143-145, in the State that is or will be occupied by the borrower as the borrower's principal dwelling; (ii) a mortgage or deed of trust on real property in the State upon which there is located an existing structure designed principally for occupancy of from one to four families that is or will be occupied by the borrower as the borrower's principal dwelling; or (iii) a mortgage or deed of trust on real property in the State upon which there is to be constructed using the loan proceeds a structure or structures designed principally for occupancy of from one to four families that, when completed, will be occupied by the borrower as the borrower's principal dwelling.

(5) The terms of the loan: (i) permit the borrower as a matter of right to defer payment of principal or interest; and (ii) allow or provide for the negative amortization of the loan balance.

(b) Except as provided in subdivision (6) of subsection (c) of this section, this section applies only to the following loans:

(1) A loan originated on or after January 1, 2005, that was at the time the loan was originated a rate spread home loan as defined in G.S. 24-1.1F.

(2) A loan secured by the borrower's principal dwelling, which loan was modified after January 1, 2005, and became at the time of such modification and as a consequence of such modification a rate spread home loan.

(3) A loan that was a nontraditional mortgage loan at the time the loan was originated.

(4) A loan secured by the borrower's principal dwelling, which loan was modified and became at the time of such modification and as a consequence of such modification a nontraditional mortgage loan.

(c) This section does not apply to any of the following:

(1) A home equity line of credit as defined in G.S. 45-81(a).

(2) A construction loan as defined in G.S. 24-10(c).

(3) A reverse mortgage as defined in G.S. 53-257 that complies with the provisions of Article 21 of Chapter 53 of the General Statutes.

(4) A bridge loan with a term of 12 months or less, such as a loan to purchase a new dwelling where the borrower plans to sell his or her current dwelling within 12 months.

(5) A loan made by a natural person who makes no more than one loan in a 12-month period and is not in the business of lending.

(6) A loan secured by a subordinate lien on the borrower's principal dwelling, unless the loan was made contemporaneously with a rate spread home loan or a nontraditional mortgage loan that is subject to the provisions of this section.

(d) In addition to any statutory or common law prohibition against deficiency judgments, the following shall apply to the foreclosure of mortgages and deeds of trust that secure loans subject to this section:

(1) For mortgages and deeds of trust recorded before January 1, 2010, the holder of the obligation secured by the foreclosed mortgage or deed of trust shall not be entitled to any deficiency judgment against the borrower for any balance owing on such obligation if: (i) the real property encumbered by the lien of the mortgage or deed of trust being foreclosed was sold by a mortgagee or trustee under a power of sale contained in the mortgage or deed of trust; and (ii) the real property sold was, at the time the foreclosure proceeding was commenced, occupied by the borrower as the borrower's principal dwelling.

(2) For mortgages and deeds of trust recorded on or after January 1, 2010, the holder of the obligation secured by the foreclosed mortgage or deed of trust

shall not be entitled to any deficiency judgment against the borrower for any balance owing on such obligation if: (i) the real property encumbered by the lien of the mortgage or deed of trust being foreclosed was sold as a consequence of a judicial proceeding or by a mortgagee or trustee under a power of sale contained in the mortgage or deed of trust; and (ii) the real property sold was, at the time the judicial or foreclosure proceeding was commenced, occupied by the borrower as the borrower's principal dwelling.

(e) The court may, in its discretion, award to the borrower the reasonable attorneys' fees actually incurred by the borrower in the defense of an action for deficiency if: (i) the borrower prevails in an action brought by the holder of the obligation secured by the foreclosed mortgage or deed of trust to recover a deficiency judgment following the foreclosure of a loan to which this section applies; and (ii) the court rules that the holder of the obligation secured by the foreclosed mortgage or deed of trust is not entitled to a deficiency judgment under the provisions of this section. The amount of attorneys' fees to be awarded shall be determined without regard to the provisions of the loan documents, the provisions of G.S. 6-21.2, or any statutory presumption as to the amount of such attorneys' fees. (2009-441, s. 1.)

§ 45-21.38B: Reserved for future codification purposes.

§ 45-21.38C. Severability.

The provisions of this Article shall be severable, and if any phrase, clause, sentence, or provision is declared to be unconstitutional or otherwise invalid or is preempted by federal law or regulation, the validity of the remainder of this Article shall not be affected thereby. (2009-441, s. 2.)

Article 2C.

Validating Sections; Limitation of Time for Attacking Certain Foreclosures.

§ 45-21.39. Limitation of time for attacking certain foreclosures on ground trustee was agent, etc., of owner of debt.

(a) No action or proceeding shall be brought or defense or counterclaim pleaded later than one year after March 14, 1941, in which a foreclosure sale which occurred prior to January 1, 1941, under a deed of trust conveying real estate as security for a debt is attacked or otherwise questioned upon the ground that the trustee was an officer, director, attorney, agent or employee of the owner of the whole or any part of the debt secured thereby, or upon the ground that the trustee and the owner of the debt or any part thereof have common officers, directors, attorneys, agents or employees.

(b) This section shall not be construed to give or create any cause of action where none existed before March 14, 1941, nor shall the limitation provided in subsection (a) hereof have the effect of barring any cause of action based upon grounds other than those mentioned in said subsection, unless the grounds set out in subsection (a) are an essential part thereof.

(c) This section shall not be construed to enlarge the time in which to bring any action or proceeding or to plead any defense or counterclaim; and the limitation hereby created is in addition to all other limitations now existing. (1941, c. 202; 1949, c. 720, s. 4.)

§ 45-21.40. Real property; validation of deeds made after expiration of statute of limitations where sales made prior thereto.

In all cases where sales of real property have been made under powers of sale contained in mortgages or deeds of trust and such sales have been made within the times which would have been allowed by the statute of limitations for the commencement of actions to foreclose such mortgages or deeds of trust, and the execution and delivery of deeds in consummation of such sales have been delayed until after the expiration of the period which would have been allowed by the statute of limitations for the commencement of actions to foreclose such mortgages or deeds of trust as a result of the filing of raised or increased bids, such deeds in the exercise of the power of sale are hereby validated and are declared to have the same effect as if they had been executed and delivered within the period allowed by the statute of limitations for the commencement of actions to foreclose such mortgages or deeds of trust. (1943, c. 16, s. 2; 1949, c. 720, s. 4.)

§ 45-21.41. Orders signed on days other than first and third Mondays validated; force and effect of deeds.

In all actions for the foreclosure of any mortgage or deed of trust which has heretofore been instituted and prosecuted before the clerk of the superior court of any county in North Carolina, wherein the judgment confirming the sale made by the commissioner appointed in said action, and ordering the said commissioner to execute a deed to the purchaser, was signed by such clerk on a day other than the first or third Monday of a month, such judgment of confirmation shall be and is hereby declared to be valid and of the same force and effect as though signed and docketed on the first or third Monday of any month, and any deed made by any commissioner or commissioners in any such action where the confirmation of sale was made on a day other than a first or third Monday of the month shall be and is hereby declared to have the same force and effect as if the same were executed and delivered pursuant to a judgment of confirmation properly signed and docketed by the clerk of the superior court on a first or third Monday of the month. (1923, c. 53, s. 1; C.S., s. 2593(a); 1949, c. 720, s. 4.)

§ 45-21.42. Validation of deeds where no order or record of confirmation can be found.

In all cases prior to the first day of March, 1974, where sales of property have been made under the power of sale contained in any deed of trust, mortgage or other instrument conveying property to secure a debt or other obligation, or where such sales have been made pursuant to an order of court in foreclosure proceedings and deeds have been executed by any trustee, mortgagee, commissioner, or person appointed by the court, conveying the property, or security, described therein, and said deed, or other instrument so executed, containing the property described therein, to the highest bidder or purchaser of said sale and such deed, or other instrument, contains recitals to the effect that said sale was reported to the clerk of the superior court, or to the court, and/or such sale was duly confirmed by the clerk of the superior court, or court, then and in that event all such deeds, conveyances, or other instruments, containing such recitals are declared to be lawful, valid and binding upon all parties to the proceedings, or parties named in such deeds of trust, mortgages, or other orders or instruments, and are hereby declared to be effective and valid to pass title for the purpose of transferring title to the purchasers at such sales with the same force and effect as if an order of confirmation had been filed in the office of the clerk of the superior court, or with the court, together with necessary reports and other decrees and to the same effect as if a record had been made in the minutes of the court of such orders, decrees and confirmations, provided that nothing contained in this section shall be construed as applicable to or affecting pending litigation. (1945, c. 984; 1949, c. 720, s. 4; 1957, c. 505; 1979, c. 242.)

§ 45-21.43. Validation of certain foreclosure sales.

In all cases where mortgages or deeds of trust on real estate with power of sale have been foreclosed pursuant to said power by proper advertisement and sale in the county where such real estate is located, notwithstanding the wording of such mortgages or deeds of trust providing for advertisement or sale, or both, in some other county, or at some other particular place in the county in which the real estate is located, which place was in fact designated in the notice of sale, all such sales are hereby fully validated, ratified and confirmed and shall be as effective to pass title to the real estate described therein as fully and to the same extent as if such mortgages or deeds of trust had provided for advertisement and sale in the county where such real estate is actually situate. (1951, c. 220; 1961, c. 537.)

§ 45-21.44. Validation of foreclosure sales when provisions of G.S. 45-21.17(2) not complied with.

In all cases prior to May 1, 1990, where mortgages or deeds of trust on real estate with power of sale have been foreclosed pursuant to said power by proper advertisement except that the date of the last publication was from seven to 20 days preceding the date of sale, all such sales are fully validated, ratified, and confirmed and shall be as effective to pass title to the real estate described therein as fully and to the same extent as if the provisions of G.S. 45-21.17(2) had been fully complied with. (1959, c. 52; 1963, c. 1157; 1971, c. 879, s. 1; 1975, c. 454, s. 2; 1985, c. 689, s. 15; 1989 (Reg. Sess., 1990), c. 1024, s. 11.1.)

§ 45-21.45. Validation of foreclosure sales where notice and hearing not provided.

In all cases where mortgages or deeds of trust on real estate with power of sale have been foreclosed pursuant to said power by proper advertisement and sale, but the mortgagor or grantor under such mortgage or deed of trust did not receive actual notice of such foreclosure or have the opportunity of a hearing prior to such foreclosure, all such sales are hereby fully validated, ratified and confirmed and shall be as effective to pass title to the real estate described therein as fully and to the same extent as if such notice and opportunity for hearing had been given, unless an action to set aside such foreclosure is commenced within one year from June 6, 1975. (1975, c. 492, s. 12.)

§ 45-21.46. Validation of foreclosure sales where posting and publication not complied with.

(a)   In all cases of foreclosure of mortgages or deeds of trust secured by real estate pursuant to power of sale which foreclosures were commenced on or subsequent to June 6, 1975, and consummated prior to June 1, 1983, in which foreclosure sales the requirements for posting and publication of notice of sale set forth in G.S. 45-21.17 were complied with but the requirements of the mortgage or deed of trust as to posting and publication of notice of sale were not complied with, are validated, ratified and confirmed and shall be effective to pass title to real estate to the same extent as though all requirements of the mortgage or deed of trust respecting posting and publication of notice of sale were complied with; unless an action to set aside such foreclosure is commenced before January 1, 1984.

(b)   All foreclosures of mortgages or deeds of trust secured by real estate pursuant to power of sale, which foreclosures were commenced on or subsequent to June 1, 1983, and consummated prior to April 1, 1985, in which foreclosure sales the requirements for posting and publication of notice of sale set forth in G.S. 45-21.17 were complied with but the requirements of the mortgage or deed of trust as to posting and publication of notice of sale were not complied with, are validated, ratified and confirmed and shall be effective to pass title to real estate to the same extent as though all requirements of the mortgage or deed of trust respecting posting and publication of notice of sale were complied with; unless an action to set aside such foreclosure is commenced in the period beginning January 1, 1984, and ending January 1, 1986. (1983, c. 582, s. 1; c. 738, s. 1; 1985, c. 341.)

§ 45-21.47. Validation of foreclosure sales when trustee is officer of owner of debt.

All sales of real property made prior to January 1, 1991, under a power of sale contained in a mortgage or deed of trust for which the trustee was an officer, director, attorney, agent, or employee of the owner of all or part of the debt secured by the mortgage or deed of trust are validated and have the same effect as if the trustee had not been an officer, director, attorney, agent, or employee of the owner of the debt unless an action to set aside the foreclosure is commenced within one year after January 1, 1991. (1983, c. 582, s. 1; 1985, c. 604; 1987, c. 277, s. 10; 1989, c. 390, s. 10; 1991, c. 489, s. 10.)

§ 45-21.48. Validation of certain foreclosure sales that did not comply with posting requirement.

A sale of real property made on or before July 2, 1985, under a power of sale contained in a mortgage or deed of trust, for which a notice of the sale was not posted at the courthouse door for 20 days immediately preceding the sale, as required by G.S. 45-21.17(1), but was posted at the courthouse door for at least 15 days immediately preceding the sale, is declared to be a valid sale to the same extent as if the notice of the sale had been posted for 20 days; unless an action to set aside the foreclosure sale is not barred by the statute of limitations and is commenced on or before October 1, 1985. (1985, c. 567, s. 2.)

§ 45-21.49. Validation of foreclosure sales when provisions of § 45-21.16A(3) not complied with.

(a)   Whenever any real property was sold under a power of sale as provided in Article 2A of Chapter 45, and the notice of sale did not describe the improvements on the property to be sold, as required under G.S. 45-21.16A(3), the sale shall not be invalidated because of such omission.

(b)   This section shall apply to all sales completed prior to June 1, 1987. (1987, c. 277, s. 10a.)

Article 3.

Mortgage Sales.

§ 45-22: Transferred to G.S. 45-21.39 by Session Laws 1949, c. 720, s. 4.

§§ 45-23 through 45-26. Repealed by Session Laws 1949, c. 720, s. 5.

§ 45-26.1. Transferred to G.S. 45-21.40 by Session Laws 1949, c. 720, s. 4.

§§ 45-27 through 45-30. Repealed by Session Laws 1949, c. 720, s. 5.

§ 45-31. Transferred to G.S. 45-21.41 by Session Laws 1949, c. 720, s. 4.

§§ 45-32 through 45-36. Transferred to G.S. 45-21.34 to 45-21.38 by Session Laws 1949, c. 720, s. 3.

§ 45-36.1. Transferred to G.S. 45-21.42 by Session Laws 1949, c. 720, s. 4.

Article 4.

Satisfaction.

§ 45-36.2. Obligation of good faith.

Every action or duty within this Article imposes an obligation of good faith in its performance or enforcement. (1953, c. 848; 2005-123, s. 1.)

§ 45-36.3. Notification by mortgagee of satisfaction of provisions of deed of trust or mortgage, or other instrument; civil penalty.

(a)   After the satisfaction of the provisions of any deed of trust or mortgage, or other instrument intended to secure with real property the payment of money or the performance of any other obligation and registered as required by law, the holder of the evidence of the indebtedness, if it is a single instrument, or a duly authorized agent or attorney of such holder shall within 60 days:

(1)   Discharge and release of record such documents and forward the cancelled documents to the grantor, trustor or mortgagor; or,

(2)   Alternatively, the holder of the evidence of the indebtedness or a duly authorized agent or attorney of such holder, at the request of the grantor, trustor or mortgagor, shall forward said instrument and the deed of trust or mortgage instrument, with payment and satisfaction acknowledged in accordance with the requirements of G.S. 45-37, to the grantor, trustor or mortgagor.

(b)   Any person, institution or agent who fails to comply with this section may be required to pay a civil penalty of not more than one thousand dollars ($1,000) in addition to reasonable attorneys' fees and any other damages awarded by the court to the grantor, trustor or mortgagor, or to a subsequent purchaser of the property from the grantor, trustor or mortgagor. A five hundred dollar ($500.00) civil penalty may be recovered by the grantor, trustor or mortgagor, and a five hundred dollar ($500.00) penalty may be recovered by the purchaser of the property from the grantor, trustor or mortgagor. If that purchaser of the property consists of more than a single grantee, then the civil penalty will be divided equally among all of the grantees. A petitioner may recover damages under this section only if he has given the mortgagee, obligee, beneficiary or other responsible party written notice of his intention to bring an action pursuant to this section. Upon receipt of this notice, the mortgagee, obligee, beneficiary or other responsible party shall have 30 days, in addition to the initial 60-day period, to fulfill the requirements of this section.

(c) Should any person, institution or agent who is not the present holder of the evidence of indebtedness be required to pay a civil penalty, attorneys' fees, or other damages under this section, they will have an action against the holder of the evidence of indebtedness for all sums they were required to pay.

(d) This section applies only if the provisions of the deed of trust, mortgage, or other instrument are satisfied before October 1, 2005. (1979, c. 681, s. 1; 1987, c. 662, ss. 1-3; 2005-123, s. 1.)

§ 45-36.4. Definitions.

As used in this Article, the following terms mean:

(1) Address for giving a notification. - For the purpose of a particular type of notification, the most recent address provided in a document by the intended recipient of the notification to the person giving the notification, unless the person giving the notification knows of a more accurate address, in which case the term means that address.

(1a) Borrower. - A person primarily liable for payment or performance of the obligation secured by the real property described in a security instrument.

(1b) Credit suspension directive. - A notification given to a secured creditor pursuant to G.S. 45-36.7A directing the secured creditor to suspend temporarily a borrower's right and ability to obtain additional credit advances in anticipation of the imminent sale of, or the imminent making of a new loan to be secured by, real property then encumbered by an existing security instrument when the anticipated transaction will involve either the satisfaction of the existing security instrument or the release of the real property from the lien of the existing security instrument.

(2) Day. - Calendar day.

(3) Document. - Information that is inscribed on a tangible medium or that is stored in an electronic or other medium and is retrievable in perceivable form.

(4) Electronic. - Relating to technology having electrical, digital, magnetic, wireless, optical, electromagnetic, or similar capabilities.

(5) Entitled person. - A person who:

a. Is a borrower;

b. Is a landowner;

c. Has contracted to purchase real property encumbered by an existing security instrument;

d. Has made or has committed to make a loan that is secured or is to be secured by real property encumbered by an existing security instrument;

e. Is a title insurance company authorized pursuant to Article 26 of Chapter 58 of the General Statutes to issue title insurance policies in the State of North Carolina that has insured or has committed to insure title to real property encumbered by an existing security instrument;

f. Is the foreclosing trustee or the high bidder in a foreclosure sale involving real property encumbered by an existing security instrument;

g. Is a qualified lien holder; or

h. Is an attorney licensed to practice law in the State of North Carolina or a bank, savings and loan association, savings bank, or credit union, but only when:

1. The attorney, bank, savings and loan association, savings bank, or credit union is or will be responsible for the disbursement of funds in connection with the sale of, or a new loan secured by, property then encumbered by an existing security instrument; and

2. A requirement of the sale or new loan transaction is or will be that the property be conveyed or encumbered free and clear of the lien of the existing security instrument.

(6) Good faith. - Honesty in fact and the observance of reasonable commercial standards of fair dealing.

(7) Landowner. - A person that, before foreclosure, has the right of redemption in the real property described in a security instrument. The term does not include a person that holds only a lien on the real property or the trustee under a deed of trust.

(8) Notification. - A document containing information required under this Article and signed by the person required to provide the information.

(9) Original parties. - With respect to a security instrument, each person named as a party to the security instrument on the face thereof as originally recorded. In identifying the original parties to a deed of trust for purposes of this Article, it is not necessary to include the original trustee or trustees named therein.

(10) Payoff amount. - The sum necessary to satisfy a secured obligation.

(11) Payoff statement. - A document containing the information specified in G.S. 45-36.7(e).

(12) Person. - An individual, corporation, business trust, estate, trust, partnership, limited liability company, association, joint venture, public corporation, government, or governmental subdivision, agency, or instrumentality, or any other legal or commercial entity.

(12a) Qualified lien holder. - A person who holds or is the beneficiary of a security interest in or lien on real property encumbered by an existing security instrument, but only if that person's security interest in or lien on the real property arises from a mortgage or deed of trust that is subordinate in priority to the lien of the existing security instrument. The term does not include a trustee under a deed of trust.

(13) Recording data. - The book and page number or document number that indicates where a document is recorded in the office of the register of deeds.

(14) Register of deeds. - Includes the register of deeds, assistant register of deeds, or deputy register of deeds.

(15) Satisfy. - With respect to a security instrument, to terminate the effectiveness of the security instrument.

(16) Secured creditor. - A person that holds or is the beneficiary of a security interest or that is authorized both to receive payments on behalf of a person that holds a security interest and to record a satisfaction of the security instrument upon receiving full performance of the secured obligation. The term does not include a trustee under a security instrument.

(17) Secured obligation. - An obligation the payment or performance of which is secured by a security interest.

(18) Security instrument. - An agreement, however denominated, that creates or provides for an interest in real property to secure payment or performance of an obligation, whether or not it also creates or provides for a lien on personal property. The term includes a deed of trust and a mortgage.

(19) Security interest. - An interest in real property created by a security instrument.

(19a) Short-pay amount. - The sum necessary to obtain the release of all or a specific portion of the real property from the lien of a security instrument without satisfying the secured obligation in full.

(19b) Short-pay statement. - A document containing the information specified in G.S. 45-36.7(e1).

(20) Sign. - With present intent to authenticate or adopt a document:

a. To execute or adopt a tangible symbol; or

b. To attach to or logically associate with the document an electronic sound, symbol, or process.

(21) State. - A state of the United States, the District of Columbia, Puerto Rico, the United States Virgin Islands, or any territory or insular possession subject to the jurisdiction of the United States.

(22) Submit for recording. - To deliver, with required fees and taxes, a document sufficient to be recorded under this Article to the register of deeds in the county in which the real property described in the related security instrument is located.

(23) Trustee. - The trustee or substitute then serving as such under the terms of a deed of trust. (2005-123, s. 1; 2011-312, s. 3.)

§ 45-36.5. Notification: manner of giving and effective date.

(a) A person gives a notification by any of the following:

(1) Depositing it with the United States Postal Service with first-class postage paid or with a commercially reasonable delivery service with cost of delivery provided, properly addressed to the recipient's address for giving a notification.

(2) Sending it by facsimile transmission, electronic mail, or other electronic transmission to the recipient's address for giving a notification, but only if the recipient agreed to receive notification in that manner.

(3) Causing it to be received at the address for giving a notification within the time that it would have been received if given pursuant to subdivision (1) of this subsection.

(b) A notification is effective on any of the following:

(1) The day after it is deposited with a commercially reasonable delivery service for overnight delivery.

(2) Three days after it is deposited with the United States Postal Service, first-class mail with postage prepaid, or with a commercially reasonable delivery service for delivery other than by overnight delivery.

(3) The day it is given, if given pursuant to subdivision (a)(2) of this section.

(4) The day it is received, if given by a method other than as provided in subdivision (a)(1) or (a)(2) of this section.

(c) If this Article or a notification given pursuant to this Article requires performance on or by a certain day and that day is a Saturday, Sunday, or legal holiday under the laws of this State or the United States, the performance is sufficient if performed on the next day that is not a Saturday, Sunday, or legal holiday. (2005-123, s. 1.)

§ 45-36.6. Document of rescission: effect; liability for wrongful recording.

(a) Definitions. - The following definitions apply in this section:

(1) Document of rescission. - A document that rescinds either (i) a release that was recorded in error or (ii) the erroneous satisfaction of a security instrument.

(2) Release. - A document that either (i) releases property from the lien of a security instrument or (ii) indicates that an obligation is no longer secured by a security instrument.

(b) If a release is recorded in error or a security instrument is erroneously satisfied of record, then the secured creditor or the person who caused the release to be recorded in error or the security instrument to be erroneously satisfied of record may execute and record a document of rescission. The document of rescission must be duly acknowledged before an officer authorized to make acknowledgments. Upon recording, the document of rescission either (i) rescinds a release that was recorded in error and deprives the release of any effect or (ii) rescinds the erroneous satisfaction of record of the security instrument and reinstates the security instrument.

(c) A recorded document of rescission has no effect on the rights of a person that:

(1) Records an interest in the real property described in a security instrument after the recording of a release that was recorded in error or the erroneous satisfaction of record of the security instrument and before the recording of the document of rescission; and

(2) Would otherwise have priority over or take free of the lien created by the security instrument as reinstated under Chapter 47 of the General Statutes.

(d) A person that erroneously or wrongfully records a document of rescission is liable to any person injured thereby for the actual loss caused by the recording and reasonable attorneys' fees and costs.

(e) A document is a document of rescission if it does all of the following:

(1) Identifies the related security instrument, including the type of security instrument, the original parties to the security instrument, the recording data for the security instrument, and the office in which the security instrument is recorded.

(2) If the document of rescission is intended to rescind a release that was recorded in error, (i) identifies the release that was recorded in error by its recording data and the office in which it is recorded, (ii) states that the release was recorded in error, and (iii) states that the release is rescinded.

(3) If the document of rescission is intended to rescind the erroneous satisfaction of record of a security instrument, (i) identifies the satisfaction document that was recorded in error by its recording data and the office in which it is recorded, (ii) states that the security instrument was erroneously satisfied of record, and (iii) states that the satisfaction of the security instrument is rescinded and the security instrument reinstated.

(4) States that the person signing the document of rescission is either (i) the secured creditor or (ii) the person who caused the release to be recorded in error or the security instrument to be erroneously satisfied of record.

(5) Is signed and acknowledged as required by law for a conveyance of an interest in real property.

(f) The register of deeds shall accept a document of rescission for recording unless one of the following applies:

(1) The document is submitted by a method or in a medium not authorized for registration by the register of deeds under applicable law.

(2) The required recording fee is not paid.

(3) The document is not signed and acknowledged as required by law for a conveyance of an interest in real property by either the secured creditor or the person who caused the release to be recorded in error or the security instrument to be erroneously satisfied of record. The register of deeds shall not be required to verify or make inquiry concerning (i) the truth of the matters stated in any document of rescission or (ii) the authority of the person executing any document of rescission to do so.

(g) No particular phrasing is required for a document of rescission that rescinds a release that was recorded in error. The following form, when properly completed, is sufficient to satisfy the requirements of subsection (e) of this section:

"DOCUMENT OF RESCISSION

(G.S. 45-36.6(e))

The security instrument to which this Document of Rescission relates is identified as follows:

Type of Security Instrument: (identify type of security instrument, such as deed of trust or mortgage)

Original Grantor(s): (identify original grantor(s), trustor(s), or mortgagor(s))

Original Secured Party(ies): (identify the original beneficiary(ies), mortgagee(s), or secured party(ies) in the security instrument)

Recording Data: The security instrument is recorded in Book _____ at Page ____ or as document number ____ in the office of the Register of Deeds for _____ County, North Carolina.

This Document of Rescission rescinds the release recorded in Book _____ at Page ____ or as document number ____ in the office of the Register of Deeds for _____ County, North Carolina. The release was recorded in error, is hereby rescinded, and is declared to be of no effect.

The undersigned is: (check applicable box)

____ The secured creditor in the security instrument identified above.

____ The person who caused the release to be recorded in error.

Date:

Signature of secured creditor or person who caused the release to be recorded in error

[Acknowledgment before officer authorized to take acknowledgments]"

(h) No particular phrasing is required for a document of rescission that rescinds the erroneous satisfaction of a security instrument. The following form, when properly completed, is sufficient to satisfy the requirements of G.S. 45-36.6(e):

"DOCUMENT OF RESCISSION

(G.S. 45-36.6(e))

The security instrument to which this Document of Rescission relates is identified as follows:

Type of Security Instrument: (identify type of security instrument, such as deed of trust or mortgage)

Original Grantor(s): (identify original grantor(s), trustor(s), or mortgagor(s))

Original Secured Party(ies): (identify the original beneficiary(ies), mortgagee(s), or secured party(ies) in the security instrument)

Recording Data: The security instrument is recorded in Book _____ at Page ____ or as document number ____ in the office of the Register of Deeds for _____ County, North Carolina.

The security instrument was erroneously satisfied of record by that satisfaction document recorded in Book _____ at Page ____ or as document number ____ in the office of the Register of Deeds for _____ County, North Carolina. The satisfaction of the security instrument is hereby rescinded, the security instrument is reinstated, and the security instrument is declared to be in full force and effect.

The undersigned is: (check applicable box)

____ The secured creditor in the security instrument identified above.

____ The person who caused the security instrument to be satisfied of record erroneously.

Date:

Signature of secured creditor or person who caused the security instrument to be satisfied of record erroneously

[Acknowledgment before officer authorized to take acknowledgments]".

(2005-123, s. 1; 2006-259, s. 52(b); 2006-264, s. 40(a); 2011-312, s. 4.)

§ 45-36.7. Payoff and short-pay statements; request and content.

(a) An entitled person, or an agent authorized by an entitled person to request a payoff or a short-pay statement, may give to the secured creditor a notification requesting a payoff statement or a short-pay statement. The notification must contain all of the following:

(1) The entitled person's name.

(2) If given by a person other than an entitled person, the name of the person giving the notification and a statement that the person is an authorized agent of the entitled person.

(3) A direction whether the statement is to be sent to the entitled person or that person's authorized agent.

(4) The address to which the creditor must send the statement.

(5) Sufficient information to enable the creditor to identify the secured obligation and the real property encumbered by the security interest.

(6) Whether the request is for a payoff statement or a short-pay statement.

(7) If the request is for a payoff statement, the specified payoff date, which may not be more than 30 days after the notification is given.

(8) If the request is for a short-pay statement, (i) the specified short-pay date, which may not be more than 30 days after the notification is given, (ii) a clear statement as to whether the request is for the short-pay amount required to release all of the real property described in the security instrument or only a portion of that property, and (iii) if the request is for the short-pay amount required to release only a portion of the real property described in the security

instrument, a description of the specific real property to be released upon payment of the short-pay amount.

(b)   If a notification under subsection (a) of this section directs the secured creditor to send the payoff statement or a short-pay statement to a person identified as an authorized agent of the entitled person, the secured creditor must send the statement to the agent, unless the secured creditor knows that the entitled person has not authorized the request.

(c)   A person who gives to a secured creditor a notification requesting a payoff statement or a short-pay statement thereby represents that the person is an entitled person or the authorized agent of an entitled person. A secured creditor may rely on that representation in providing a payoff statement or a short-pay statement unless the secured creditor knows that the requesting person is neither an entitled person nor the authorized agent of an entitled person. A secured creditor has no duty to make inquiry as to whether, or to verify that, the person requesting a payoff statement or a short-pay statement is an entitled person or the authorized agent of an entitled person.

(d)   Within 10 days after the effective date of a notification that complies with subsection (a) of this section, the secured creditor shall issue a payoff statement or a short-pay statement and send it as directed pursuant to subdivision (a)(3) of this section in the manner prescribed in G.S. 45-36.5 for giving a notification. A secured creditor that sends a payoff statement or a short-pay statement to the entitled person or the authorized agent may not claim that the notification did not satisfy subsection (a) of this section. If the person to whom the notification is given once held an interest in the secured obligation but has since assigned that interest, the person need not send a payoff statement or a short-pay statement but shall give (i) a notification of the assignment to the person to whom the payoff statement or a short-pay statement otherwise would have been sent, providing the name and address of the assignee, or (ii) a notification to the person to whom the payoff statement or a short-pay statement otherwise would have been sent, stating that the recipient claims no interest in the security instrument or the secured obligation, that the secured obligation was assigned, but that the identity and address of the assignee is not known.

(e)   A payoff statement must contain:

(1)   The date on which it was prepared and the payoff amount as of that date, including the amount by type of each fee, charge, or other sum included within the payoff amount;

(2) The information reasonably necessary to calculate the payoff amount as of the requested payoff date, including the per diem interest amount; and

(3) The payment cutoff time, if any, the address or place where payment must be made, and any limitation as to the authorized method of payment.

(e1) A short-pay statement must contain:

(1) The information reasonably necessary to calculate the short-pay amount as of the requested short-pay date, including the per diem interest amount, if any;

(2) The payment cutoff time, if any, the address or place where payment of the short-pay amount must be made, and any limitation as to the authorized method of payment;

(3) Any conditions precedent that must be satisfied to obtain the release of the property identified in the request for the short-pay statement from the lien of the security instrument; and

(4) Confirmation of the specific real property to be released from the lien of the security instrument upon receipt of the timely payment of the short-pay amount and satisfaction of the other conditions precedent to the release of that property.

Unless the short-pay statement expressly provides otherwise, all persons liable for payment or performance of the obligations secured by the security instrument will remain liable for the secured obligations to the extent the short-pay amount is not sufficient to satisfy the secured obligations in full.

(f) A payoff statement or a short-pay statement may contain the amount of any fees authorized under this section not included in the payoff amount. A secured creditor may require the payment in full of any fees authorized under this section before issuing a payoff statement or a short-pay statement.

(g) A secured creditor may not qualify a payoff amount or state that it is subject to change before the payoff date unless the payoff statement provides information sufficient to permit the entitled person or the person's authorized agent to request an updated payoff amount at no charge and to obtain that updated payoff amount during the secured creditor's normal business hours on the payoff date or the immediately preceding business day. A secured creditor may not qualify a short-pay amount or state that it is subject to change before the short-pay date unless the short-pay statement provides information sufficient to permit the entitled person or the person's authorized agent to request an updated short-pay amount at no charge and to obtain that updated short-pay amount during the secured creditor's normal business hours on the short-pay date or the immediately preceding business day.

(h)   A secured creditor must provide upon request one payoff statement or one short-pay statement without charge during any six-month period. A secured creditor may charge a fee of twenty-five dollars ($25.00) for each additional payoff statement and one hundred dollars ($100.00) for each additional short-pay statement requested during that six-month period. However, a secured creditor may not charge a fee for providing an updated payoff amount or short-pay amount under subsection (g) of this section or a corrected payoff statement or short-pay statement under G.S. 45-36.8(a).

(i)   Unless the security instrument provides otherwise, a secured creditor is not required to send a payoff statement or a short-pay statement by means other than first-class mail. If the creditor agrees to send a statement by another means, it may charge a reasonable fee for complying with the requested manner of delivery.

(j)   Except as otherwise provided in G.S. 45-36.12, if a secured creditor to which a notification has been given pursuant to subsection (a) of this section does not send a timely payoff statement that substantially complies with subsection (e) of this section or a short-pay statement that substantially complies with subsection (e1) of this section, the creditor is liable to the entitled person for any actual damages caused by the failure, but not punitive damages. A creditor that does not pay the damages provided in this subsection within 30 days after receipt of a notification demanding payment shall also be liable for reasonable attorneys' fees and costs.

(k)   This section does not apply unless (i) the notification requesting a payoff statement is given on or after October 1, 2005, and (ii) the notification requesting a short-pay statement is given on or after October 1, 2011. (2005-123, s. 1; 2011-312, s. 5.)

§ 45-36.7A. Credit suspension directives.

(a) A credit suspension directive may be given to a secured creditor by any of the following:

(1) Any borrower.

(2) The legal representative of any borrower.

(3) The attorney for any borrower.

(4) An attorney licensed to practice law in the State of North Carolina or a bank, savings and loan association, savings bank, or credit union, but only when (i) the attorney, bank, savings and loan association, savings bank, or credit union is responsible for the disbursement of funds in connection with the sale of, or a new loan secured by, real property then encumbered by an existing security instrument; (ii) a requirement of the sale or new loan transaction is that the property be conveyed or encumbered free and clear of the lien of the existing security instrument; and (iii) the credit suspension directive is given to the secured creditor contemporaneously with a notification requesting a payoff statement or a short-pay statement in anticipation of and in preparation for the imminent settlement of the sale or new loan transaction.

(b) A credit suspension directive must contain all of the following:

(1) The name and authority of the person giving the directive.

(2) Sufficient information to enable the creditor to identify the secured obligation, the identity of the borrower, and the real property encumbered by the security interest.

(3) The specified payoff date, which may not be more than 30 days after the notification is given.

(4) A clear and unambiguous directive to the secured creditor to suspend through and including the payoff date the borrower's right and ability to obtain any additional credit advances which, if made, would be secured by the security instrument.

(c) If the person who gives a credit suspension directive to a secured creditor is a person listed in subdivision (a)(4) of this section, that person shall also (i) give a copy of the credit suspension directive to the borrower and (ii) provide an additional notification to the borrower that provides substantially as follows:

"NOTICE TO BORROWER

You have a loan with (name of lender) secured by a mortgage or deed of trust on real property located at (address of property).

We will be responsible for disbursing funds in connection with a scheduled sale of the property or a new loan that will be secured by the property. A requirement of the sale or new loan transaction is that the property be conveyed or encumbered free and clear of the existing mortgage or deed of trust that secures your loan.

As permitted by North Carolina law, we are sending the (enclosed/attached/following/foregoing) notification to your lender directing that it temporarily suspend your right and ability to obtain credit advances in anticipation of the settlement of the sale or loan. The notification accompanies a request asking the amount that must be sent to your lender to pay your loan in full and cancel the mortgage or deed of trust that secures your loan (or, if your loan will not be paid in full, to release the property from the mortgage or deed of trust that secures your loan). The information your lender provides us may be inaccurate if you obtain additional credit advances before the scheduled settlement date of the sale or new loan transaction.

When your lender receives our directive, it will temporarily suspend your right and ability to obtain credit advances. The period of suspension will continue through and including (anticipated payoff date), the anticipated payoff date, regardless of whether the settlement of the sale or new loan transaction occurs as scheduled. The suspension will not affect your responsibility to continue making payments to your lender during the suspension period. You should not attempt to obtain additional credit advances from your lender during the suspension period.

You may instruct us at any time during the suspension period to withdraw the credit suspension directive we are sending your lender, and we are required by law to comply. However, if you do so, you may jeopardize the settlement of the sale or new loan transaction because the payoff or release information provided by your lender may become inaccurate.

When proceeds from a sale or new loan transaction are used to pay an existing loan in full, lenders typically close the loan account, thereby terminating their borrower's ability to obtain additional credit advances. You should contact your lender to determine whether you will be able to obtain additional credit advances after the settlement of the sale or new loan transaction.

If you have questions about this notice or our action, please contact (name of contact person or department) by calling us at (phone number) or writing to us at (mailing address).

(Name of attorney, bank, savings and loan association, savings bank, or credit union)"

(d)   Upon receipt of a credit suspension directive, a secured creditor shall:

(1)   Subject to subsection (e) of this section, suspend the borrower's right and ability to obtain credit advances which, if made, would be secured by the security instrument. The period of suspension shall continue through and including the payoff date stated in the credit suspension directive.

(2)   Apply all sums subsequently paid during the period of suspension by or on behalf of the borrower in connection with the secured obligation, including sums paid to the secured creditor by a person responsible for the disbursement of funds in connection with the sale of, or a new loan secured by, real property

then encumbered by a security instrument, to the satisfaction of the secured obligation, regardless of whether the amount or amounts paid are sufficient to pay the secured obligation and other sums secured by the security instrument in full. Sums paid to the secured creditor in excess of the amount required to pay the secured obligation and other sums secured by the security instrument in full shall be refunded by the secured creditor to or at the direction of the person who paid the excess amount.

(e) Notwithstanding a secured creditor's receipt of a credit suspension directive, a secured creditor may do any of the following, all of which shall be secured by the security instrument:

(1) The secured creditor may advance sums and incur expenses (i) for insurance, taxes, and assessments, (ii) to protect the secured creditor's interest under the security instrument, (iii) to preserve and protect the value or condition of the real property encumbered by the security instrument, or (iv) to complete the construction of improvements on the real property encumbered by the security instrument.

(2) The secured creditor may permit the borrower to obtain a credit advance, but only if the credit advance was initiated or approved before the secured creditor received the credit suspension directive.

(f) If the person giving a credit suspension directive is not a borrower, then the person giving a credit suspension directive shall be conclusively deemed the borrower's agent acting with full authority from the borrower to issue the credit suspension directive on the borrower's behalf.

(g) A credit suspension directive may be withdrawn at any time by the person who gave the directive. If the person who gives a credit suspension directive to a secured creditor is a person listed in subdivision (a)(4) of this section, that person shall promptly notify the secured creditor that the credit suspension directive is withdrawn (i) if instructed by the borrower at any time to withdraw the directive or (ii) if the anticipated sale or new loan transaction is cancelled. Upon receipt of a notice from the person who originally gave the credit suspension directive that the credit suspension directive is withdrawn, the secured creditor may reinstate the borrower's right and ability to obtain credit advances. (2011-312, s. 6.)

§ 45-36.8. Understated payoff statement or short-pay statement: correction; effect.

(a)   If a secured creditor determines that the payoff amount it provided in a payoff statement or the short-pay amount it provided in a short-pay statement was understated, the creditor may send a corrected payoff or short-pay statement. If the entitled person or the person's authorized agent receives and has a reasonable opportunity to act upon a corrected payoff statement or short-pay statement before making payment, the corrected statement supersedes an earlier statement.

(b)   A secured creditor that sends a payoff statement containing an understated payoff amount or a short-pay statement containing an understated short-pay amount may not deny the accuracy of the payoff amount or short-pay amount as against any person that reasonably and detrimentally relies upon the understated payoff amount or short-pay amount.

(c)   This Article does not:

(1)   Affect the right of a secured creditor to recover any sum that it did not include in a payoff amount or a short-pay amount from any person liable for payment of the secured obligation; or

(2)   Limit any claim or defense that a person liable for payment of a secured obligation may have under law other than this Article. (2005-123, s. 1; 2011-312, s. 7.)

§ 45-36.9. Secured creditor to submit satisfaction or release for recording; liability for failure.

(a)   A secured creditor shall submit for recording a satisfaction of a security instrument within 30 days after the creditor receives full payment or performance of the secured obligation. If a security instrument secures a line of credit or future advances, the secured obligation is fully performed only if, in addition to full payment, the secured creditor has received (i) a notification requesting the creditor to terminate the line of credit, (ii) a credit suspension directive, or (iii) a notification containing a clear and unambiguous statement sufficient to terminate the effectiveness of the provision for future advances in the security instrument including, but not limited to, a request to terminate an equity line of credit given pursuant to G.S. 45-82.2 or a notice regarding future advances given pursuant to G.S. 45-82.3.

(a1) If the conditions stated in a short-pay statement are fully satisfied on or before the short-pay date stated in the short-pay statement, including the payment in full of the short-pay amount and the satisfaction of all other conditions precedent to the release set forth in the short-pay statement, then within 30 days after the short-pay date the secured creditor shall release the property which is the subject of the short-pay statement from the lien of the security instrument. The release of the property may be accomplished by a deed of release, an instrument of full or partial reconveyance, a partial release recorded pursuant to G.S. 45-36.22, the satisfaction of record of the security instrument by any of the means authorized in G.S. 45-37(a), or by any other lawful means.

(b) Except as otherwise provided in G.S. 45-36.12, a secured creditor that is required to submit a satisfaction of a security instrument or a release for recording pursuant to this section and does not do so by the end of the period specified in subsection (a) or (a1) of this section is liable to the landowner for any actual damages caused by the failure, but not punitive damages.

(c) Except as otherwise provided in subsection (d) of this section and in G.S. 45-36.12, a secured creditor that is required to submit a satisfaction of a security instrument or a release for recording pursuant to this section and does not do so by the end of the period specified in subsection (a) or (a1) of this section is also liable to the landowner for one thousand dollars ($1,000) and any reasonable attorneys' fees and court costs incurred if, after the expiration of the period specified in subsection (a) or (a1) of this section, all of the following occur:

(1) The landowner gives the secured creditor a notification, by any method authorized by G.S. 45-36.5 that provides proof of receipt, demanding that the secured creditor submit a satisfaction or release for recording.

(2) The secured creditor does not submit a satisfaction or release for recording within 30 days after the secured creditor's receipt of the notification.

(3) The security instrument is not satisfied of record by any of the methods provided in G.S. 45-37(a) or the release is not filed within 30 days after the secured creditor's receipt of the notification.

The right to receive the additional one thousand dollars ($1,000) is personal to the landowner who gives the secured creditor notification under this subsection and may not be assigned.

(d)   Subsection (c) of this section does not apply if the secured creditor received full payment or performance of the secured obligation before October 1, 2005.

(e)   Repealed by Session Laws 2011-246, s. 3, effective October 1, 2011. (2005-123, s. 1; 2011-246, s. 3; 2011-312, s. 8; 2013-204, s. 2.1.)

§ 45-36.10. Content and effect of satisfaction.

(a)   A document is a satisfaction of a security instrument if it does all of the following:

(1)   Identifies the type of security instrument, the original parties to the security instrument, the recording data for the security instrument, and the office in which the security instrument is recorded.

(2)   States that the person signing the satisfaction is the secured creditor.

(3)   Reserved.

(4)   Contains language terminating the effectiveness of the security instrument.

(5)   Is signed by the secured creditor and acknowledged as required by law for a conveyance of an interest in real property.

(b)   The register of deeds shall accept for recording a satisfaction of a security instrument, unless one of the following applies:

(1)   The document is submitted by a method or in a medium not authorized for registration by the register of deeds under applicable law.

(2)   The document is not signed by the secured creditor and acknowledged as required by law for a conveyance of an interest in real property. The register of deeds shall not be required to verify or make inquiry concerning (i) the truth of

the matters stated in any satisfaction document, or (ii) the authority of the person executing any satisfaction document to do so.

(c) The recording of a satisfaction of a security instrument does not by itself extinguish any liability of a person for payment or performance of the secured obligation. (2005-123, s. 1.)

§ 45-36.11. Satisfaction: form.

(a) Standard Form. - No particular phrasing is required for a satisfaction of a security instrument. The following form, when properly completed, is sufficient to satisfy the requirements of G.S. 45-36.10(a):

"SATISFACTION OF SECURITY INSTRUMENT

(G.S. 45-36.10; G.S. 45-37(a)(7))

The undersigned is now the secured creditor in the security instrument identified as follows:

Type of Security Instrument: (identify type of security instrument, such as deed of trust or mortgage)

Original Grantor(s): (Identify original grantor(s), trustor(s), or mortgagor(s))

Original Secured Party(ies): (Identify the original beneficiary(ies), mortgagee(s), or secured party(ies) in the security instrument)

Recording Data: The security instrument is recorded in Book ____ at Page ____ or as document number _____ in the office of the Register of Deeds for _____ County, North Carolina.

This satisfaction terminates the effectiveness of the security instrument.

Date: _____

_____

(Signature of secured creditor)

[Acknowledgment before officer authorized to take acknowledgments]"

(b)   Alternate Form. - A secured creditor who would like to indicate that the underlying obligation secured by the instrument has been extinguished may use the following form, which, when properly completed, is also sufficient to satisfy the requirements of G.S. 45-36.10(a):

"SATISFACTION OF SECURITY INSTRUMENT

(G.S. 45-36.10; G.S. 45-37(a)(7))

The undersigned is now the secured creditor in the security instrument identified as follows:

Type of Security Instrument: (identify type of security instrument, such as deed of trust or mortgage)

Original Grantor(s): (Identify original grantor(s), trustor(s), or mortgagor(s))

Original Secured Party(ies): (Identify the original beneficiary(ies), mortgagee(s), or secured party(ies) in the security instrument)

Recording Data: The security instrument is recorded in Book ____ at Page ____ or as document number _____ in the office of the Register of Deeds for _____ County, North Carolina.

This satisfaction terminates the effectiveness of the security instrument and extinguishes the underlying obligation secured by the instrument.

Date: _____
_____
(Signature of secured creditor)

[Acknowledgment before officer authorized to take acknowledgments]".

(2005-123, s. 1; 2012-150, s. 1.)

§ 45-36.12. Limitation of secured creditor's liability.

A secured creditor is not liable under this Article if it:

(1)   Established a reasonable procedure to achieve compliance with its obligations under this Article;

(2)   Complied with that procedure in good faith; and

(3)   Was unable to comply with its obligations because of circumstances beyond its control. (2005-123, s. 1.)

§ 45-36.13. Eligibility to serve as satisfaction agent.

No person other than an attorney licensed to practice law in the State of North Carolina may serve as a satisfaction agent under this Article. (2005-123, s. 1.)

§ 45-36.14. Affidavit of satisfaction: notification to secured creditor.

(a)   If a secured creditor has not submitted for recording a satisfaction of a security instrument and the security instrument has not been satisfied of record by any of the methods provided by G.S. 45-37(a) within the period specified in G.S. 45-36.9(a), a satisfaction agent acting for and with authority from the landowner may give the secured creditor a notification that the satisfaction agent intends to submit for recording an affidavit of satisfaction of the security instrument. The notification must include all of the following:

(1)   The identity and mailing address of the satisfaction agent.

(2)   Identification of the security instrument for which a recorded satisfaction is sought, including the names of the original parties to, and the recording data for, the security instrument.

(3)   A statement that the satisfaction agent has reasonable grounds to believe that:

a.   The person to whom the notification is being given is the secured creditor; and

b. The secured creditor has received full payment or performance of the secured obligation.

(4) A statement that the security instrument has not been satisfied of record.

(5) A statement that the satisfaction agent, acting with the authorization of the owner of the real property described in the security instrument, intends to sign and submit for recording an affidavit of satisfaction of the security instrument unless, within 30 days after the effective date of the notification:

a. The secured creditor submits a satisfaction of the security instrument for recording;

b. The satisfaction agent receives from the secured creditor a notification stating that the secured obligation remains unsatisfied;

c. The satisfaction agent receives from the secured creditor a notification stating that the secured creditor has assigned the security instrument and identifying the name and address of the assignee; or

d. The security instrument is satisfied of record by any of the methods provided in G.S. 45-37(a).

(b) A notification under subsection (a) of this section must be sent by a method authorized by G.S. 45-36.5 that provides proof of receipt to the secured creditor's address for giving a notification for the purpose of requesting a payoff statement or, if the satisfaction agent cannot ascertain that address, to the secured creditor's address for notification for any other purpose.

(c) This Article does not require a person to agree to serve as a satisfaction agent.

(d) A satisfaction agent does not have to give the notification described in this section if (i) the secured creditor has authorized the satisfaction agent to sign and submit an affidavit of satisfaction; (ii) the satisfaction agent has in his or her possession the instruments described in G.S. 45-36.15(a)(3), (a)(4), or (a)(5); or (iii) after diligent inquiry, the satisfaction agent has been unable to determine the identity of the secured creditor because, for example, the last known secured creditor no longer exists and the satisfaction agent has been unable to identify any successor-in-interest to the last known secured creditor. (2005-123, s. 1; 2013-204, s. 2.2.)

§ 45-36.15. Affidavit of satisfaction: authorization to submit for recording.

(a) Subject to subsections (b) and (c) of this section, a satisfaction agent may sign and submit for recording an affidavit of satisfaction of a security instrument complying with G.S. 45-36.16 if the satisfaction agent has reasonable grounds to believe that the secured creditor has received full payment or performance of the secured obligation and one or more of the following apply:

(1) The secured creditor has not, to the knowledge of the satisfaction agent, submitted for recording a satisfaction of a security instrument or otherwise caused the security instrument to be satisfied of record pursuant to any of the methods provided in G.S. 45-37(a) within 30 days after the effective date of a notification complying with G.S. 45-36.14(a).

(2) The secured creditor has authorized the satisfaction agent to sign and submit for recording an affidavit of satisfaction.

(3) The satisfaction agent has in his or her possession the original security instrument and the original bond, note, or other instrument secured thereby, with an endorsement of payment and satisfaction appearing thereon made by one or more of the following: (i) the secured creditor; (ii) the trustee or substitute trustee, if the security instrument is a deed of trust; (iii) an assignee of the secured creditor; or (iv) any bank, savings and loan association, savings bank, or credit union chartered under the laws of North Carolina or any other state or the United States having an office or branch in North Carolina, when so endorsed in the name of the institution by an officer thereof.

(4) The satisfaction agent has in his or her possession the original security instrument intended to secure the payment of money or the performance of any other obligation, together with the original bond, note, or other instrument secured, or the original security instrument alone if the security instrument itself sets forth the obligation secured or other obligation to be performed and does not call for or recite any note, bond, or other instrument secured by it if, at the time the affidavit of satisfaction is to be signed and submitted, all such instruments are more than 10 years old counting from the maturity date of the

last obligation secured. If the instrument or instruments secured by the security instrument have an endorsement of partial payment, satisfaction, performance, or discharge within the period of 10 years, the period of 10 years shall be counted from the date of the most recent endorsement.

(5) The satisfaction agent has in his or her possession the original security instrument given to secure the bearer or holder of any negotiable instruments transferable solely by delivery, together with all the evidences of indebtedness secured thereby, marked paid and satisfied in full and signed by the bearer or holder thereof.

(6) After diligent inquiry, the satisfaction agent has been unable to determine the identity of the secured creditor because, for example, the last known secured creditor no longer exists and the satisfaction agent has been unable to identify any successor-in-interest to the last known secured creditor.

(b) A satisfaction agent may not sign and submit for recording an affidavit of satisfaction of a security instrument if it has received a notification under G.S. 45-36.14(a)(5)b. stating that the secured obligation remains unsatisfied.

(c) Unless the satisfaction agent has in his or her possession the instruments described in subdivision (a)(3), (a)(4), or (a)(5) of this section or the satisfaction agent is unable to determine the identity of the secured creditor because, for example, the last known assignee of the security instrument no longer exists and the satisfaction agent has been unable to identify any successor-in-interest to the last known assignee, a satisfaction agent who receives a notification under G.S. 45-36.14(a)(5)c. stating that the security instrument has been assigned may not submit for recording an affidavit of satisfaction of the security instrument without first:

(1) Giving a notification of intent to submit for recording an affidavit of satisfaction to the identified assignee at the identified address; and

(2) Complying with G.S. 45-36.14 with respect to the identified assignee. (2005-123, s. 1; 2013-204, s. 2.3.)

§ 45-36.16. Affidavit of satisfaction: content.

An affidavit of satisfaction of a security instrument must comply with all of the following:

(1)   Identify the type of security instrument, the original parties to the security instrument, the secured creditor, the recording data for the security instrument, and the office in which the security instrument is recorded.

(2)   State the basis upon which the person signing the affidavit is a satisfaction agent.

(3)   Reserved.

(4)   State that the person signing the affidavit has reasonable grounds to believe that the secured creditor has received full payment or performance of the secured obligation.

(4a)   Reserved.

(4b)   Reserved.

(5)   State one or more of the following, as applicable:

a.   The person signing the affidavit, acting with the authority of the owner of the real property described in the security instrument, gave notification to the secured creditor in the manner prescribed by G.S. 45-36.14 of his or her intention to sign and submit for recording an affidavit of satisfaction. More than 30 days have elapsed since the effective date of that notification, and the person signing the affidavit (i) has no knowledge that the secured creditor has submitted a satisfaction for recording and (ii) has not received a notification that the secured obligation remains unsatisfied.

b.   The secured creditor authorized the person signing the affidavit to sign and record an affidavit of satisfaction.

c.   The person signing the affidavit has in his or her possession the original security instrument and the original bond, note, or other instrument secured thereby, with an endorsement of payment and satisfaction appearing thereon made by one or more of the following: (i) the secured creditor; (ii) the trustee or substitute trustee, if the security instrument is a deed of trust; (iii) an assignee of the secured creditor; or (iv) a bank, savings and loan association, savings bank, or credit union chartered under the laws of North Carolina or any other state or the United States having an office or branch in North Carolina, endorsed in the name of the institution by an officer thereof.

d. The person signing the affidavit has in his or her possession the original security instrument intended to secure the payment of money or the performance of any other obligation together with the original bond, note, or other instrument secured thereby, or the original security instrument alone if the security instrument itself sets forth the obligation secured or other obligation to be performed and does not call for or recite any note, bond, or other instrument secured by it. All such instruments are more than 10 years old counting from the maturity date of the last obligation secured. If the instrument or instruments secured by the security instrument have an endorsement of partial payment, satisfaction, performance, or discharge within the period of 10 years, the period of 10 years has been counted from the date of the most recent endorsement.

e. The person signing the affidavit has in his or her possession the original security instrument given to secure the bearer or holder of any negotiable instruments transferable solely by delivery, together with all the evidences of indebtedness secured thereby, marked paid and satisfied in full and signed by the bearer or holder thereof.

f. After diligent inquiry, the person signing the affidavit has been unable to determine the identity of the secured creditor.

(6), (7) Repealed by Session Laws 2013-204, s. 2.4, effective June 26, 2013.

(8) Be signed and (i) acknowledged as required by law for a conveyance of an interest in real property or (ii) sworn to or affirmed before an officer authorized to administer oaths and affirmations.

(9) Copies of all or any part or parts of the instruments described in subdivision (5) of this section may be attached to and recorded with the affidavit of satisfaction. (2005-123, s. 1; 2013-204, s. 2.4.)

§ 45-36.17. Affidavit of satisfaction: form.

No particular phrasing of an affidavit of satisfaction is required. The following form of affidavit, when properly completed, is sufficient to satisfy the requirements of G.S. 45-36.16:

"AFFIDAVIT OF SATISFACTION

(G.S. 45-36.16, 45-36.17, 45-36.18)

_____

(Date of Affidavit)

The undersigned hereby states as follows:

1. I am an attorney licensed to practice law in the State of North Carolina.

2. I am signing this Affidavit of Satisfaction to evidence full payment or performance of the obligations secured by real property covered by the following security instrument (the "security instrument"), which I believe is currently or was most recently held by _____ (the "secured creditor"):

Type of security instrument:_____

Original Grantor(s):_____

___

Original Secured Party(ies):_____

Recording Data: The security instrument is recorded in Book_____

at Page _____ or as document number _____

in the Office of the Register of Deeds for _____ County, North Carolina.

3. I have reasonable grounds to believe that the secured creditor has received full payment or performance of the balance of the obligations secured by the security instrument.

4. [Check appropriate box]

[ ] Acting with authorization from the owner of the real property described in the security instrument, I gave notification to the secured creditor in the manner prescribed by G.S. 45-36.14 of my intention to sign and record an affidavit of satisfaction of the security instrument if, within 30 days after the effective date of the notification, the secured creditor did not submit a satisfaction of the security interest for recording or give notification that the secured obligation remains unsatisfied. The 30-day period has elapsed. I have no knowledge that the secured creditor has submitted a satisfaction for recording, and I have not received notification that the secured obligation remains unsatisfied.

[ ] I have been authorized by the secured creditor to execute and record this Affidavit of Satisfaction.

[ ] I have in my possession the original security instrument and the original bond, note, or other instrument secured thereby, with an endorsement of payment and satisfaction appearing thereon made by one or more of the following: (i) the secured creditor; (ii) the trustee or substitute trustee, if the security instrument is a deed of trust; (iii) an assignee of the secured creditor; or (iv) a bank, savings and loan association, savings bank, or credit union chartered under the laws of North Carolina or any other state or the United States having an office or branch in North Carolina, endorsed in the name of the institution by an officer thereof.

[ ] I have in my possession the original security instrument together with the original bond, note, or other instrument secured thereby, or the original security instrument alone if the security instrument itself sets forth the obligation secured or other obligation to be performed and does not call for or recite any note, bond, or other instrument secured by it. All such instruments are more than 10 years old counting from the maturity date of the last obligation secured. If the instrument or instruments secured by the security instrument have an endorsement of partial payment, satisfaction, or performance or discharge within the period of 10 years, the period of 10 years has been counted from the date of the most recent endorsement.

[ ] I have in my possession the original security instrument given to secure the bearer or holder of any negotiable instruments transferable solely by delivery, together with all the evidences of indebtedness secured thereby, marked paid and satisfied in full and signed by the bearer or holder thereof.

[ ] After diligent inquiry, I have been unable to determine the identity of the secured creditor.

5. (If applicable) Attached to and filed with this Affidavit of Satisfaction are copies of all or part(s) of the following instruments: (Describe attached copies)

This Affidavit of Satisfaction constitutes a satisfaction of the security instrument pursuant to G.S. 45-36.18.

_____

(Signature of Satisfaction Agent)

[Acknowledgment, oath, or affirmation before officer authorized to take acknowledgments and administer oaths and affirmations]"

(2005-123, s. 1; 2013-204, s. 2.5.)

§ 45-36.18. Affidavit of satisfaction: effect.

(a) Upon recording, an affidavit substantially complying with the requirements of G.S. 45-36.16 constitutes a satisfaction of the security instrument described in the affidavit.

(b) The recording of an affidavit of satisfaction of a security instrument does not by itself extinguish any liability of a person for payment or performance of the secured obligation.

(c) The register of deeds may not refuse to accept for recording an affidavit of satisfaction of a security instrument unless:

(1) The affidavit is submitted by a method or in a medium not authorized for registration by the register of deeds under applicable law; or

(2) The affidavit is not signed by the satisfaction agent and either (i) acknowledged as required by law for a conveyance of an interest in real property or (ii) sworn to or affirmed before an officer authorized to administer oaths and affirmations. The register of deeds shall not be required to verify or make inquiry concerning (i) the truth of the matters stated in any affidavit of satisfaction, or (ii) the authority of the person executing any affidavit of satisfaction to do so. (2005-123, s. 1; 2013-204, s. 2.6.)

§ 45-36.19. Liability of satisfaction agent.

(a) Except as otherwise provided in subsection (b) of this section, a satisfaction agent or any person purporting to be a satisfaction agent that records or submits for recording an affidavit of satisfaction of a security instrument erroneously or with knowledge that the statements contained in the affidavit are false is liable to the secured creditor for any actual damages caused by the recording and reasonable attorneys' fees and costs.

(b) A satisfaction agent that records or submits for recording an affidavit of satisfaction of a security instrument erroneously is not liable if the agent properly complied with this Article, gave notification to the secured creditor in the manner prescribed by G.S. 45-36.14, and the secured creditor did not respond in a timely manner to the notification pursuant to G.S. 45-36.14(a)(5).

(c) If a satisfaction agent or any person purporting to be a satisfaction agent records or submits for recording an affidavit of satisfaction of a security instrument with knowledge that the statements contained in the affidavit are false, this section does not preclude any of the following:

(1) A court from awarding punitive damages on account of the conduct.

(2) The secured creditor from proceeding against the satisfaction agent or person purporting to be a satisfaction agent under law of this State other than this Article.

(3) The enforcement of any criminal statute prohibiting the conduct. (2005-123, s. 1; 2013-204, s. 2.7.)

§ 45-36.20. Trustee's satisfaction of deed of trust: content and effect.

(a) Upon recording, a trustee's satisfaction substantially complying with the requirements of this section constitutes a satisfaction of the deed of trust described in the trustee's satisfaction.

(b) The recording of a trustee's satisfaction does not by itself extinguish any liability of a person for payment or performance of the secured obligation.

(c) This section applies only if the security instrument is a deed of trust. This section is not exclusive. Deeds of trust may also be satisfied of record by methods other than the filing of a trustee's satisfaction.

(d) Document is a trustee's satisfaction of a deed of trust if it complies with all of the following:

(1) Identifies the original parties to the deed of trust, the recording data for the deed of trust, and the office in which the deed of trust is recorded.

(2) States that the person signing the trustee's satisfaction is then serving as trustee or substitute trustee under the terms of the deed of trust.

(3) Contains language terminating the effectiveness of the deed of trust.

(4) Is signed by the trustee or substitute trustee then serving under the terms of the deed of trust and acknowledged as required by law for a conveyance of an interest in real property.

(e) The register of deeds shall accept for recording a trustee's satisfaction of a deed of trust, unless:

(1) The trustee's satisfaction is submitted by a method or in a medium not authorized for registration by the register of deeds under applicable law; or

(2) The trustee's satisfaction is not signed by the trustee or substitute trustee and acknowledged as required by law for a conveyance of an interest in real property. The register of deeds shall not be required to verify or make inquiry concerning (i) the truth of the matters stated in any trustee's satisfaction, or (ii) the authority of the person executing any trustee's satisfaction to do so. (2005-123, s. 1.)

§ 45-36.21. Trustee's satisfaction of deed of trust: form.

(a)   Standard Form. - No particular phrasing is required for a trustee's satisfaction of a deed of trust. The following form, when properly completed, is sufficient to satisfy the requirements of G.S. 45-36.20:

"TRUSTEE'S SATISFACTION OF DEED OF TRUST

(G.S. 45-36.20; G.S. 45-37(a)(7))

The undersigned is now serving as the trustee or substitute trustee under the terms of the deed of trust identified as follows:

Original Grantor(s): (Identify original grantor(s) or trustor(s))

Original Secured Party(ies): (Identify the original beneficiary(ies) or secured party(ies) in the deed of trust)

Recording Data: The deed of trust is recorded in Book ____ at Page ____ or as document number _____ in the office of the Register of Deeds for _____ County, North Carolina.

This satisfaction terminates the effectiveness of the deed of trust.

Date: _____

_____

(Signature of trustee or substitute trustee)

[Acknowledgment before officer authorized to take acknowledgments]"

(b)   Alternate Form. - A trustee and secured creditor who would like to indicate that the underlying obligation secured by the deed of trust has been extinguished may use the following form, which, when properly completed, is also sufficient to satisfy the requirements of G.S. 45-36.20:

"TRUSTEE'S SATISFACTION OF DEED OF TRUST

AND

CREDITOR'S RELEASE

(G.S. 45-36.20; G.S. 45-37(a)(7))

The undersigned is now serving as the trustee or substitute trustee under the terms of the deed of trust identified as follows:

Original Grantor(s): (Identify original grantor(s) or trustor(s))

Original Secured Party(ies): (Identify the original beneficiary(ies) or secured party(ies) in the deed of trust)

Recording Data: The deed of trust is recorded in Book ____ at Page ____ or as document number _____ in the office of the Register of Deeds for _____ County, North Carolina.

This satisfaction terminates the effectiveness of the deed of trust.

Date: _____

_____

(Signature of trustee or substitute trustee)

[Acknowledgment before officer authorized to take acknowledgments]

The obligation secured by the deed of trust has been extinguished.

Date: _____

_____

(Signature of secured creditor)

[Acknowledgment before officer authorized to take acknowledgments]".

(2005-123, s. 1; 2012-150, s. 2.)

§ 45-36.22. Partial release: content and effect; form.

(a) A document is a partial release if it does all of the following:

(1) Identifies the type of security instrument, the original parties to the security instrument, the recording data for the security instrument, and the office in which the security instrument is recorded.

(2) States that the person signing the partial release is the secured creditor or, if the security instrument is a deed of trust, that the person or persons signing the partial release is or are the secured creditor, the trustee, or both the secured creditor and the trustee.

(3) Contains language releasing property or an interest in property from the lien of the security instrument.

(4) Is signed and acknowledged as required by law for a conveyance of an interest in real property by the secured creditor or, if the security instrument is a deed of trust, by the secured creditor, the trustee, or both the secured creditor and the trustee.

(b) The register of deeds shall accept a partial release for recording unless one of the following applies:

(1) The document is submitted by a method or in a medium not authorized for registration by the register of deeds under applicable law.

(2) The required recording fee is not paid.

(3) The document is not signed and acknowledged as required by law for a conveyance of an interest in real property by the secured creditor or, if the security instrument is a deed of trust, by the secured creditor, the trustee, or both the secured creditor and the trustee. The register of deeds shall not be required to verify or make inquiry concerning the truth of the matters stated in any partial release or the authority of the person executing any partial release to do so.

(c) Upon recording, a partial release shall release from the lien of the security instrument the property or interest in property as is expressly described and released. With respect only to the specific property or interest in property identified and released by a partial release, the partial release shall (i) operate and have the same effect as a duly executed and recorded deed of release or reconveyance of the property or interest in the property; (ii) release and discharge all of the secured creditor's interest in the property or property interest arising from the security instrument; and (iii) if the security instrument is a deed of trust, release and discharge all the interest of the trustee in the property or property interest arising from the deed of trust. The security instrument shall otherwise remain in full force and effect, and the remainder of the property and interests in property described in and encumbered by the security instrument shall remain subject to the lien of the security instrument.

(d)   The recording of a partial release does not by itself extinguish any liability of a person for payment or performance of the secured obligation.

(e)   The provisions of this section are not exclusive. Property and interests in property may be released from the lien of a security instrument by methods other than the filing of a partial release.

(f)   Unless the deed of trust provides otherwise, the trustee in a deed of trust is not a necessary party to a partial release.

(g)   No particular phrasing is required for a partial release. The following form, when properly completed, is sufficient to satisfy the requirements of G.S. 45-36.22(a):

"PARTIAL RELEASE

(G.S. 45-36.22)

The security instrument that is the subject of this Partial Release is identified as follows:

Type of Security Instrument: (identify type of security instrument, such as deed of trust or mortgage)

Original Grantor(s): (identify original grantor(s), trustor(s), or mortgagor(s))

Original Secured Party(ies): (identify the original beneficiary(ies), mortgagee(s), or secured party(ies) in the security instrument)

Recording Data: The security instrument is recorded in Book _____ at Page _____ or as document number _____ in the office of the Register of Deeds for _____ County, North Carolina.

The person or persons signing this Partial Release is/are: (check appropriate box)

[ ]   The secured creditor.

[ ]   The trustee or substitute trustee.

[ ]   The secured creditor and the trustee or substitute trustee.

The following described property or interest in property (and no other) is released from the lien of the security instrument: (identify legal description of property or interest in property to be released)

Date:

Signature(s) of secured creditor and/or trustee

[Acknowledgment before officer authorized to take acknowledgments]". (2011-312, s. 9.)

§ 45-36.23. Obligation release: content and effect.

(a)   A document is an obligation release if it does all of the following:

(1)   Identifies the type of security instrument, the original parties to the security instrument, the recording data for the security instrument, and the office in which the security instrument is recorded.

(2)   States that the person signing the obligation release is the owner and holder of the obligation or obligations to be released.

(3)   Identifies one or more of the specific obligations that are secured by the security instrument and contains language confirming that, with respect to each such secured obligation, the obligation is no longer secured by the security instrument.

(4)   Is signed and acknowledged as required by law for a conveyance of an interest in real property by the owner and holder of the specific obligation or obligations to be released.

(b) The register of deeds shall accept an obligation release for recording unless one of the following applies:

(1) The document is submitted by a method or in a medium not authorized for registration by the register of deeds under applicable law.

(2) The required recording fee is not paid.

(3) The document is not signed and acknowledged as required by law for a conveyance of an interest in real property by the owner and holder of the obligation or obligations to be released. The register of deeds shall not be required to verify or make inquiry concerning (i) the truth of the matters stated in any obligation release or (ii) the authority of the person executing any obligation release to do so.

(c) From and after the date an obligation release is recorded, the obligation or obligations specifically identified and released in the obligation release (and only such obligation or obligations) shall no longer be secured by the security instrument, without regard to whether the obligation has been paid in full and satisfied. Unless the obligation release states that the secured obligation has been paid in full and satisfied, the recording of an obligation release does not by itself extinguish any liability of a person for payment or performance of the obligation or obligations released.

(d) Secured obligations that are not specifically identified and released in an obligation release remain secured by the security instrument, and the recording of an obligation release does not extinguish any liability of a person for payment or performance of the remaining secured obligation or obligations. The recording of an obligation release has no effect on the lien of the security instrument on the real property described in the security instrument.

(e) Unless the deed of trust provides otherwise, the trustee in a deed of trust is not a necessary party to an obligation release.

(f) No particular phrasing is required for an obligation release. The following form, when properly completed, is sufficient to satisfy the requirements of G.S. 45-36.23(a):

"OBLIGATION RELEASE

(G.S. 45-36.23)

The undersigned is now the owner and holder of the obligation(s) to be released by this instrument. As used in this release, the term "Security Instrument" refers to the security instrument identified as follows:

Type of Security Instrument: (identify type of security instrument, such as deed of trust or mortgage)

Original Grantor(s): (identify original grantor(s), trustor(s), or mortgagor(s))

Original Secured Party(ies): (identify the original beneficiary(ies), mortgagee(s), or secured party(ies) in the security instrument)

Recording Data: The security instrument is recorded in Book ____ at Page ____ or as document number _____ in the office of the Register of Deeds for _____ County, North Carolina.

Secured obligations that are no longer secured. Each of the following obligations is no longer secured by the Security Instrument, without regard to whether the obligation has been paid in full and satisfied: (identify with particularity each secured obligation that will no longer be secured by the Security Instrument)

(Optional provision which may be used in addition to or in lieu of the paragraph above:)

Secured obligations that have been paid in full and satisfied. Each of the following obligations has been paid in full and satisfied and is consequently no longer secured by the Security Instrument: (identify with particularity each secured obligation that has been paid in full and satisfied and is consequently no longer secured by the Security Instrument)

Date:

Signature of owner and holder of the obligation(s) to be released

[Acknowledgment before officer authorized to take acknowledgments]". (2011-312, s. 10.)

§ 45-36.24. Expiration of lien of security instrument.

(a) Maturity Date. - For purposes of this section:

(1) If a secured obligation is for the payment of money:

a. If all remaining sums owing on the secured obligation are due and payable in full on a date specified in the secured obligation, the maturity date of the secured obligation is the date so specified. If no such date is specified in the secured obligation, the maturity date of the secured obligation is the last date a payment on the secured obligation is due and payable under the terms of the secured obligation.

b. If all remaining sums owing on the secured obligation are due and payable in full on demand or on a date specified in the secured obligation, whichever first occurs, the maturity date of the secured obligation is the date so specified. If all sums owing on the secured obligation are due and payable in full on demand and no alternative date is specified in the secured obligation for payment in full, the maturity date of the secured obligation is the date of the secured obligation.

c. The maturity date of the secured obligation is "stated" in a security instrument if (i) the maturity date of the secured obligation is specified as a date certain in the security instrument, (ii) the last date a payment on the secured obligation is due and payable under the terms of the secured obligation is specified in the security instrument, or (iii) the maturity date of the secured obligation or the last date a payment on the secured obligation is due and payable under the terms of the secured obligation can be ascertained or determined from information contained in the security instrument, such as, for example, from a payment schedule contained in the security instrument.

(2) If the secured obligation is for the performance of some obligation other than the payment of money:

a. If the secured obligation is required to be performed by a date specified in the secured obligation, the maturity date of the secured obligation is the date so specified.

b. If the obligation is to be performed on demand or before a date specified in the secured obligation, whichever first occurs, the maturity date of the secured obligation is the date so specified. If the obligation is to be performed on demand and no alternative date for performance is specified in the secured obligation, the maturity date of the secured obligation is the date of the secured obligation.

c. The maturity date of the secured obligation is "stated" in a security instrument if (i) the maturity date of the secured obligation is specified as a date certain in the security instrument or (ii) the maturity date of the secured obligation can be ascertained or determined from information contained in the security instrument.

(b) Automatic Lien Expiration. - Except as provided in subsection (g) of this section, unless the lien of a security instrument has been extended in the manner prescribed in subsection (c), (d), or (e) of this section, the security instrument has been foreclosed, or the security instrument has been satisfied of record pursuant to G.S. 45-37, the lien of a security instrument automatically expires, and the security instrument is conclusively deemed satisfied of record pursuant to G.S. 45-37, at the earliest of the following times:

(1) If the security instrument was first recorded before October 1, 2011:

a. If the maturity date of the secured obligation is stated in the security instrument, 15 years after the maturity date.

b. If the maturity date of the secured obligation is not stated in the security instrument, 35 years after the date the security instrument was recorded in the office of the register of deeds.

c. Without regard to whether the maturity date of the secured obligation is stated in the security instrument, 15 years from whichever of the following occurs last:

1. The date when the conditions of the security instrument were required by its terms to have been performed.

2. The date of maturity of the last installment of debt or interest secured thereby.

3. The date an affidavit or separate instrument was recorded pursuant to the provisions of G.S. 45-37(b), if any such affidavit or separate instrument was

recorded before October 1, 2011, and before the lien of the security instrument expired.

(2) If the security instrument was first recorded on or after October 1, 2011:

a. If the maturity date of the secured obligation is stated in the security instrument, 15 years after the maturity date.

b. If the maturity date of the secured obligation is not stated in the security instrument, 35 years after the date the security instrument was recorded in the office of the register of deeds.

(c) Methods To Extend a Lien. - The lien of a recorded security instrument may be extended one or more times by recording (i) a lien maturity extension agreement or (ii) a notice of maturity date. If more than one lien maturity extension agreement or notice of maturity date is recorded, the most recently recorded lien maturity extension agreement or notice of maturity date controls in determining when the lien of a security instrument expires. A lien maturity extension agreement or notice of maturity date is ineffective unless recorded before the lien expires. The lien of the original security instrument may not be extended to a date more than 50 years after the date the security instrument was originally recorded in the office of the register of deeds without the written agreement of the then owner of the property encumbered by the lien of the security instrument.

(d) Lien Maturity Extension Agreement. -

(1) The lien of a recorded security instrument may be extended to a date specified in a lien maturity extension agreement, provided the lien maturity extension agreement is recorded before the lien expires. When a lien maturity extension agreement has been duly recorded, the lien of the security instrument will expire on the date specified in the lien maturity extension agreement.

(2) A document (including any document that modifies, amends, or restates a security instrument) is a lien maturity extension agreement if it does all of the following:

a. Identifies the type of security instrument, the original parties to the security instrument, the recording data for the security instrument, and the office in which the security instrument is recorded.

b. States the date to which the lien of the security instrument is extended.

c. Is signed and acknowledged as required by law for a conveyance of an interest in real property by the secured creditor and the then owner of the property encumbered by the lien of the security instrument.

(3) No particular phrasing is required for a lien maturity extension agreement. The following form, when properly completed, is sufficient to satisfy the requirements for a lien maturity extension agreement:

"LIEN MATURITY EXTENSION AGREEMENT

(G.S. 45-36.24(d))

_____ is now the secured creditor under the security instrument identified as follows:

Type of Security Instrument: (identify type of security instrument, such as deed of trust or mortgage)

Original Grantor(s): (identify original grantor(s), trustor(s), or mortgagor(s))

Original Secured Party(ies): (identify the original beneficiary(ies), mortgagee(s), or secured party(ies) in the security instrument)

Recording Data: The security instrument is recorded in Book ____ at Page ____ or as document number ____ in the office of the Register of Deeds for _____ County, North Carolina.

_____ is now the owner of the real property encumbered by the lien of the security instrument.

Pursuant to G.S. 45-36.24(d), the lien of the security instrument is extended to and including _____ (specify date).

Date: _____

_____   _____

Signature of Current Owner   Signature of Secured Creditor

of Real Property

[Acknowledgments before officer authorized to take acknowledgments]"

(e)   Notice of Maturity Date. -

(1)   The lien of a recorded security instrument may be extended by a notice of maturity date, provided the notice of maturity date is recorded before the lien expires.

(2)   When a notice of maturity date signed only by the secured creditor has been duly recorded, the lien of the security instrument will expire at the earliest of the following times: (i) 15 years after the maturity of the secured obligation as stated in the notice of maturity date or (ii) 50 years after the date the security instrument was originally recorded in the office of the register of deeds. A document signed only by the secured creditor is a notice of maturity date if it does all of the following:

a.   Identifies the type of security instrument, the original parties to the security instrument, the recording data for the security instrument, and the office in which the security instrument is recorded.

b.   States that the person signing the notice of maturity date is the secured creditor.

c.   States the maturity date of the secured obligation.

d.   Is signed and acknowledged as required by law for a conveyance of an interest in real property by the secured creditor.

(3)   When a notice of maturity date signed by the secured creditor and by the then owner of the property encumbered by the lien of the security instrument has been duly recorded, the lien of the security instrument will expire 15 years after the maturity date of the secured obligation as stated in the notice of maturity. A document (including any document that modifies, amends, or restates a security instrument) signed by the secured creditor and by the then owner of the property encumbered by the lien of the security instrument is a notice of maturity date if it:

a. Identifies the type of security instrument, the original parties to the security instrument, the recording data for the security instrument, and the office in which the security instrument is recorded.

b. States the maturity date of the secured obligation.

c. Is signed and acknowledged as required by law for a conveyance of an interest in real property by the secured creditor and the then owner of the property encumbered by the lien of the security instrument.

(4) No particular phrasing is required for a notice of maturity date. The following form, when properly completed, is sufficient to satisfy the requirements for a notice of maturity date signed only by the secured creditor:

"NOTICE OF MATURITY DATE

(G.S. 45-36.24(e))

The undersigned is now the secured creditor under the security instrument identified as follows:

Type of Security Instrument: (identify type of security instrument, such as deed of trust or mortgage)

Original Grantor(s): (identify original grantor(s), trustor(s), or mortgagor(s))

Original Secured Party(ies): (identify the original beneficiary(ies), mortgagee(s), or secured party(ies) in the security instrument)

Recording Data: The security instrument is recorded in Book ____ at Page ____ or as document number ____ in the office of the Register of Deeds for _____ County, North Carolina.

The maturity date of the secured obligation is _____ (specify date).

Date: _____

_____

Signature(s) of secured creditor

[Acknowledgment before officer authorized to take acknowledgments]"

(f)   Exception. - The register of deeds shall accept a lien maturity extension agreement or a notice of maturity date for recording and index the document as a subsequent instrument in accordance with G.S. 161-14.1, unless one of the following applies:

(1)   The document is submitted by a method or in a medium not authorized for registration by the register of deeds under applicable law.

(2)   The required recording fee is not paid.

(3)   The document is not signed and acknowledged as required by law for a conveyance of an interest in real property. The register of deeds shall not be required to verify or make inquiry concerning (i) the truth of the matters stated in the document, (ii) whether the parties to the document are in fact the secured creditor and the then owner of the real property encumbered by the lien of the security instrument, or (iii) the authority of any person executing the document to do so.

(g)   Foreclosure Proceedings. - No proceeding may be commenced to foreclose the lien of a security instrument unless the proceeding is commenced prior to the date on which the lien of the security instrument expires. However, if a proceeding to foreclose the lien of a security instrument is commenced before the lien of the security instrument expires, the lien created by the security instrument shall continue until final disposition of the proceeding. This provision shall not be construed as extending the lien or the right to bring or maintain any action for which a shorter period may be provided by law.

(h)   No Shortening of Lien Without Secured Creditor's Consent. - Subject to the provisions of G.S. 45-37, the duration of the lien of a security instrument may not be shortened without the consent of the secured creditor.

(i)   No Release or Satisfaction Necessary. - No release, satisfaction, or other instrument is necessary to discharge the lien of a security instrument that has expired; however, nothing in this section shall be construed as affecting or preventing the execution and recordation of any such release, satisfaction, or other document.

(j) Trustee in a Deed of Trust. - For purposes of this section, the trustee or substitute trustee in a deed of trust (i) shall not be considered the owner of the property encumbered by the lien of the deed of trust and (ii) shall not be a necessary party to a lien maturity extension agreement or notice of maturity date.

(k) Applicability. - This section applies to all security instruments, whether recorded before, on, or after October 1, 2011, except the following:

(1) Any security instrument securing the payment of money or securing the performance of any other obligation or obligations conclusively presumed to have been fully paid and performed pursuant to the provisions of G.S. 45-37(b) prior to October 1, 2011.

(2) Any security instrument made or given by any railroad company, or any agreement of conditional sale, equipment trust agreement, lease, chattel mortgage, or other instrument relating to the sale, purchase, or lease of railroad equipment or rolling stock, or of other personal property. (2011-312, s. 11; 2013-204, s. 2.8.)

§ 45-37. Satisfaction of record of security instruments.

(a) Subject to the provisions of G.S. 45-36.9(a) and G.S. 45-73 relating to security instruments which secure future advances, any security instrument intended to secure the payment of money or the performance of any other obligation registered as required by law may be satisfied of record and thereby discharged and released of record in the following manner:

(1) Security instruments satisfied of record prior to October 1, 2005, pursuant to this subdivision as it was in effect prior to October 1, 2005, shall be deemed satisfied of record, discharged, and released.

(2) Security instruments satisfied of record prior to October 1, 2011, pursuant to this subdivision as it was in effect prior to October 1, 2011, shall be deemed satisfied of record, discharged, and released.

(3) Security instruments satisfied of record prior to October 1, 2011, pursuant to this subdivision as it was in effect prior to October 1, 2011, shall be deemed satisfied of record, discharged, and released.

(4) Security instruments satisfied of record prior to October 1, 2011, pursuant to this subdivision as it was in effect prior to October 1, 2011, shall be deemed satisfied of record, discharged, and released.

(5) Security instruments satisfied of record prior to October 1, 2005, pursuant to this subdivision as it was in effect prior to October 1, 2005, shall be deemed satisfied of record, discharged, and released.

(6) Security instruments satisfied of record prior to October 1, 2005, pursuant to this subdivision as it was in effect prior to October 1, 2005, shall be deemed satisfied of record, discharged, and released.

(7) By recording:

a. A satisfaction document that satisfies the requirements of G.S. 45-36.10,

b. An affidavit of satisfaction that satisfies the requirements of G.S. 45-36.16, or

c. A trustee's satisfaction that satisfies the requirements of G.S. 45-36.20, but only if the security instrument is a deed of trust.

The register of deeds shall not be required to verify or make inquiry concerning (i) the truth of the matters stated in any satisfaction document, affidavit of satisfaction, or trustee's satisfaction, or (ii) the authority of the person executing any satisfaction document, affidavit, or trustee's satisfaction to do so.

(b) It shall be conclusively presumed that the conditions of any security instrument recorded before October 1, 2011, securing the payment of money or securing the performance of any other obligation or obligations have been complied with or the debts secured thereby paid or obligations performed, as against creditors or purchasers for valuable consideration from the mortgagor or grantor, from and after the expiration of 15 years from whichever of the following occurs last:

(1) The date when the conditions of the security instrument were required by its terms to have been performed, or

(2) The date of maturity of the last installment of debt or interest secured thereby;

provided that on or before October 1, 2011, and before the lien has expired pursuant to this subsection, the holder of the indebtedness secured by the security instrument or party secured by any provision thereof may file an affidavit with the register of deeds which affidavit shall specifically state:

(1)   The amount of debt unpaid, which is secured by the security instrument; or

(2)   In what respect any other condition thereof shall not have been complied with; or

may record a separate instrument signed by the secured creditor and witnessed by the register of deeds stating:

(1)   Any payments that have been made on the indebtedness or other obligation secured by the security instrument including the date and amount of payments and

(2)   The amount still due or obligations not performed under the security instrument.

The effect of the filing of the affidavit or the recording of a separate instrument made as herein provided shall be to postpone the effective date of the conclusive presumption of satisfaction to a date 15 years from the filing of the affidavit or from the recording of the separate instrument. There shall be only one postponement of the effective date of the conclusive presumption provided for herein. The register of deeds shall record and index the affidavit provided for herein or the separate instrument made as herein provided as a subsequent instrument in accordance with G.S. 161-14.1. This subsection shall not apply to any security instrument made or given by any railroad company, or to any agreement of conditional sale, equipment trust agreement, lease, chattel mortgage or other instrument relating to the sale, purchase or lease of railroad equipment or rolling stock, or of other personal property.

The lien of any security instrument that secured the payment of money or the performance of any other obligation or obligations and that was conclusively presumed to have been fully paid and performed prior to October 1, 2011, pursuant to the provisions of this subsection is conclusively deemed to have expired and shall be of no further force or effect. No release, satisfaction, or other instrument is necessary to discharge the lien of a security instrument that has expired; however, nothing in this section shall be construed as affecting or preventing the execution and recordation of any such release, satisfaction, or other document.

This subsection shall apply only to security instruments securing the payment of money or securing the performance of any other obligation or obligations that were conclusively presumed pursuant to this subsection to have been fully paid and performed prior to October 1, 2011. All other security instruments shall be subject to the provisions of G.S. 45-36.24.

(c)   Repealed by Session Laws 1991, c. 114, s. 4.

(d)   Repealed by Session Laws 2005-123, s. 1.

(e)   Any transaction subject to the provisions of the Uniform Commercial Code, Chapter 25 of the General Statutes, is controlled by the provisions of that act and not by this section.

(f)   Whenever this section requires a signature or endorsement, that signature or endorsement shall be followed by the name of the person signing or endorsing the document printed, stamped, or typed so as to be clearly legible.

(g)   The satisfaction of record of a security instrument pursuant to this section shall operate and have the same effect as a duly executed and recorded deed of release or reconveyance of the property described in the security instrument and shall release and discharge (i) all the interest of the secured creditor in the real property arising from the security instrument and, (ii) if the security instrument is a deed of trust, all the interest of the trustee or substitute trustee in the real property arising from the deed of trust. (1870-1, c. 217; Code, s. 1271; 1891, c. 180; 1893, c. 36; 1901, c. 46; Rev., s. 1046; 1917, c. 49, s. 1; c. 50, s. 1; C.S., s. 2594; 1923, c. 192, s. 1; c. 195; 1935, c. 47; 1945, c. 988; 1947, c. 880; 1951, c. 292, s. 1; 1967, c. 765, ss. 1-5; 1969, c. 746; 1975, c. 305; 1985, c. 219; 1987, c. 405, s. 1; c. 620, s. 1; 1989, c. 434, s. 1; 1991, c. 114, s. 4; 1995, c. 292, ss. 1, 2, 5; 1995 (Reg. Sess., 1996), c. 604, s. 1; 2005-123, s. 1; 2006-226, s. 12; 2006-259, s. 2; 2006-264, s. 40(b); 2011-246, s. 4; 2011-312, s. 12.)

§ 45-37.1. Validation of certain entries of cancellation made by beneficiary or assignee instead of trustee.

In all cases where, prior to January 1, 1930, it appears from the margin or face of the record in the office of the register of deeds of any county in this State that the original beneficiary named in any deed of trust, trust indenture, or other instrument intended to secure the payment of money and constituting a lien on real estate, or his assignee of record, shall have made an entry purporting to fully satisfy and discharge the lien of such instrument, and such entry has been signed by the original payee and beneficiary in said deed of trust, or other security instrument, or by his assignee of record, or by his or their properly constituted officer, agent, attorney, or legal representatives, and has been duly witnessed by the register of deeds or his deputy, all such entries of cancellation and satisfaction are hereby validated and made full, sufficient and complete to release, satisfy and discharge the lien of such instrument, and shall have the same effect as if such entry had been made and signed by the trustee named in said deed of trust, or other security instrument, or by his duly appointed successor or substitute. (1945, c. 986.)

§ 45-37.2. Indexing satisfactions and other documents relating to security instruments.

(a)   The register of deeds shall record and index the following instruments in accordance with G.S. 161-14.1:

(1)   A substitution of trustee.

(2)   A document of rescission recorded pursuant to G.S. 45-36.6.

(3)   A deed of release or reconveyance.

(4)   A partial release recorded pursuant to G.S. 45-36.22.

(5)   An obligation release recorded pursuant to G.S. 45-36.23.

(6)   A satisfaction document, affidavit of satisfaction, or trustee's satisfaction recorded pursuant to G.S. 45-37(a)(7).

(7) A lien maturity extension agreement or notice of maturity date recorded pursuant to G.S. 45-36.24.

No fee shall be charged by the register of deeds for recording a satisfaction document, affidavit of satisfaction, or a trustee's satisfaction.

(b) G.S. 161-14.1 (1963, c. 1021, s. 1; 1967, c. 765, s. 6; 1987, c. 620, s. 2; 1991, c. 114, s. 2; 1993, c. 425, s. 3; 1995, c. 292, s. 6; 2005-123, s. 1; 2011-246, s. 5; 2011-312, s. 13.)

§ 45-38. Recording of foreclosure.

In case of foreclosure of any deed of trust, or mortgage, the trustee, mortgagee, or the trustee's or mortgagee's attorney shall record a notice of foreclosure that includes the date when, and the person to whom, a conveyance was made by reason of the foreclosure. In the event the entire obligation secured by a mortgage or deed of trust is satisfied by a sale of only a part of the property embraced within the terms of the mortgage or deed of trust, the trustee, mortgagee, or the trustee's or mortgagee's attorney shall indicate in the notice of foreclosure which property was sold.

A notice of foreclosure shall consist of a separate instrument, or that part of the original deed of trust or mortgage rerecorded, reciting the information required hereinabove, the names of the original parties to the original instrument foreclosed, and the recording data for the instrument foreclosed. A notice of foreclosure shall be indexed by the register of deeds in accordance with G.S. 161-14.1. (1923, c. 192, s. 2; C.S., s. 2594(a); 1949, c. 720, s. 2; 1963, c. 1021, s. 2; 1971, c. 985; 1991, c. 114, s. 3; 1993, c. 305, s. 24; 2005-123, s. 1; 2006-226, s. 13.)

§ 45-39: Repealed by Session Laws 1949, c. 720, s. 5.

§ 45-40: Repealed by Session Laws 2005-123, s. 1, effective October 1, 2005.

§ 45-41. Recorded deed of release of mortgagee's representative.

The personal representative of any mortgagee or trustee in any mortgage or deed of trust which has heretofore or which may hereafter be registered in the manner required by the laws of this State may satisfy of record, discharge and release the same and all property thereby conveyed by deed of quitclaim, release or conveyance executed, acknowledged and recorded as is now prescribed by law for the execution, acknowledgment and registration of deeds and mortgages in this State. (1909, c. 283, s. 1; C.S., s. 2596; 2005-123, s. 1.)

§ 45-42. Satisfaction of corporate mortgages by corporate officers.

All security instruments executed to a corporation may be satisfied and so marked of record as by law provided for the satisfaction of security instruments, by any officer of the corporation indicating the office held. For the purposes of recordation and satisfaction, such signature shall be deemed to be a certification by the signer that he is an officer and is authorized to execute the satisfaction on behalf of such corporation. Where security instruments were marked "satisfied" on the records before the twenty-third day of February, 1909, by any president, secretary, treasurer or cashier of any corporation by such officer writing his own name and affixing thereto the title of his office in such corporation, such satisfaction is validated, and is as effective to all intents and purposes as if a deed of release duly executed by such corporation had been made, acknowledged and recorded. (1909, c. 283, ss. 2, 3; C.S., s. 2597; 1935, c. 271; 1963, c. 193; 1991, c. 647, s. 6; 2005-123, s. 1.)

§ 45-42.1. Corporate cancellation of lost mortgages by register of deeds.

Upon affidavit of the secretary and treasurer of a corporation showing that the records of such corporation show that such corporation has fully paid and satisfied all of the notes secured by a security instrument executed by such corporation and such payment and satisfaction was made more than 25 years ago, and that such security instrument was made to a corporation which ceased to exist more than 25 years ago, and such affidavit shall further state that the records of such corporation show that no payments have been made on such secured obligation by the corporation executing such security instrument for 25 years, the register of deeds of the county in which such security instrument is recorded is authorized to record the affidavit. The register of deeds shall index the affidavit according to G.S. 161-22 using the names of parties stated in the affidavit and shall make reference to the recording data of the original security instrument as stated in the affidavit opposite the name of each party so indexed. Upon recording such affidavit, the said security instrument shall be deemed to be cancelled and satisfied of record: Provided, that this section shall not apply to any mortgagor corporation except those in which the State of North Carolina owns more than a majority of the capital stock and shall not apply to any security instrument in which the principal amount secured thereby exceeds the sum of fifteen thousand dollars ($15,000): Provided, such cancellation shall not bar any action to foreclose such security instrument instituted within 90 days after the same is cancelled. (1945, c. 1090; 1991, c. 114, s. 7; 2005-123, s. 1.)

§ 45-42.2: Reserved for future codification purposes.

§ 45-42.3. Automatic release of real property from ancillary security instruments.

(a) The following definitions shall apply in this section:

(1) Ancillary security instrument. - An assignment of leases with respect to the real property, an assignment of rents from or arising out of the real property, a financing statement covering fixtures on the real property that is filed in the office of the register of deeds in the county in which the real property is located, and any other document or instrument that assigns, or creates a lien on, an interest in the real property.

(2) Real property. - The real property described in and encumbered by the lien of a security instrument.

(b) Except as provided in subsection (c) of this section, (i) the expiration of the lien of a security instrument pursuant to G.S. 45-36.24 or the satisfaction of a security instrument of record pursuant to G.S. 45-37 shall be deemed automatically to release the real property from the operation of all ancillary security instruments that secure the same obligation or obligations secured by the security instrument and (ii) the recording of a partial release pursuant to

G.S. 45-36.22 or the recording of a deed of release shall be deemed automatically to release the real property described in the partial release or deed of release from the operation of all ancillary security instruments that secure the same obligation or obligations secured by the security instrument.

(c) Subsection (b) of this section shall not apply to an ancillary security instrument if (i) the ancillary security instrument secures obligations other than, or in addition to, the obligation or obligations secured by the security instrument; (ii) the security instrument, the ancillary security instrument, or the document recorded in the office of the register of deeds to satisfy the security instrument of record expressly states that the satisfaction of the security instrument of record shall not release the real property from the operation of that particular ancillary security instrument or from ancillary security instruments in general; or (iii) the security instrument, the ancillary security instrument, the partial release, or the deed of release expressly states that the partial release or deed of release shall not release real property from the operation of that particular ancillary security instrument or ancillary security instruments in general. (2011-312, s. 14.)

Article 5.

Miscellaneous Provisions.

§ 45-43. Real estate mortgage loans; commissions.

Any individual or corporation authorized by law to do a real estate mortgage loan business may make or negotiate loans of money on notes secured by mortgages or deeds of trust on real estate bearing legal interest payable semiannually at maturity or otherwise, and in addition thereto, may charge, collect and receive such commission or fee as may be agreed upon for making or negotiation of any such loan, not exceeding, however, an amount equal to one and one-half percent (1 1/2%) of the principal amount of the loan for each year over which the repayment of the said loan is extended: Provided, however, the repayment of such loan shall be in annual installments extending over a period of not less than three nor more than 15 years, and that no annual installment, other than the last, shall exceed thirty-three and one-third percent (33 1/3%) of the principal amount of loans which are payable in installments extending over a period of as much as three years and less than four years, twenty-five percent (25%) of the principal amount of loans which are payable in installments extending over a period of not less than four years nor more than five years, and fifteen percent (15%) of the principal amount of loans which are payable in installments extending over a period of more than five years and not more than 15 years. This section shall only apply to the counties of Ashe, Buncombe, Caldwell, Forsyth, Gaston, Henderson, McDowell, Madison, Rutherford, Watauga, and Yancey. (Ex. Sess. 1924, c. 35; 1925, cc. 28, 209; Pub. Loc. 1925, c. 592, modified by 1927, c. 5; Pub. Loc. 1927, c. 187.)

§§ 45-43.1 through 45-43.5. Repealed by Session Laws 1971, c. 1229, s. 1.

§ 45-44. Mortgages held by insurance companies, banks, building and loan associations, or other lending institutions.

A mortgage or deed of trust held by an insurance company, bank, building and loan association, or other lending institution shall be deemed, for the purposes of any regulatory statute applicable to such institutions, to be a first lien on the property despite the existence of prior mortgages or other liens on the same property in all cases where sufficient funds for the discharge of such prior mortgages or other liens shall have been deposited with such lending institution in trust solely for such purpose. Such funds may be deposited either in cash or in obligations of the State of North Carolina or of the United States maturing in sufficient amount on or before the date or dates that the indebtedness secured by such prior mortgages or other liens is to be paid. (1957, c. 1350.)

§ 45-45. Spouse of mortgagor included among those having right to redeem real property.

Any married person has the right to redeem real property conveyed by his or her spouse's mortgages, deeds of trust and like security instruments and upon such redemption, to have an assignment of the security instrument and the uncancelled obligation secured thereby. (1959, c. 879, s. 13.)

§ 45-45.1. Release of mortgagor by dealings between mortgagee and assuming grantee.

Except where otherwise provided in the mortgage or deed of trust or in the note or other instrument secured thereby, or except where the mortgagor, or grantor of a deed of trust otherwise consents:

(1) Whenever real property which is encumbered by a mortgage or deed of trust is sold and the grantee assumes and agrees to pay such mortgage or deed of trust, and thereafter the mortgagee or secured creditor under the deed of trust gives the grantee a legally binding extension of time, or releases the grantee from liability on the obligation, the mortgagor or grantor of the deed of trust is released from any further liability on the obligation.

(2) Whenever real property which is encumbered by a mortgage or deed of trust is sold and the grantee assumes and agrees to pay such mortgage or deed of trust, and thereafter the mortgagee or secured creditor under the deed of trust or trustee acting in his behalf releases any of the real property included in the mortgage or deed of trust, the mortgagor or grantor of the deed of trust is released to the extent of the value of the property released, which shall be the value at the time of the release or at the time an action is commenced on the obligation secured by the mortgage or deed of trust, whichever value is the greater.

(3) Whenever real property which is encumbered by a mortgage or deed of trust is sold expressly subject to the mortgage or deed of trust, but the grantee does not assume the same, and thereafter the mortgagee or secured creditor under the deed of trust makes a binding extension of time of the mortgage or deed of trust, the mortgagor or grantor of the deed of trust is released to the extent of the value of the property at the time of the extension agreement.

(4) Whenever real property which is encumbered by a mortgage or deed of trust is sold expressly subject to the mortgage or deed of trust, but the grantee does not assume the same, and thereafter the mortgagee or secured creditor under the deed of trust, or trustee acting in his behalf, releases any of the real property included in the mortgage or deed of trust, the mortgagor or grantor of the deed of trust is released to the extent of the value of the property released, which shall be the value at the time of the release or at the time an action is commenced on the obligation secured by the mortgage or deed of trust, whichever value is the greater. (1961, c. 356.)

§ 45-45.2. Transfer taxes not applicable.

Notwithstanding any other provision of law, no excise tax on instruments conveying an interest in real property, except that levied by Article 8E of Chapter 105 of the General Statutes, shall apply to instruments conveying an interest in property as the result of foreclosure or in lieu of foreclosure to the holder of the security interest being foreclosed or subject to being foreclosed. (1987, c. 685.)

§ 45-45.3. Trustee in a deed of trust.

(a)   The following definitions apply in this section:

(1)   Secured creditor. - The holder, owner, or assignee of the obligation secured by a deed of trust.

(2)   Trustee. - The trustee or substitute trustee then serving as such under the terms of a deed of trust.

(b)   Unless the deed of trust provides otherwise, all of the following may be done without the knowledge, consent, or joinder of the trustee:

(1)   Pursuant to G.S. 45-36.23, an obligation may be declared by the owner and holder of the obligation to be no longer secured by the deed of trust.

(2)   Property may be released from the lien of a deed of trust by the secured creditor.

(3)   The lien of a deed of trust may be released or subordinated by the secured creditor.

(4)   The terms of a deed of trust may be modified by the secured creditor and the then record owner of the property encumbered by the lien of the deed of trust.

(5)   The deed of trust may be satisfied of record by the secured creditor.

(c) Except in matters relating to the foreclosure of the deed of trust or the exercise of a power of sale under the terms of the deed of trust, the trustee is neither a necessary nor a proper party to any civil action or proceeding involving (i) title to the real property encumbered by the lien of the deed of trust or (ii) the priority of the lien of the deed of trust. Examples of civil actions or proceedings in which the trustee is neither a necessary nor a proper party include, but are not limited to, civil actions or proceedings relating to:

(1) Condemnation.

(2) Bankruptcy.

(3) The establishment or correction of title to real property, including, but not limited to, actions to quiet title, reform land records, or resolve boundary line disputes.

(4) Fraudulent conveyances.

(5) The creation or enforcement of an attachment or judgment lien.

(6) The foreclosure of a lien other than the lien of the deed of trust, regardless of whether the lien is superior or subordinate to the lien of the deed of trust, including, but not limited to, the foreclosure of mortgages, other deeds of trust, tax liens, and assessment liens.

(7) The establishment, perfection, or enforcement of a mechanic's or materialman's lien.

(8) The creation or enforcement of a constructive trust, resulting trust, or equitable lien relating to the property.

(9) The partition of real property.

(10) The interpretation or enforceability of a will, trust, or estate.

(11) A subrogation claim or other equitable claim or defense involving the priority or enforceability of a deed of trust.

(12) Determination or enforcement of rights and obligations involving easements or restrictive covenants.

(d) If a trustee is improperly joined as a party to an action or proceeding when this section provides that the trustee is neither a necessary nor a proper party to that action or proceeding, then:

(1) Upon motion duly made by any party to the action or proceeding, the trustee shall be dismissed from the action or proceeding;

(2) Regardless of whether the trustee makes an appearance in the action or proceeding, no entry of a default or default judgment shall be entered against the trustee; and

(3) If the trustee makes an appearance in the action or proceeding, each person who improperly joined the trustee as a party to the action or proceeding shall be jointly and severally liable to the trustee for all the expenses and costs incurred by the trustee in the defense of the action or proceeding or in obtaining the trustee's dismissal from the action or proceeding, including the reasonable attorneys' fees actually incurred by the trustee.

(e) Except as expressly provided in this section, this section is not in derogation of case law and statutory provisions that vest legal title to property conveyed by a deed of trust in the trustee named therein. (2011-312, s. 15.)

Article 6.

Uniform Trust Receipts Act.

§§ 45-46 through 45-66: Repealed by Session Laws 1965, c. 700, s. 2.

Article 7.

Instruments to Secure Future Advances and Future Obligations.

§ 45-67. Definitions.

The following definitions apply in this Article:

(1) Advance. - A disbursement of funds or other action that increases the outstanding principal balance owing on an obligation for the payment of money.

(2) Security instrument. - A mortgage, deed of trust, or other instrument relating to real property securing an obligation or obligations to a person, firm, or corporation specifically named in such instrument for the payment of money. (1969, c. 736, s. 1; 1989, c. 496, s. 1; 2009-197, s. 1.)

§ 45-68. Requirements.

A security instrument, otherwise valid, shall secure the following so as to give priority as provided in G.S. 45-70:

(1) Recodified as subdivision (1b).

(1a) Existing obligations that are specifically or generally identified, described, or referenced in the security instrument as being secured thereby, and all advances made at or prior to the registration of the security instrument.

(1b) Future advances and future obligations that are specifically or generally identified, described, or referenced in the security instrument as being secured thereby that may from time to time be made or incurred, but only if the security instrument shows all of the following:

a. That the security instrument is given wholly or partly to secure future advances and/or future obligations.

b. The maximum principal amount that may be secured by the security instrument at any one time.

c. The period within which future advances may be made and future obligations may be incurred, which period shall not extend more than 30 years beyond the date of the security instrument or, if the security agreement is not dated, the date the security instrument is registered.

(2), (3) Repealed by Session Laws 2009-197, s. 2, effective October 1, 2009. (1969, c. 736, s. 1; 1985, c. 457; 1989, c. 496, s. 2; 2009-197, s. 2; 2011-312, s. 16.)

§ 45-69. Fluctuation of obligations within maximum amount.

Unless the security instrument provides to the contrary, if the maximum amount secured by the security instrument has not been advanced or if any obligation secured thereby is paid or is reduced by partial payment, further advances may be made and additional obligations secured by the security instrument may be incurred from time to time within the time limit fixed by the security instrument. Such further advances and obligations, together with interest thereon, shall be secured to the same extent as original advances and obligations under the security instrument, if the provisions of G.S. 45-68 are complied with. (1969, c. 736, s. 1; 2009-197, s. 3; 2011-312, s. 17.)

§ 45-70. Priority of security instrument.

(a) Subject to subsections (a1), (c), and (d) of this section, any security instrument that conforms to the requirements of this Article shall, from the time and date of registration thereof, have the same priority to the extent of all future advances and future obligations secured by it, and all interest accruing thereon, as if all the advances had been made, all the obligations incurred, and all the interest accrued at the time the security instrument was registered.

(a1) Subject to subsections (c) and (d) of this section, if at any time the aggregate outstanding principal balance of the obligation or obligations secured by a security instrument that conforms to the requirements of this Article exceeds the maximum principal amount that may be secured by the security instrument at any one time, then, unless the security instrument provides otherwise, the amount in excess and the interest accrued on the amount in excess shall be secured by the security instrument, but (i) the amount in excess and the interest accrued on the amount in excess shall not be afforded the priority provided in subsection (a) of this section and (ii) the priority of the lien of the security instrument with respect to the amount in excess and the interest accrued on the amount in excess shall be determined by other applicable law.

(b) Repealed by Session Laws 1989, c. 496, s. 3.

(c) All payments made, sums advanced, and expenses incurred by the secured creditor (i) for insurance, taxes, and assessments, (ii) to protect the secured creditor's interest under the security instrument, or (iii) to preserve and protect the value or condition of the real property encumbered by the security instrument shall be secured by the security instrument and shall have the same priority as if they had been paid, advanced, or incurred at the time the security instrument was registered. The provisions of G.S. 45-68 shall not be applicable to such payments, advances, or expenses, nor shall accrued interest or such payments, advances, or expenses be considered in computing the principal amount that is secured by the security instrument at any one time.

(d) Notwithstanding any other provision of this Article, any security instrument hereafter executed which secures an obligation or obligations of an electric or telephone membership corporation incorporated or domesticated in North Carolina to the United States of America or any of its agencies, or to any other financing institution, or of an electric or gas utility operating in North Carolina, shall from the time and date of registration of said security instrument have the same priority to the extent of (i) all future obligations incurred by the membership corporation or utility to any mortgagee or beneficiary named in the security instrument, together with interest thereon, (ii) all future advances secured by it, together with interest thereon, and (iii) all payments made, sums advanced, and expenses incurred by the secured creditor of the types described in subsection (c) of this section, as if they all had been accrued, paid, made, advanced, and incurred at the time of the registration of the security instrument, regardless of whether the security instrument meets the requirements of G.S. 45-68. (1969, c. 736, s. 1; 1971, c. 565; 1979, c. 594; 1989, c. 496, s. 3; 2009-197, s. 4; 2011-312, s. 18.)

§ 45-71. Satisfaction of the security instrument.

Upon payment of all the obligations secured by a security instrument which conforms to the requirements of this Article and upon termination of all obligation to make advances, and upon written demand made by the maker of the security instrument, his successor in interest, or anyone claiming under him, the holder of the security instrument is hereby authorized to and shall make a written entry upon the security instrument showing payment and satisfaction of the instrument, which entry he shall date and sign. When the security instrument secures notes, bonds, or other undertakings for the payment of money which have not already been entered on the security instrument as paid, the holder of the security instrument, unless payment was made to him, may require the exhibition of all such evidences of indebtedness secured by the instrument marked paid before making his entry showing payment and satisfaction. (1969, c. 736, s. 1.)

§ 45-72. Termination of future optional advances.

(a) The holder of a security instrument conforming to the provisions of this Article shall, at the request of the maker of the security instrument or his successor in title promptly furnish to him a statement duly executed and acknowledged in such form as to meet the requirements for the execution and acknowledgment of deeds, setting forth in substance the following:

"This is to certify that the total outstanding balance of all obligations, the payment of which is secured by that certain instrument executed by_____, dated_____, recorded in book _____ at page _____ in the office of the Register of Deeds of _____ County, North Carolina, is $_____, of which amount $_____ represents principal.

No future advances will be made under the aforesaid instrument, except such expense as it may become necessary to advance to preserve the security now held.

This _____ day of _____ , 19_____ .

_____

(Signature and Acknowledgment)"

(b) Such statement, when duly executed and acknowledged, shall be entitled to probate and registration, and upon filing for registration shall be effective from the date of the statement. It shall have the effect of limiting the lien or encumbrance of the holder of the security instrument to the amount therein stated, plus any necessary advances made to preserve the security, and interest on the unpaid principal. It shall bar any further advances under the security instrument therein referred to except such as may be necessary to preserve the security then held as provided in G.S. 45-70(c). (1969, c. 736, s. 1; 1989, c. 496, s. 4; 1999-456, s. 59.)

§ 45-73. Cancellation of record; presentation of notes described in security instrument sufficient.

The provisions of G.S. 45-37 apply to discharge of record of instruments executed under this Article. (1969, c. 736, s. 1; 2011-246, s. 6.)

§ 45-74. Article not exclusive.

The provisions of this Article shall not be deemed exclusive. Nothing in this Article shall invalidate or overrule any rule of validity or priority applicable to any security instrument failing to comply with the provisions of this Article. (1969, c. 736, s. 1; 2011-312, s. 19.)

§§ 45-75 through 45-79. Reserved for future codification purposes.

Article 8.

Instruments to Secure Certain Home Loans.

§ 45-80. Priority of security instruments securing certain home loans.

(a) Notwithstanding any other provision of law, a deed of trust or mortgage which secures a loan that complies with subsection (b) below shall have priority and continue to have priority from the time and date of registration thereof to the extent of all principal and interest secured by said deed of trust or mortgage notwithstanding that the loan may be renewed or extended one or more times and notwithstanding that the interest rate may be increased or decreased from time to time. Interest which accrues pursuant to changes in the interest rate made pursuant to a method agreed to as provided in subsection (b) below (whenever such changes are made) shall be secured and have priority from the registration of the deed of trust or mortgage and not from the time changes are made.

(b) With respect to a loan referred to in subsection (a) above:

(1) The parties must provide in a written instrument agreed to by the borrower at or before registration of the deed of trust or mortgage that the loan may be renewed or extended in accordance with stated terms and that the interest rate may be increased or decreased according to a stated method; and

(2) The loan must be a loan described in G.S. 24-1.1A(a)(1) or (2).

(c) The provisions of this section shall not be deemed exclusive and no deed of trust or mortgage or other security instrument which is otherwise valid shall be invalidated by failure to comply with the provisions of this section. (1979, 2nd Sess., c. 1182.)

Article 9.

Instruments to Secure Equity Lines of Credit.

§ 45-81. Definitions.

The following definitions apply in this Article:

(1) Authorized person. - Any borrower; the legal representative of any borrower; the attorney for any borrower; a title insurance company authorized pursuant to Article 26 of Chapter 58 of the General Statutes to issue title insurance policies in the State of North Carolina, but only when the company is acting in connection with a title insurance policy issued or to be issued with respect to property then encumbered by an existing equity line security instrument; or an attorney licensed to practice law in the State of North Carolina or a bank, savings and loan association, savings bank, or credit union, but only when (i) the attorney, bank, savings and loan association, savings bank, or credit union is or was responsible for the disbursement of funds in connection with the sale of, or a new loan secured by, property then encumbered by an existing equity line security instrument and (ii) a requirement of the sale or new loan transaction is or was that the property be conveyed or encumbered free and clear of the lien of the existing equity line security instrument.

(2) Borrower. - A person primarily liable for payment or performance of an equity line of credit.

(3) Equity line of credit. - An agreement in writing between a lender and a borrower for an extension of credit pursuant to which (i) at any time within a specified period not to exceed 30 years the borrower may request and the lender is obligated to provide advances up to an agreed aggregate limit; (ii) any repayments of principal by the borrower within the specified period will reduce the amount of advances counted against the aggregate limit; and (iii) the borrower's obligation to the lender is secured by an equity line security instrument.

(4) Equity line security instrument. - An agreement, however denominated, that (i) creates or provides for an interest in real property to secure payment or performance of an equity line of credit, whether or not it also creates or provides for a lien on personal property; (ii) shows on its face the maximum principal amount which may be secured at any one time; and (iii) shows on its face that it secures an equity line of credit governed by the provisions of this Article. The term "equity line security instrument" includes a deed of trust and a mortgage.

(5) Lender is obligated. - The lender is contractually bound to provide advances. The contract must set forth any events of default by the borrower, or other events not within the lender's control, which may relieve the lender from his obligation, and must state whether or not the lender has reserved the right to cancel or terminate the obligation.

(6) Notice regarding future advances. - A written notice submitted under G.S. 45-82.3 to a lender that prevents certain advances made pursuant to an equity line of credit from being secured by the related equity line security instrument.

(7) Owner. - Any person owning a present or future interest in the real property encumbered by an equity line security instrument, but does not mean the trustee in a deed of trust or the owner or holder of a mortgage, deed of trust, mechanic's or materialman's lien, judgment lien, or any other lien on, or security interest in, the real property.

(8) Person. - An individual, corporation, business trust, estate, trust, partnership, limited liability company, association, joint venture, public corporation, government, or governmental subdivision, agency, or instrumentality, or any other legal or commercial entity.

(9) Qualified lien holder. - A person who has a mortgage or deed of trust on property already encumbered by an existing equity line security instrument,

where that person's mortgage or deed of trust was recorded after the existing equity line security instrument and it appears from warranties or otherwise that the person's mortgage or deed of trust was not intended to be subordinate to the existing equity line security instrument. The term does not include a trustee under a deed of trust.

(10) Request to terminate an equity line of credit; and termination request. - A written request submitted under G.S. 45-82.2 to a lender to terminate an equity line of credit. Each of the following shall be deemed a termination request: (i) a notification given pursuant to G.S. 45-36.9(a) requesting the lender to terminate the equity line of credit, (ii) a notification given pursuant to G.S. 45-36.9(a) containing a statement sufficient to terminate the effectiveness of the provision for future advances in the equity line security instrument, and (iii) a written request made by or on behalf of a borrower to a lender pursuant to G.S. 45-37 to satisfy a related equity line security instrument as a matter of public record. (1985, c. 207, s. 2; 1995, c. 237, s. 1; 2011-312, s. 20.)

§ 45-82. Priority of equity line security instrument.

An equity line security instrument shall, from the time and date of its registration, have the same priority to the extent of all advances secured by it as if the advances had been made at the time of the registration of the equity line security instrument, notwithstanding the fact that from time to time during the term of the equity line of credit no balance is outstanding. Interest that accrues on the equity line of credit and all payments made, sums advanced, and expenses incurred by the lender (i) for insurance, taxes, and assessments, (ii) to protect the lender's interest under the equity line security instrument, or (iii) to preserve and protect the value or condition of the property encumbered by the equity line security instrument shall be secured by the equity line security instrument and shall have the same priority as if they had been accrued, paid, advanced, and incurred at the time the equity line security instrument was registered. The accrued interest, payments, advances, and expenses shall not be considered in computing the principal amount that is secured by the equity line security instrument at any one time. (1985, c. 207, s. 2; 2011-312, s. 21.)

§ 45-82.1. Extension of period for advances.

(a) The period for advances agreed to pursuant to G.S. 45-81(3) may be extended by written agreement of the lender and borrower executed and registered prior to expiration or termination of the equity line of credit or the borrower's obligation to repay any outstanding indebtedness. Any extended period shall not exceed 30 years from the end of the preceding period for advances.

(b) If a lender and borrower extend the period for advances by registering a certificate as described in subsection (c) of this section, advances that are made after the period for advances provided in the original recorded equity line security instrument or any previously recorded extension shall have priority from a date not later than the date of registration of the certificate described in subsection (c) of this section.

(c) The priority provided in subsection (b) of this section shall be accorded only if the lender, the borrower, and, if different than the borrower, the then owners of the real property encumbered by the equity line security instrument execute a certificate evidencing the extension and register the certificate in the office of the register of deeds where the equity line security instrument is registered. The failure of any owner to execute the certificate shall affect only that owner's interest in the property, and executions by other owners shall have full effect to the extent of their interests in the property.

(d) No particular phrasing is required for a certificate of extension under this section. The following form, when properly completed, is sufficient to satisfy the requirements of subsection (c) of this section:

"Certificate of Extension of Period for Advances Under Equity Line of Credit

(G.S. 45-82.1)

_____ is now the lender and secured creditor in the security instrument identified as follows:

Type of Security Instrument: (identify type of security instrument, such as deed of trust or mortgage)

Original Grantor(s): (identify original grantor(s), trustor(s), or mortgagor(s))

Original Secured Party(ies): (identify the original beneficiary(ies), mortgagee(s), or secured party(ies) in the security instrument)

Recording Data: The security instrument is recorded in Book _____ at Page _____ or as document number _____ in the office of the Register of Deeds for _____ County, North Carolina.

The borrower(s) is/are the following: _____.

The current owner(s) of the property described in the security instrument is/are: _____.

The parties have agreed to extend to _____ (insert date) the period within which the borrower may request advances as set forth in G.S. 45-82.1.

Date: _____

_____

Signature of secured creditor

_____

_____

Signature of borrower(s)   Signature of property
owner(s) (if different)

[Acknowledgment before officer authorized to take acknowledgments]". (1995, c. 237, s. 2; 2011-312, s. 22.)

§ 45-82.2. Request to terminate an equity line of credit.

(a) Upon receipt of a request from an authorized person to terminate an equity line of credit, the lender shall (i) terminate the borrower's right to obtain advances under the borrower's equity line of credit; (ii) apply all sums subsequently paid by or on behalf of the borrower in connection with the equity line of credit to the satisfaction of the equity line of credit and other sums secured by the related equity line security instrument; and (iii) when the balance of all outstanding sums secured by the related equity line security instrument becomes zero, satisfy the related equity line security instrument as a matter of public record pursuant to G.S. 45-37. A request to terminate an equity line of credit shall be conclusively deemed to have been submitted by or on behalf of a borrower if it is submitted by an authorized person.

(b) No particular phrasing is required for a request to terminate an equity line of credit. The following form, when properly completed, is sufficient to serve as a request to terminate an equity line of credit:

"REQUEST TO TERMINATE AN EQUITY LINE OF CREDIT

(G.S. 45-82.2)

To: (name of lender)

This is a request to terminate an equity line of credit submitted pursuant to G.S. 45-82.2. For purposes of this request:

1. The borrower(s) is/are: (identify one or more of the borrowers)

2. The account number of the equity line of credit is: (specify the account number of the equity line of credit, if known by the person submitting the request)

3. The street address of the property is: (provide the street address of the property encumbered by the security instrument identified in 4.)

4. The equity line of credit is secured by the security instrument identified as follows:

Type of Security Instrument: (identify type of security instrument, such as deed of trust or mortgage)

Original Grantor(s): (identify original grantor(s), trustor(s), or mortgagor(s))

Original Secured Party(ies): (identify the original beneficiary(ies), mortgagee(s), or secured party(ies) in the security instrument)

Recording Data: The security instrument is recorded in Book _____ at Page _____ or as document number _____ in the office of the Register of Deeds for _____ County, North Carolina.

I request and direct that you (i) terminate the borrower's right to obtain advances under the borrower's equity line of credit; (ii) apply all sums subsequently paid by or on behalf of the borrower in connection with the equity line of credit to the satisfaction of the equity line of credit and other sums secured by the related security instrument; and (iii) when the balance of all outstanding sums secured by the related security instrument becomes zero, satisfy the security instrument identified above as a matter of public record pursuant to G.S. 45-37.

I certify that I am:

[ ]   The borrower (or one of the borrowers, if there is more than one).

[ ]   The legal representative of a borrower.

[ ]   The attorney for a borrower.

[ ]   A title insurance company that satisfies the requirements of G.S. 45-81(1).

[ ]   An attorney licensed to practice law in the State of North Carolina that satisfies the requirements of G.S. 45-81(1).

[ ]   A bank, savings and loan association, savings bank, or credit union that satisfies the requirements of G.S. 45-81(1).

Date:

Signature of person submitting the request"

(c)   If the person who gives a lender a request to terminate an equity line of credit is a title insurance company described in G.S. 45-81(1), that person shall give a copy of the request to the borrower accompanied by a notice that provides substantially as follows:

"NOTICE TO BORROWER

You have an equity line of credit with (name of lender) secured by a mortgage or deed of trust on real property located at (address of property).

We are a title insurance company that has issued or has agreed to issue a title insurance policy on that property. As permitted by North Carolina law, we are sending the (enclosed/attached/following/foregoing) request to your lender asking that your equity line of credit be terminated. Our reason for making this request is:

(specify reason it is appropriate for the title insurance company to request the termination of the borrower's equity line of credit)

When your lender receives our request, your lender will terminate and close your equity line of credit, and you will no longer be able to obtain credit advances. However, termination of your equity line of credit will not release you from liability for the account. All sums your lender subsequently receives in connection with your equity line of credit (including any sums we may send to your lender) will be applied by your lender to the satisfaction of your account. When the balance of your account becomes zero, your lender will be required to cancel the mortgage or deed of trust as a matter of public record.

If you have questions about this notice or our action, please contact (name of contact person or department) by calling us at (phone number) or writing to us at (mailing address).

(Name of title insurance company)"

(d)   If the person who gives a lender a request to terminate an equity line of credit is an attorney, bank, savings and loan association, savings bank, or credit union described in G.S. 45-81(1), that person shall give a copy of the request to the borrower accompanied by a notice that provides substantially as follows:

"NOTICE TO BORROWER

You have an equity line of credit with (name of lender) secured by a mortgage or deed of trust on real property located at (address of property).

We were responsible for disbursing funds in connection with the sale of the property or a new loan secured by the property. A requirement of the sale or new loan transaction was that the property be conveyed or encumbered free and clear of the existing mortgage or deed of trust that secures your equity line of credit.

As permitted by North Carolina law, we are sending the (enclosed/attached/following/foregoing) request to your lender asking that your equity line of credit be terminated. Our reason for making this request is to ensure that the mortgage or deed of trust on the property will be cancelled once your equity line of credit is paid in full.

When your lender receives our request, your lender will terminate and close your equity line of credit, and you will no longer be able to obtain credit advances. However, termination of your equity line of credit will not release you from liability for the account. All sums your lender subsequently receives in connection with your equity line of credit (including any sums we send to your lender in connection with the closing of the sale of the property or the new loan) will be applied by your lender to the satisfaction of your account. When the balance of your account becomes zero, your lender will be required to cancel the mortgage or deed of trust as a matter of public record.

If you have questions about this notice or our action, please contact (name of contact person or department) by calling us at (phone number) or writing to us at (mailing address).

(Name of attorney, bank, savings and loan association, savings bank, or credit union)" (2011-312, s. 23.)

§ 45-82.3. Notice regarding future advances.

(a) A notice regarding future advances may be submitted to a lender by an authorized person, an owner of the property, or a qualified lien holder.

(b) Except as provided in subsection (c) of this section, an advance made by a lender to a borrower pursuant to an equity line of credit will not be secured by the related equity line security instrument if the advance occurs after the lender receives and has had not less than one complete business day to act on a notice regarding future advances.

(c) Notwithstanding a lender's receipt of a notice regarding future advances, the following shall be secured by the equity line security instrument and shall have the same priority as if they had been owing, accrued, paid, advanced, or incurred at the time the equity line security instrument was registered:

(1) Sums owing to the lender under the equity line of credit at the time the lender receives the notice regarding future advances (including accrued interest), all interest that thereafter accrues on the equity line of credit, and all

payments made, sums advanced, and expenses incurred by the lender before or after the lender receives the notice regarding future advances (i) for insurance, taxes, and assessments, (ii) to protect the lender's interest under the equity line security instrument, or (iii) to preserve and protect the value or condition of the real property encumbered by the equity line security instrument.

(2) Any advance made by the lender to a borrower pursuant to an equity line of credit that occurs within one complete business day after the lender receives the notice regarding future advances.

(3) Any advance made by the lender to a borrower pursuant to an equity line of credit that occurs more than one complete business day after the lender receives the notice regarding future advances, but only if the advance was initiated or approved before the lender received the notice regarding future advances.

(d) Receipt by a lender of a notice regarding future advances shall be conclusively deemed to be an action by the borrower adversely affecting the lender's security for the equity line of credit. Upon receipt of a notice regarding future advances, the lender may terminate the borrower's right and ability to obtain additional advances under the equity line of credit.

(e) No particular phrasing is required for a notice regarding future advances. The following form, when properly completed, is sufficient to serve as a notice regarding future advances:

"NOTICE REGARDING FUTURE ADVANCES

(G.S. 45-82.3)

To: (name of lender)

This is a notice regarding future advances submitted pursuant to G.S. 45-82.3. For purposes of this notice:

1. The borrower(s) is/are: (identify borrower(s))

2. The account number of the equity line of credit is: (specify the account number of the equity line of credit, if known by the person submitting the notice)

3. The street address of the property is: (provide the street address of the property encumbered by the security instrument identified in 4.)

4. The equity line of credit is secured by the security instrument identified as follows:

Type of Security Instrument: (identify type of security instrument, such as deed of trust or mortgage)

Original Grantor(s): (identify original grantor(s), trustor(s), or mortgagor(s))

Original Secured Party(ies): (identify the original beneficiary(ies), mortgagee(s), or secured party(ies) in the security instrument)

Recording Data: The security instrument is recorded in Book ____ at Page ____ or as document number _____ in the office of the Register of Deeds for _____ County, North Carolina.

Except as provided in G.S. 45-82.3(c), subsequent advances made by you under the equity line of credit will not be secured by the security instrument identified above.

I certify that I am:

[ ] The borrower (or one of the borrowers, if there is more than one).

[ ] The legal representative of a borrower.

[ ] The attorney for a borrower.

[ ] An owner of the property encumbered by the security instrument identified above.

[ ] A title insurance company that satisfies the requirements of G.S. 45-81(1).

[ ] An attorney licensed to practice law in the State of North Carolina that satisfies the requirements of G.S. 45-81(1).

[ ] A bank, savings and loan association, savings bank, or credit union that satisfies the requirements of G.S. 45-81(1).

[ ]   A qualified lien holder as defined in G.S. 45-81(9).

Date:

Signature of person submitting the request"

(f)   If the person who gives a lender a notice regarding future advances is (i) a title insurance company described in G.S. 45-81(1); (ii) an attorney, bank, savings and loan association, savings bank, or credit union described in G.S. 45-81(1), (iii) an owner as defined in G.S. 45-81(7), other than an owner who is also a borrower, or (iv) a qualified lien holder described in G.S. 45-81(9), then that person shall give a copy of the notice regarding future advances to the borrower accompanied by a notice that provides substantially as follows:

"NOTICE TO BORROWER

You have an equity line of credit with (name of lender) secured by a mortgage or deed of trust on real property located at (address of property).

As permitted by North Carolina law, we are sending the (enclosed/attached/following/foregoing) Notice Regarding Future Advances to your lender. Subject to certain exceptions, the notice prevents any new credit advances you obtain under your equity line of credit from being secured by the mortgage or deed of trust that currently secures its repayment. Our reason for giving your lender the notice is to limit the amount secured by the mortgage or deed of trust that secures your equity line of credit and to prevent that amount from increasing.

When your lender receives our notice, your lender may elect to terminate your right and ability to obtain additional advances under your equity line of credit. However, termination of your right and ability to obtain additional advances will not release you from liability for the account. You should contact your lender to determine whether you will be able to obtain additional credit advances from your lender.

If you have questions about this notice or our action, please contact (name of contact person or department) by calling us at (phone number) or writing to us at (mailing address).

(Name of insurance company, attorney, bank, savings and loan association, savings bank, credit union, owner, or qualified lien holder)". (2011-312, s. 24.)

§ 45-82.4. Prepayment penalty.

Except as provided in G.S. 24-9(c), no prepayment penalty may be charged with respect to an equity line of credit. (2011-312, s. 25.)

§ 45-83. Future advances statute shall not apply.

The provisions of Article 7 of this Chapter shall not apply to an equity line of credit or the equity line security instrument securing it, if the equity line security instrument shows on its face that it secures an equity line of credit governed by the provisions of this Article. (1985, c. 207, s. 2; 2011-312, s. 26.)

§ 45-84. Article not exclusive.

Except as otherwise provided in G.S. 45-83, the provisions of this Article are not exclusive. Nothing in this Article shall invalidate or overrule any rule of validity or priority applicable to any mortgage, deed of trust, or other security instrument failing to comply with the provisions of this Article. (1985, c. 207, s. 2; 2011-312, s. 27.)

§ 45-85. Reserved for future codification purposes.

§ 45-86. Reserved for future codification purposes.

§ 45-87. Reserved for future codification purposes.

§ 45-88. Reserved for future codification purposes.

§ 45-89. Reserved for future codification purposes.

Article 10.

Mortgage Debt Collection and Servicing.

§ 45-90. Definitions.

As used in this Article, the following definitions apply:

(1) Home loan. - A loan secured by real property located in this State used, or intended to be used, by an individual borrower or individual borrowers in this State as a dwelling, regardless of whether the loan is used to purchase the property or refinance the prior purchase of the property or whether the proceeds of the loan are used for personal, family, or business purposes.

(2) Servicer. - A "servicer" as defined in the Real Estate Settlement Procedures Act, 12 U.S.C. § 2605(i). A licensed attorney, who in the practice of law or performing as a trustee, accepts payments related to a loan closing, default, foreclosure, or settlement of a dispute or legal claim related to a loan, shall not be considered a servicer for the purposes of this Article. (2007-351, s. 5.)

§ 45-91. Assessment of fees; processing of payments; publication of statements.

A servicer must comply as to every home loan, regardless of whether the loan is considered in default or the borrower is in bankruptcy or the borrower has been in bankruptcy, with the following requirements:

(1) Any fee that is incurred by a servicer shall be both:

a. Assessed within 45 days of the date on which the fee was incurred. Provided, however, that attorney or trustee fees and costs incurred as a result of a foreclosure action shall be assessed within 45 days of the date they are charged by either the attorney or trustee to the servicer.

b. Explained clearly and conspicuously in a statement mailed to the borrower at the borrower's last known address within 30 days after assessing the fee, provided the servicer shall not be required to take any action in violation of the provisions of the federal bankruptcy code. The servicer shall not be required to send such a statement for a fee that: (i) results from a service that is affirmatively requested by the borrower, (ii) is paid for by the borrower at the time the service is provided, and (iii) is not charged to the borrower's loan account.

(2) All amounts received by a servicer on a home loan at the address where the borrower has been instructed to make payments shall be accepted and credited, or treated as credited, within one business day of the date received, provided that the borrower has made the full contractual payment and has provided sufficient information to credit the account. If a servicer uses the scheduled method of accounting, any regularly scheduled payment made prior to the scheduled due date shall be credited no later than the due date. Provided, however, that if any payment is received and not credited, or treated as credited, the borrower shall be notified within 10 business days by mail at the borrower's last known address of the disposition of the payment, the reason the payment was not credited, or treated as credited to the account, and any actions necessary by the borrower to make the loan current.

(2a) The notification required by subdivision (2) of this section is not necessary if (i) the servicer complies with the terms of any agreement or plan made with the borrower and has applied and credited payments received in the manner required, and (ii) the servicer is applying and crediting payments to the borrower's account in compliance with all applicable State and federal laws, including bankruptcy laws, and if at least one of the following occurs:

a. The borrower has entered into a written loss mitigation, loan modification, or forebearance agreement with the servicer that itemizes all amounts due and specifies how payments will be applied and credited;

b. The borrower has elected to participate in an alternative payment plan, such as a biweekly payment plan, that specifies as part of a written agreement how payments will be applied and credited; or

c. The borrower is making payments pursuant to a bankruptcy plan.

(3) Failure to charge the fee or provide the information within the allowable time and in the manner required under subdivision (1) of subsection (a) of this section constitutes a waiver of such fee.

(4) All fees charged by a servicer must be otherwise permitted under applicable law and the contracts between the parties. Nothing herein is intended to permit the application of payments or method of charging interest which is less protective of the borrower than the contracts between the parties and other applicable law.

(5) The obligations of mortgage servicers set forth in G.S. 53-243.11. (2007-351, s. 5; 2008-227, s. 1; 2008-228, s. 19.)

§ 45-92. Obligation of servicer to handle escrow funds.

Any servicer that exercises the authority to collect escrow amounts on a home loan held or to be held for the borrower for insurance, taxes, and other charges with respect to the property shall collect and make all payments from the escrow account, so as to ensure that no late penalties are assessed or other negative consequences result. The provisions of this section shall apply regardless of whether the loan is delinquent or in default unless the servicer has a reasonable basis to believe that recovery of these funds will not be possible or the loan is more than 90 days in default. (2007-351, s. 5.)

§ 45-93. Borrower requests for information.

The servicer shall make reasonable attempts to comply with a borrower's request for information about the home loan account and to respond to any dispute initiated by the borrower about the loan account, as provided in this section. The servicer shall maintain, until the home loan is paid in full, otherwise satisfied, or sold, written or electronic records of each written request for information regarding a dispute or error involving the borrower's account. Specifically, the servicer is required to do all of the following:

(1) Provide a written statement to the borrower within 10 business days of receipt of a written request from the borrower that includes or otherwise enables the servicer to identify the name and account of the borrower and includes a statement that the account is or may be in error or otherwise provides sufficient detail to the servicer regarding information sought by the borrower. The borrower is entitled to one such statement in any six-month period free of charge, and additional statements shall be provided if the borrower pays the servicer a reasonable charge for preparing and furnishing the statement not to exceed twenty-five dollars ($25.00). The statement shall include the following information if requested:

a. Whether the account is current or, if the account is not current, an explanation of the default and the date the account went into default.

b. The current balance due on the loan, including the principal due, the amount of funds (if any) held in a suspense account, the amount of the escrow balance (if any) known to the servicer, and whether there are any escrow deficiencies or shortages known to the servicer.

c. The identity, address, and other relevant information about the current holder, owner, or assignee of the loan.

d. The telephone number and mailing address of a servicer representative with the information and authority to answer questions and resolve disputes.

(2) Provide the following information and/or documents within 25 business days of receipt of a written request from the borrower that includes or otherwise enables the servicer to identify the name and account of the borrower and includes a statement that the account is or may be in error or otherwise provides sufficient detail to the servicer regarding information sought by the borrower:

a. A copy of the original note, or if unavailable, an affidavit of lost note.

b. A statement that identifies and itemizes all fees and charges assessed under the loan transaction and provides a full payment history identifying in a clear and conspicuous manner all of the debits, credits, application of and disbursement of all payments received from or for the benefit of the borrower, and other activity on the home loan including escrow account activity and suspense account activity, if any. The period of the account history shall cover at a minimum the two-year period prior to the date of the receipt of the request for information. If the servicer has not serviced the home loan for the entire two-year time period the servicer shall provide the information going back to the date on which the servicer began servicing the home loan. For purposes of this subsection, the date of the request for the information shall be presumed to be no later than 30 days from the date of the receipt of the request. If the servicer claims that any delinquent or outstanding sums are owed on the home loan prior to the two-year period or the period during which the servicer has serviced the loan, the servicer shall provide an account history beginning with the month that the servicer claims any outstanding sums are owed on the loan up to the date of the request for the information. The borrower is entitled to one such statement in any six-month period free of charge. Additional statements shall be provided if the borrower pays the servicer a reasonable charge for preparing and furnishing the statement not to exceed fifty dollars ($50.00).

(3) Promptly correct errors relating to the allocation of payments, the statement of account, or the payoff balance identified in any notice from the borrower provided in accordance with subdivision (2) of this section, or discovered through the due diligence of the servicer or other means. (2007-351, s. 5.)

§ 45-94. Remedies.

In addition to any equitable remedies and any other remedies at law, any borrower injured by any violation of this Article may bring an action for recovery of actual damages, including reasonable attorneys' fees. The Commissioner of Banks, the Attorney General, or any party to a home loan may enforce the provisions of this section. With the exception of an action by the Commissioner of Banks or the Attorney General, at least 30 days before a borrower or a borrower's representative institutes a civil action for damages against a servicer for a violation of this Article, the borrower or a borrower's representative shall notify the servicer in writing of any claimed errors or disputes regarding the borrower's home loan that forms the basis of the civil action. The notice must be sent to the address as designated on any of the servicer's bills, statements, invoices, or other written communication, and must enable the servicer to identify the name and loan account of the borrower. For purposes of this section, notice shall not include a complaint or summons. Nothing in this section shall limit the rights of a borrower to enjoin a civil action, or make a counterclaim, cross-claim, or plead a defense in a civil action. A servicer will not be in violation of this Article if the servicer shows by a preponderance of evidence that:

(1) The violation was not intentional or the result of bad faith; and

(2) Within 30 days after discovering or being notified of an error, and prior to the institution of any legal action by the borrower against the servicer under this section, the servicer corrected the error and compensated the borrower for any fees or charges incurred by the borrower as a result of the violation. (2007-351, s. 5; 2008-228, s. 20; 2013-412, s. 8.)

§ 45-95. Severability.

The provisions of this Article shall be severable, and if any phrase, clause, sentence, or provision is declared to be invalid or is preempted by federal law or regulation, the validity of the remainder of this section shall not be affected thereby. If any provision of this Article is declared to be inapplicable to any specific category, type, or kind of points and fees, the provisions of this Article shall nonetheless continue to apply with respect to all other points and fees. (2007-351, s. 5.)

§ 45-96: Reserved for future codification purposes.

§ 45-97: Reserved for future codification purposes.

§ 45-98: Reserved for future codification purposes.

§ 45-99: Reserved for future codification purposes.

Article 11.

Emergency Program to Reduce Home Foreclosures.

§ 45-100. Title.

This Article shall be known as the Emergency Program to Reduce Home Foreclosures Act. (2008-226, s. 1; 2010-168, s. 9; 2012-79, s. 2.17(g).)

§ 45-101. Definitions.

The following definitions apply throughout this Article:

(1)	Act as a mortgage servicer. - To engage, whether for compensation or gain from another or on its own behalf, in the business of receiving any scheduled periodic payments from a borrower pursuant to the terms of any mortgage loan, including amounts for escrow accounts, and making the payments of principal and interest and such other payments with respect to the amounts received from the borrower as may be required pursuant to the mortgage loan, the mortgage servicing loan documents, or servicing contract.

(1a)	Repealed by Session Laws 2010-168, s. 1, effective November 1, 2010.

(1b)	Home loan. - A loan that has all of the following characteristics:

a.	The loan is not (i) an equity line of credit as defined in G.S. 24-9, (ii) a construction loan as defined in G.S. 24-10, (iii) a reverse mortgage transaction, or (iv) a bridge loan with a term of 12 months or less, such as a loan to purchase a new dwelling where the borrower plans to sell a current dwelling within 12 months.

b.	The borrower is a natural person.

c.	The debt is incurred by the borrower primarily for personal, family, or household purposes.

d.	The principal amount of the loan does not exceed the conforming loan size limit for a single-family dwelling as established from time to time by Fannie Mae.

e. The loan is secured by (i) a security interest in a manufactured home, as defined in G.S. 143-145, in the State which is or will be occupied by the borrower as the borrower's principal dwelling, (ii) a mortgage or deed of trust on real property in the State upon which there is located an existing structure designed principally for occupancy of from one to four families that is or will be occupied by the borrower as the borrower's principal dwelling, or (iii) a mortgage or deed of trust on real property in the State upon which there is to be constructed using the loan proceeds a structure or structures designed principally for occupancy of from one to four families which, when completed, will be occupied by the borrower as the borrower's principal dwelling.

f. A purpose of the loan is to (i) purchase the dwelling, (ii) construct, repair, rehabilitate, remodel, or improve the dwelling or the real property on which it is located, (iii) satisfy and replace an existing obligation secured by the same real property, or (iv) consolidate existing consumer debts into a new home loan.

(1c) Housing Finance Agency. - The North Carolina Housing Finance Agency.

(2) Mortgage lender. - A person engaged in the business of making mortgage loans for compensation or gain.

(3) Mortgage servicer. - A person who directly or indirectly acts as a mortgage servicer as that term is defined in subdivision (1) of this section or who otherwise meets the definition of the term "servicer" in the Real Estate Settlement Procedures Act, 12 U.S.C. § 2605(i), with respect to mortgage loans.

(3a) Repealed by Session Laws 2010-168, s. 1, effective November 1, 2010.

(4) Repealed by Session Laws 2010-168, s. 1, effective November 1, 2010. (2008-226, s. 1; 2009-457, s. 3; 2010-168, ss. 1, 9; 2011-288, s. 1; 2012-79, s. 2.17(g).)

§ 45-102. Pre-foreclosure notice for home loans.

At least 45 days prior to the filing of a notice of hearing in a foreclosure proceeding on a primary residence, mortgage servicers of home loans shall send written notice by mail to the last known address of the borrower to inform the borrower of the availability of resources to avoid foreclosure, including:

(1)   An itemization of all past due amounts causing the loan to be in default.

(2)   An itemization of any other charges that must be paid in order to bring the loan current.

(3)   A statement that the borrower may have options available other than foreclosure and that the borrower may discuss available options with the mortgage lender, the mortgage servicer, or a counselor approved by the U.S. Department of Housing and Urban Development.

(4)   The address, telephone number, and other contact information for the mortgage lender, the mortgage servicer, or the agent for either of them who is authorized to attempt to work with the borrower to avoid foreclosure.

(5)   The name, address, telephone number, and other contact information for one or more HUD-approved counseling agencies operating to assist borrowers in North Carolina to avoid foreclosure.

(6)   The address, telephone number, and other contact information for the State Home Foreclosure Prevention Project of the Housing Finance Agency. (2008-226, s. 1; 2010-168, ss. 1, 9; 2012-79, s. 2.17(a), (g).)

§ 45-103. Pre-foreclosure information to be filed with the Administrative Office of the Courts for home loans.

(a)   Within three business days of mailing the notice required by G.S. 45-102, the mortgage servicer shall file certain information with the Administrative Office of the Courts. The filing shall be in an electronic format, as designated by the Administrative Office of the Courts, and shall contain the name and address of the borrower, the due date of the last scheduled payment made by the borrower, and the date the notice was mailed to the borrower. The Administrative Office of the Courts shall establish an internal database to track information required by this section. The Housing Finance Agency shall design and develop the State Home Foreclosure Prevention Project database, in consultation with the Administrative Office of the Courts. Only the Administrative

Office of the Courts, the Housing Finance Agency, and the clerk of court as provided by G.S. 45-107 shall have access to the database.

(b) As permitted by applicable State and federal law, optional information may be requested from the mortgage servicer to facilitate further review by the State Home Foreclosure Prevention Project described in G.S. 45-104. This optional information shall be used by the State Home Foreclosure Prevention Project to prioritize efforts to reach borrowers most likely to avoid foreclosure and to prevent delay for defaults where foreclosure is unavoidable.

(c) Repealed by Session Laws 2010-168, s. 1, effective November 1, 2010. (2008-226, s. 1; 2010-168, ss. 1, 9; 2011-288, s. 2; 2012-79, s. 2.17(b), (g).)

§ 45-104. State Home Foreclosure Prevention Project and Fund.

(a) The purpose of the State Home Foreclosure Prevention Project is to seek solutions to avoid foreclosures for home loans. The Project may include input from HUD-approved housing counselors, community organizations, the Credit Union Division and other State agencies, mortgage lenders, mortgage servicers, and other partners. The Housing Finance Agency shall administer the Project.

(b) There is established a State Home Foreclosure Prevention Trust Fund to be managed and maintained by the Housing Finance Agency. The funds shall be held separate from any other funds received by the Housing Finance Agency in trust for the operation of the State Home Foreclosure Prevention Project.

(c) Upon the filing of the information required under G.S. 45-103, the mortgage servicer shall pay a fee of seventy-five dollars ($75.00) to the State Home Foreclosure Prevention Trust Fund. The fee shall not be charged more than once for a home loan covered by this act. The Housing Finance Agency shall collect the fee. Upon receipt of the fee the Housing Finance Agency shall deposit the funds into the State Home Foreclosure Prevention Trust Fund. The Housing Finance Agency shall manage the State Home Foreclosure Prevention Trust Fund.

(d) The Housing Finance Agency shall use funds from the State Home Foreclosure Prevention Trust Fund to compensate performance-based service contracts or other contracts and grants necessary to implement the purposes of this act in the following manner:

(1) An amount, not to exceed the greater of two million two hundred thousand dollars ($2,200,000) or thirty percent (30%) of the funds per year, to cover the administrative costs of the operation of the program by the Housing Finance Agency, including managing on behalf of the Administrative Office of the Courts the database identified in G.S. 45-103, expenses associated with informing homeowners of State resources available for foreclosure prevention, expenses associated with connecting homeowners to available resources, and assistance to homeowners and counselors in communicating with mortgage servicers.

(2) An amount, not to exceed the greater of three million four hundred thousand dollars ($3,400,000) or forty percent (40%) per year, to make grants to or reimburse nonprofit housing counseling agencies for providing foreclosure prevention counseling services to homeowners involved in the State Home Foreclosure Prevention Project.

(3) An amount, not to exceed thirty percent (30%) of the total funds collected per year, to make grants to or reimburse nonprofit legal service providers for services rendered on behalf of homeowners in danger of defaulting on a home loan to avoid foreclosure, limited to legal representation such as negotiation of loan modifications or other loan work-out solutions, defending homeowners in foreclosure or representing homeowners in bankruptcy proceedings, and research and counsel to homeowners regarding the status of their home loans.

(4) Any funds remaining in the State Home Foreclosure Prevention Trust Fund as of June 30, 2011, and any funds remaining in the State Home Foreclosure Prevention Trust Fund upon the expiration of each subsequent fiscal year shall be directed to the North Carolina Housing Trust Fund.

(e) The Housing Finance Agency shall have the discretion to enter into an agreement to administer funds under subdivisions (2) and (3) of subsection (d) of this section in a manner that complements or supplements other State and federal programs directed to prevent foreclosures for homeowners participating in the State Home Foreclosure Prevention Project.

(f) The Housing Finance Agency shall report to the General Assembly describing the operation of the program established by this act not later than

May 1 of each year until the funds are completely disbursed from the State Home Foreclosure Prevention Trust Fund. Information in the report shall be presented in aggregate form and may include the number of clients helped, the effectiveness of the funds in preventing home foreclosure, recommendations for further efforts needed to reduce foreclosures, and provide any other aggregated information the Housing Finance Agency determines is pertinent or that the General Assembly requests. (2008-226, ss. 1, 5; 2010-168, ss. 1, 9; 2011-288, s. 3; 2012-79, s. 2.17(c), (f), (g).)

§ 45-105. Extension of foreclosure process.

The Housing Finance Agency shall review information provided in the database created by G.S. 45-103 to determine which home loans are appropriate for efforts to avoid foreclosure. If the Housing Finance Agency reasonably believes, based on a full review of the loan information, the mortgage servicer's loss mitigation efforts, the borrower's capacity and interest in staying in the home, and other appropriate factors, that further efforts by the State Home Foreclosure Prevention Project offer a reasonable prospect to avoid foreclosure on primary residences, the Executive Director of the Housing Finance Agency shall have the authority to extend one time under this Article the allowable filing date for any foreclosure proceeding on a primary residence by up to 30 days beyond the earliest filing date established by the pre-foreclosure notice. If the Executive Director of the Housing Finance Agency makes the determination that a loan is subject to this section, the Housing Finance Agency shall notify the borrower, mortgage servicer, and the Administrative Office of the Courts. (2008-226, s. 1; 2010-168, ss. 1, 9; 2011-288, s. 4; 2012-79, s. 2.17(d), (g).)

§ 45-106. Use and privacy of records.

The data provided to the Administrative Office of the Courts pursuant to G.S. 45-103 shall be exclusively for the use and purposes of the State Home Foreclosure Prevention Project developed by the Commissioner of Banks and administered by the Housing Finance Agency in accordance with G.S. 45-104. The information provided to the database is not a public record, except that a mortgage lender and a mortgage servicer shall have access to the information submitted only with regard to its own loans. Provision of information to the Administrative Office of the Courts for use by the State Home Foreclosure

Prevention Project shall not be considered a violation of G.S. 53B-8. A mortgage servicer shall be held harmless for any alleged breach of privacy rights of the borrower with respect to the information the mortgage servicer provides in accordance with this Article. (2008-226, s. 1; 2010-168, ss. 1, 9; 2011-288, s. 5; 2012-79, s. 2.17(e), (g).)

§ 45-107. Foreclosure filing.

(a) For the duration of the program authorized by this Article, foreclosure notices filed on home loans on or after November 1, 2010, shall contain a certification by the filing party that the pre-foreclosure notice required by G.S. 45-102 and the pre-foreclosure information required by G.S. 45-103 were provided in accordance with this Article and that the periods of time established by the Article have elapsed.

(b) The clerk of superior court or other judicial officer may have access to the pre-foreclosure database to confirm information provided in subsection (a) of this section. A materially inaccurate statement in the certification shall be cause for dismissal without prejudice of any foreclosure proceeding on a primary residence initiated by the mortgage servicer and for payment by the filing party of costs incurred by the borrower in defending the foreclosure proceeding. (2008-226, s. 1; 2010-168, ss. 1, 9; 2012-79, s. 2.17(g).)

Chapter 45A.

Good Funds Settlement Act.

§ 45A-1. Short title.

This Chapter shall be known as the Good Funds Settlement Act. (1995 (Reg. Sess., 1996), c. 714, s. 1.)

§ 45A-2. Applicability.

This Chapter applies only to real estate transactions involving a one-to four-family residential dwelling or a lot restricted to residential use. (1995 (Reg. Sess., 1996), c. 714, s. 1.)

§ 45A-3. Definitions.

As used in this Chapter, unless the context otherwise requires:

(1)   "Bank" means a financial institution, including but not limited to a national bank, state chartered bank, savings bank, or credit union that is insured by the Federal Deposit Insurance Corporation or a comparable agency of the federal or state government.

(2)   "Borrower" means the maker of the promissory note evidencing the loan to be delivered at the closing.

(3)   "Cashier's check" means a check that is drawn on a bank, is signed by an officer or employee of the bank on behalf of the bank as drawer, is a direct obligation of the bank, and is provided to a customer of the bank or acquired from the bank for remittance purposes.

(4)   "Certified check" means a check with respect to which the drawee bank certifies by signature on the check of an officer or other authorized employee of the bank that (i) the signature of the drawer on the check is genuine and the bank has set aside funds that are equal to the amount of the check and will be used to pay the check or (ii) the bank will pay the check upon presentment.

(5)   "Closing" means the time agreed upon by the purchaser, seller, and lender (if applicable), when the execution and delivery of the documents necessary to consummate the transaction contemplated by the parties to the contract occurs, and includes a loan closing.

(6)   "Closing funds" means the gross or net proceeds of the real estate transaction, including any loan funds, to be disbursed by the settlement agent as part of the disbursement of settlement proceeds on behalf of the parties.

(7)   "Collected funds" means funds deposited and irrevocably credited to a settlement agent's account used to fund the disbursement of settlement proceeds which account is a trust account, escrow account, or an account held by a company or its subsidiary which is licensed and supervised by the North Carolina Commissioner of Banks.

(8) "Disbursement of settlement proceeds" means the payment of all closing funds from the transaction by the settlement agent to the persons or entities entitled to that payment.

(9) "Lender" means any person or entity engaged in making or originating loans secured by mortgages or deeds of trust on real estate.

(10) "Loan closing" means the time agreed upon by the borrower and lender, as applicable, when the execution and delivery of loan documents by the borrower occurs.

(11) "Loan documents" means the note evidencing the debt due to the lender, the deed of trust or mortgage to secure that debt to the lender, and any other documents required by the lender to be executed by the borrower as part of the loan closing transaction.

(12) "Loan funds" means the gross or net proceeds of the loan to be disbursed by the settlement agent as part of the disbursement of settlement proceeds on behalf of the borrower and lender.

(13) "Party" or "parties" means the seller, purchaser, borrower, lender, and settlement agent, as applicable to the subject transaction.

(14) "Settlement" means the time when the settlement agent has received the duly executed deed, deed of trust or mortgage, and other loan documents and funds required to carry out the terms of the contracts between the parties.

(15) "Settlement agent" means the person or persons responsible for conducting the settlement and disbursement of the settlement proceeds, and includes any individual, corporation, partnership, or other entity conducting the settlement and disbursement of the closing funds.

(16) "Teller's check" means a check provided to a customer of a bank or acquired from a bank for remittance purposes, that is drawn by the bank, and drawn on another bank or payable through or at a bank. (1995 (Reg. Sess., 1996), c. 714, s. 1.)

§ 45A-4. Duty of settlement agent.

(a) The settlement agent shall cause recordation of the deed, if any, the deed of trust or mortgage, or other loan documents required to be recorded at settlement. The settlement agent shall not disburse any of the closing funds prior to the recordation of any deeds or loan documents required to be filed by the lender, if applicable, and verification that the closing funds used to fund disbursement are deposited in the settlement agent's trust or escrow account in one or more forms prescribed by this Chapter. Unless otherwise provided in this Chapter, a settlement agent shall not cause a disbursement of settlement proceeds unless those settlement proceeds are collected funds.
Notwithstanding that a deposit made by a settlement agent to its trust or escrow account does not constitute collected funds, the settlement agent may cause a disbursement of settlement proceeds from its trust or escrow account in reliance on that deposit if the deposit is in one or more of the following forms:

(1) A certified check;

(2) A check issued by the State, the United States, a political subdivision of the State, or an agency or instrumentality of the United States, including an agricultural credit association;

(3) A cashier's check, teller's check, or official bank check drawn on or issued by a financial institution insured by the Federal Deposit Insurance Corporation or a comparable agency of the federal or state government;

(4) A check drawn on the trust account of an attorney licensed to practice in the State of North Carolina;

(5) A check or checks drawn on the trust or escrow account of a real estate broker licensed under Chapter 93A of the General Statutes;

(6) A personal or commercial check or checks in an aggregate amount not exceeding five thousand dollars ($5,000) per closing if the settlement agent making the deposit has reasonable and prudent grounds to believe that the deposit will be irrevocably credited to the settlement agent's trust or escrow account;

(7) A check drawn on the account of or issued by a mortgage banker licensed under Article 19A of Chapter 53 of the General Statutes that has posted with the Commissioner of Banks a surety bond in the amount of at least three hundred thousand dollars ($300,000). The surety bond shall be in a form

satisfactory to the Commissioner and shall run to the State for the benefit of any settlement agent with a claim against the licensee for a dishonored check.

(b) (For applicability date, see note) If the settlement agent receives information from the lender as provided in G.S. 45A-5(b) or otherwise has actual knowledge that a mortgage broker or other person acted as a mortgage broker in the origination of the loan, the settlement agent shall place an entry on page 1 of the deed of trust showing the name of the mortgage broker or other person who acted as a mortgage broker in the origination of the loan. Information pertaining to the identity of the mortgage broker or other person who acted as a mortgage broker in the origination of the loan shall not be considered confidential information. The terms "mortgage broker" and "act as a mortgage broker" shall have the same meaning as provided in G.S. 53-243.01. (1995 (Reg. Sess., 1996), c. 714, s. 1; 2001-420, ss. 1, 2; 2007-176, s. 1.)

§ 45A-5. Duty of lender, purchaser, or seller.

(a) The lender, purchaser, or seller shall, at or before closing, deliver closing funds, including the gross or net loan funds, if applicable, to the settlement agent either in the form of collected funds or in the form of a negotiable instrument described in G.S. 45A-4(a)(1) through (7), provided that the lender, purchaser, or seller, as applicable, shall cause that negotiable instrument to be honored upon presentment for payment to the bank or other depository institution upon which the instrument is drawn. However, in the case of a refinancing, or any other loan where a right of rescission applies, the lender shall, no later than the business day after the expiration of the rescission period required under the federal Truth-in-Lending Act, 15 U.S.C. § 1601, et seq., cause disbursement of loan funds to the settlement agent in one or more of the forms prescribed by provisions in this Chapter.

(b) (For applicability date, see note) The lender shall include in the loan closing instructions to the settlement agent the name of the mortgage broker or other person, if any, who acted as a mortgage broker in the origination of the loan. (1995 (Reg. Sess., 1996), c. 714, s. 1; 2007-176, s. 2.)

§ 45A-6. Validity of loan documents.

Failure to comply with the provisions of this Chapter shall not govern the validity or enforceability of any document, including a deed or any loan document, executed and delivered at any settlement occurring after October 1, 1996. (1995 (Reg. Sess., 1996), c. 714, s. 1.)

§ 45A-7. Penalty.

Any party violating this Chapter is liable to any other party suffering a loss due to that violation for that other party's actual damages plus reasonable attorneys' fees. In addition, any party violating this Chapter shall pay to the party or parties suffering a loss an amount equal to one thousand dollars ($1,000) or double the amount of interest payable on any loan for the first 60 days after the loan closing, whichever amount is greater. (1995 (Reg. Sess., 1996), c. 714, s. 1.)

§ 45A-8. Embezzlement of closing funds by settlement agent.

(a) All closing funds received by a settlement agent are trust or escrow funds received by the settlement agent in a fiduciary capacity.

(b) A settlement agent in the disbursement of settlement proceeds shall account for and pay the closing funds to the parties or entities identified for payment of the closing funds pursuant to the settlement agreement approved by the parties to the transaction.

(c) Except as to such portions of the closing funds representing the settlement agent's fees and expenses, a settlement agent shall be subject to the embezzlement provisions of G.S. 14-90. (2009-348, s. 2.)

§ 45A-9. Interest on settlement agent's real estate trust and escrow accounts.

(a) A settlement agent who maintains a trust or escrow account for purposes of receiving and disbursing closing funds and loan funds shall pay any interest earned on funds held in those accounts to the North Carolina State Bar to be used for the purposes authorized by the North Carolina State Bar under the Interest on Lawyers' Trust Account Program.

(b) The North Carolina State Bar shall adopt rules for the collection and disbursement of funds required to be paid to the North Carolina State Bar under subsection (a) of this section. (2011-336, s. 3.)

Chapter 46.

Partition.

Article 1.

Partition of Real Property.

§ 46-1. Partition is a special proceeding.

Partition under this Chapter shall be by special proceeding, and the procedure shall be the same in all respects as prescribed by law in special proceedings, except as modified herein. (1868-9, c. 122, s. 33; Code, s. 1923; Rev., s. 2485; C.S., s. 3213.)

§ 46-2. Venue in partition.

The proceeding for partition, actual or by sale, must be instituted in the county where the land or some part thereof lies. If the land to be partitioned consists of one tract lying in more than one county, or consists of several tracts lying in different counties, proceedings may be instituted in either of the counties in which a part of the land is situated, and the court of such county wherein the proceedings for partition are first brought shall have jurisdiction to proceed to a final disposition of said proceedings, to the same extent as if all of said land was situate in the county where the proceedings were instituted. (1868-9, c. 122, s. 7; Code, s. 1898; Rev., s. 2486; C.S., s. 3214; Ex. Sess. 1924, c. 62, s. 1.)

§ 46-2.1. Summons.

(a) In partition proceedings initiated under this Chapter, the period of time for answering a summons is provided in G.S. 1-394.

(b) Written notice shall be included in the petition in a manner reasonably calculated to make the respondent aware of the following:

(1) That the respondent has the right to seek the advice of an attorney and that free legal services may be available to the respondent by contacting Legal Aid of North Carolina or other legal services organizations.

(2) That pursuant to G.S. 6-21 the court has the authority, in its discretion, to order reasonable attorneys' fees to be paid as a part of the costs of the proceeding. (2009-362, s. 3.)

§ 46-3. Petition by cotenant or personal representative of cotenant.

One or more persons claiming real estate as joint tenants or tenants in common or the personal representative of a decedent joint tenant, or tenant in common, when sale of such decedent's real property to make assets is alleged and shown as required by G.S. 28A-17-3, may have partition by petition to the superior court. (1868-9, c. 122, s. 1; Code, s. 1892; Rev., s. 2487; C.S., s. 3215; 1963, c. 291, s. 2; 1985, c. 689, s. 16.)

§ 46-3.1. Court's authority to make orders pending final determination of proceeding.

Pending final determination of the proceeding, on application of any of the parties in a proceeding to partition land, the court may make such orders as it considers to be in the best interest of the parties, including but not limited to orders relating to possession, payment of secured debt or other liens on the property, occupancy and payment of rents, and to include the appointment of receivers pursuant to G.S. 1-502(6). (1981, c. 584, s. 1.)

§ 46-4. Surface and minerals in separate owners; partitions distinct.

When the title to the mineral interests in any land has become separated from the surface in ownership, the tenants in common or joint tenants of such mineral interests may have partition of the same, distinct from the surface, and without joining as parties the owner or owners of the surface; and the tenants in common or joint tenants of the surface may have partition of the same, in manner provided by law, distinct from the mineral interest and without joining as parties the owner or owners of the mineral interest. In all instances where the mineral interests and surface interest have thus become separated in ownership, the owner or owners of the mineral interests shall not be compelled to join in a partition of the surface interests, nor shall the owner or owners of the surface interest be compelled to join in a partition of the mineral interest, nor shall the rights of either owner be prejudiced by a partition of the other interests. (1905, c. 90; Rev., s. 2488; C.S., s. 3216.)

§ 46-5. Petition by judgment creditor of cotenant; assignment of homestead.

When any person owns a judgment duly docketed in the superior court of a county wherein the judgment debtor owns an undivided interest in fee in land as a tenant in common, or joint tenant, and the judgment creditor desires to lay off the homestead of the judgment debtor in the land and sell the excess, if any, to satisfy his judgment, the judgment creditor may institute before the clerk of the court of the county wherein the land lies a special proceeding for partition of the land between the tenants in common, making the judgment debtor, the other tenants in common and all other interested persons parties to the proceeding by summons. The proceeding shall then be in all other respects conducted as other special proceedings for the partition of land between tenants in common. Upon the actual partition of the land the judgment creditor may sue out execution on his judgment, as allowed by law, and have the homestead of the judgment debtor allotted to him and sell the excess, as in other cases where the homestead is allotted under execution. The remedy provided for in this section shall not deprive the judgment creditor of any other remedy in law or in equity which he may have for the enforcement of his judgment lien. (1905, c. 429; Rev., s. 2489; C.S., s. 3217.)

§ 46-6. Unknown or unlocatable parties; summons, notice, and representation.

(a) If, upon the filing of a petition for partition, it be made to appear to the court by affidavit or otherwise that there are any persons interested in the premises whose names are unknown to and cannot after due diligence be ascertained by the petitioner, the court shall order notices to be given to all such persons by a publication of the petition, or of the substance thereof, with the order of the court thereon, in one or more newspapers to be designated in the order. The notice by publication shall include a description of the property which includes the street address, if any, or other common designation for the property, if any, and may include the legal description of the property.

(b)   Before or after such general notice by publication if any person interested in the premises and entitled to notice fails to appear, the court shall appoint some disinterested person to represent the owner of any shares in the property to be divided, the ownership of which is unknown or unlocatable and unrepresented. (1887, c. 284; Rev., s. 2490; C.S., s. 3218; 2009-512, s. 1.)

§ 46-7. Commissioners appointed.

The superior court shall appoint three disinterested commissioners to divide and apportion such real estate, or so much thereof as the court may deem best, among the several tenants in common, or joint tenants. Provided, in cases where the land to be partitioned lies in more than one county, then the court may appoint such additional commissioners as it may deem necessary from counties where the land lies other than the county where the proceedings are instituted. (1868-9, c. 122, s. 1; Code, s. 1892; Rev., s. 2487; C.S., s. 3219; Ex. Sess. 1924, c. 62, s. 2.)

§ 46-7.1. Compensation of commissioners.

The clerk of the superior court shall fix the compensation of commissioners for the partition or division of lands according to the provisions of G.S. 1-408. (1949, c. 975; 1953, c. 48.)

§ 46-8. Oath of commissioners.

The commissioners shall be sworn by a magistrate, the sheriff or any deputy sheriff of the county, or any other person authorized to administer oaths, to do justice among the tenants in common in respect to such partition, according to their best skill and ability. (1868-9, c. 122, s. 2; Code, s. 1893; Rev., s. 2492; C.S., s. 3220; 1945, c. 472; 1971, c. 1185, s. 8.)

§ 46-9. Delay or neglect of commissioner penalized.

If, after accepting the trust, any of the commissioners unreasonably delay or neglect to execute the same, every such delinquent commissioner shall be liable for contempt and may be removed, and shall be further liable to a penalty of fifty dollars ($50.00), to be recovered by the petitioner. (1868-9, c. 122, s. 10; Code, s. 1901; Rev., s. 2498; C.S., s. 3221.)

§ 46-10. Commissioners to meet and make partition; equalizing shares.

The commissioners, who shall be summoned by the sheriff, must meet on the premises and partition the same among the tenants in common, or joint tenants, according to their respective rights and interests therein, by dividing the land into equal shares in point of value as nearly as possible, and for this purpose they are empowered to subdivide the more valuable tracts as they may deem best, and to charge the more valuable dividends with such sums of money as they may think necessary, to be paid to the dividends of inferior value, in order to make an equitable partition. (1868-9, c. 122, s. 3; Code, s. 1894; 1887, c. 284, s. 2; Rev., s. 2491; C.S., s. 3222; 1995, c. 379, s. 14(b).)

§ 46-11. Owelty to bear interest.

The sums of money due from the more valuable dividends shall bear interest until paid. (1868-9, c. 122, s. 8; Code, s. 1899; Rev., s. 2496; C.S., s. 3223.)

§ 46-12. Owelty from infant's share due at majority.

When a minor to whom a more valuable dividend shall fall is charged with the payment of any sum, the money shall not be payable until such minor arrives at the age of 18 years, but the general guardian, if there be one, must pay such sum whenever assets shall come into his hands, and in case the general guardian has assets which he did not so apply, he shall pay out of his own proper estate any interest that may have accrued in consequence of such failure. (1868-9, c. 122, s. 9; Code, s. 1900; Rev., s. 2497; C.S., s. 3224; 1971, c. 1231, s. 1.)

§ 46-13. Partition where shareowners unknown or title disputed; allotment of shares in common.

If there are any of the tenants in common, or joint tenants, whose names are not known or whose title is in dispute, the share or shares of such persons shall be set off together as one parcel. If, in any partition proceeding, two or more appear as defendants claiming the same share of the premises to be divided, or if any part of the share claimed by the petitioner is disputed by any defendant or defendants, it shall not be necessary to decide on their respective claims before the court shall order the partition or sale to be made, but the partition or sale shall be made, and the controversy between the contesting parties may be afterwards decided either in the same or an independent proceeding. If two or more tenants in common, or joint tenants, by petition or answer, request it, the commissioners may, by order of the court, allot their several shares to them in common, as one parcel, provided such division shall not be injurious or detrimental to any cotenant or joint tenant. (1868-9, c. 122, s. 3; Code, s. 1894; 1887, c. 284, ss. 2, 4; Rev., ss. 2491, 2511; C.S., s. 3225; 1937, c. 98.)

§ 46-14. Judgments in partition of remainders binding on parties thereto.

Where land is conveyed by deed, or devised by will, upon contingent remainder, executory devise, or other limitation, any judgment of partition rendered in an action or special proceeding in the superior court authorizing a division or partition of said lands, and to which the life tenant or tenants, and all other persons then in being, or not in being, take such land as if the contingency had then happened, are parties, and those unborn being duly represented by guardian ad litem, such judgment of partition authorizing division or partition of said lands among the respective tenants and remaindermen or executory devisees, will be valid and binding upon all parties thereto and upon all other persons not then in being. (1933, c. 215, s. 1; 1959, c. 1274, s. 1.)

§ 46-15. Repealed by Session Laws 1959, c. 879, s. 14.

§ 46-16. Partial partition; balance sold or left in common.

In all proceedings under this Chapter actual partition may be made of a part of the land sought to be partitioned and a sale of the remainder; or a part only of any land held by tenants in common, or joint tenants, may be partitioned and the remainder held in cotenancy. (1887, c. 214, s. 1; Rev., s. 2506; C.S., s. 3227.)

§ 46-17. Report of commissioners; contents; filing.

The commissioners, within a reasonable time, not exceeding 90 days after the notification of their appointment, shall make a full and ample report of their proceedings, under the hands of any two of them, specifying therein the manner of executing their trust and describing particularly the land or parcels of land divided, and the share allotted to each tenant in severalty, with the sum or sums charged on the more valuable dividends to be paid to those of inferior value. The report shall be filed in the office of the superior court clerk: Provided, that the clerk of the superior court may, in the clerk's discretion, for good cause shown, extend the time for the filing of the report of said commissioners for an additional period not exceeding 60 days. This proviso shall be applicable to proceedings now pending for the partition of real property. (1868-9, c. 122, s. 5; Code, s. 1896; Rev., s. 2494; C.S., s. 3228; 1949, c. 16; 2009-362, s. 1.)

§ 46-17.1. Dedication of streets.

Upon motion of any party or the commissioners appointed to make division, the clerk may authorize the commissioners to propose and report the dedication of such portions of the land as are necessary as a means of access to any share, or is otherwise advisable for public or private highways, streets or alleys, and such proposal shall be acted upon by the clerk as a part of the report and, if approved, shall constitute a dedication. No interest of a minor or other person under disability shall be affected thereby until such dedication is approved by a judge of the superior court. (1969, c. 45.)

§ 46-18. Map embodying survey to accompany report.

The commissioners are authorized to employ the county surveyor or, in his absence or if he be connected with the parties, some other surveyor, who shall make out a map of the premises showing the quantity, courses and distances of each share, which map shall accompany and form a part of the report of the commissioners. (1868-9, c. 122, s. 4; Code, s. 1895; Rev., s. 2493; C.S., s. 3229.)

§ 46-19. Confirmation and impeachment of report.

(a) If no exception to the report of the commissioners is filed within 10 days, the same shall be confirmed. Any party after confirmation may impeach the proceedings and decrees for mistake, fraud or collusion by petition in the cause: Provided, innocent purchasers for full value and without notice shall not be affected thereby.

(b) If an exception to the report of commissioners is filed, the clerk shall do one of the following:

(1) Confirm the report;

(2) Recommit the report for correction or further consideration;

(3) Vacate the report and direct a reappraisal by the same commissioners; or

(4) Vacate the report, discharge the commissioners, and appoint new commissioners to view the premises and make a partition of them.

(c) Appeal from the clerk to superior court of an order of confirmation of the report of commissioners is governed by G.S. 1-301.2 except that the judge may take only the actions specified in subsection (b) of this section and may not adjudge a partition of the land different from that made by the commissioners.

(1868-9, c. 122, s. 5; Code, s. 1896; Rev., s. 2494; C.S., s. 3230; 1947, c. 484, s. 2; 1999-216, s. 11.)

§ 46-20. Report and confirmation enrolled and registered; effect; probate.

Such report, when confirmed, together with the decree of confirmation, shall be enrolled and certified to the register of deeds and registered in the office of the county where such real estate is situated, and shall be binding among and between the claimants, their heirs and assigns. It shall not be necessary for the clerk of court to probate the certified papers required to be registered by this section. (1868-9, c. 122, s. 6; Code, s. 1897; Rev., s. 2495; C.S., s. 3231; 1965, c. 804.)

§ 46-21. Clerk to docket owelty charges; no release of land and no lien.

In case owelty of partition is charged in favor of certain parts of said land and against certain other parts, the clerk shall enter on the judgment docket the said owelty charges in like manner as judgments are entered on said docket, persons to whom parts are allotted in favor of which owelty is charged being marked plaintiffs on the judgment docket, and persons to whom parts are allotted against which owelty is charged being marked defendants on said docket; said entry on said docket shall contain the title of the special proceeding in which the land was partitioned, and shall refer to the book and page in which the said special proceeding is recorded; when said owelty charges are paid said entry upon the judgment docket shall be marked satisfied in like manner as judgments are cancelled and marked satisfied; and the clerk shall be entitled to the same fees for entering such judgment of owelty as he is entitled to for docketing other judgments: Provided, that the docketing of said owelty charges as hereinbefore set out shall not have the effect of releasing the land from the owelty charged in said special proceeding: Provided, any judgment docketed under this section shall not be a lien on any property whatever, except that upon which said owelty is made a specific charge. (1911, c. 9, s. 1; C.S., s. 3232.)

Article 2.

Partition Sales of Real Property.

§ 46-22. Sale in lieu of partition.

(a) Subject to G.S. 46-22.1(b), the court shall order a sale of the property described in the petition, or of any part, only if it finds, by a preponderance of the evidence, that an actual partition of the lands cannot be made without substantial injury to any of the interested parties, after having considered evidence in favor of actual partition and evidence in favor of a sale presented by any of the interested parties.

(b) In determining whether an actual partition would cause "substantial injury" to any of the interested parties, the court shall consider the following:

(1) Whether the fair market value of each cotenant's share in an actual partition of the property would be materially less than the amount each cotenant would receive from the sale of the whole.

(2) Whether an actual partition would result in material impairment of any cotenant's rights.

(b1) The court, in its discretion, shall consider the remedy of owelty where such remedy can aid in making an actual partition occur without substantial injury to the parties.

(c) The court shall make specific findings of fact and conclusions of law supporting an order of sale of the property.

(d) The party seeking a sale of the property shall have the burden of proving substantial injury under the provisions of this section. (1868-9, c. 122, ss. 13, 31; Code, ss. 1904, 1921; Rev., s. 2512; C.S., s. 3233; 1985, c. 626, s. 1; 2009-512, s. 2.)

§ 46-22.1. Mediation.

(a) Persons interested in the premises may agree at anytime to mediation of a partition. A list of mediators certified by the Dispute Resolution Commission may be obtained from the clerk or from the Commission through the Administrative Office of the Courts.

(b)   When a partition sale is requested, the court or the clerk may order mediation before considering whether to order a sale. The provisions of G.S. 7A-38.1 and G.S. 7A-38.3B shall apply. (2009-512, s. 3.)

§ 46-23. Remainder or reversion sold for partition; outstanding life estate.

The existence of a life estate in any land shall not be a bar to a sale for partition of the remainder or reversion thereof, and for the purposes of partition the tenants in common or joint tenants shall be deemed seized and possessed as if no life estate existed. But this shall not interfere with the possession of the life tenant during the existence of his estate. (1887, c. 214, s. 2; Rev., s. 2508; C.S., s. 3234.)

§ 46-24. Life tenant as party; valuation of life estate.

In all proceedings for partition of land whereon there is a life estate, the life tenant may join in the proceeding and on a sale the interest on the value of the share of the life tenant shall be received and paid to such life tenant annually; or in lieu of such annual interest, the value of such share during the probable life of such life tenant shall be ascertained and paid out of the proceeds to such life tenant absolutely. (1887, c. 214, s. 3; Rev., s. 2509; C.S., s. 3235.)

§ 46-25. Sale of standing timber on partition; valuation of life estate.

When two or more persons own, as tenants in common, joint tenants or copartners, a tract of land, either in possession, or in remainder or reversion, subject to a life estate, or where one or more persons own a remainder or reversionary interest in a tract of land, subject to a life estate, then in any such case in which there is standing timber upon any such land, a sale of said timber trees, separate from the land, may be had upon the petition of one or more of said owners, or the life tenant, for partition among the owners thereof, including the life tenant, upon such terms as the court may order, and under like proceedings as are now prescribed by law for the sale of land for partition: Provided, that when the land is subject to a life estate, the life tenant shall be made a party to the proceedings, and shall be entitled to receive his or her portion of the net proceeds of sales, to be ascertained under the mortality tables established by law: Provided further, that prior to a judgment allowing a life tenant to sell the timber there must be a finding that the cutting is in keeping with good husbandry and that no substantial injury will be done to the remainder interest. (1895, c. 187; Rev., s. 2510; C.S., s. 3236; 1949, c. 34; 1975, c. 476, s. 1; 1997-133, s. 3.)

§ 46-26. Sale of mineral interests on partition.

In case of the partition of mineral interests, in all instances where it is made to appear to the court that it would be for the best interests of the tenants in common, or joint tenants, of such interests to have the same sold, or if actual partition of the same cannot be had without injury to some or all of such tenants (in common), then it is lawful for and the duty of the court to order a sale of such mineral interests and a division of the proceeds as the interests of the parties may appear. (1905, c. 90, s. 2; Rev., s. 2507; C.S., s. 3237.)

§ 46-27. Sale of land required for public use on cotenant's petition.

When the lands of joint tenants or tenants in common are required for public purposes, one or more of such tenants, or their guardian for them, may file a petition verified by oath, in the superior court of the county where the lands or any part of them lie, setting forth therein that the lands are required for public purposes, and that their interests would be promoted by a sale thereof. Whereupon the court, all proper parties being before it, and the facts alleged in the petition being ascertained to be true, shall order a sale of such lands, or so much thereof as may be necessary. The expenses, fees and costs of this proceeding shall be paid in the discretion of the court. Mediator fees and costs of mediation shall be assessed in accordance with G.S. 7A-38.3B. (1868-9, c. 122, s. 16; Code, s. 1907; Rev., s. 2518; C.S., s. 3238; 1949, c. 719, s. 2; 2005-67, s. 4.)

§ 46-28. Sale procedure.

(a) The procedure for a partition sale shall be the same as is provided in Article 29A of Chapter 1 of the General Statutes, except as provided herein.

(b) The commissioners shall certify to the court that at least 20 days prior to sale a copy of the notice of sale was sent by first class mail to the last known address of all petitioners and respondents who previously were served by personal delivery or by registered or certified mail. The commissioners shall also certify to the court that at least ten days prior to any resale pursuant to G.S. 46-28.1(e) a copy of the notice of resale was sent by first class mail to the last known address of all parties to the partition proceeding who have filed a written request with the court that they be given notice of any resale. An affidavit from the commissioners that copies of the notice of sale and resale were mailed to all parties entitled to notice in accordance with this section shall satisfy the certification requirement and shall also be deemed prima facie true. If after hearing it is proven that a party seeking to revoke the order of confirmation of a sale or subsequent resale was mailed notice as required by this section prior to the date of the sale or subsequent resale, then that party shall not prevail under the provisions of G.S. 46-28.1(a)(2)a. and b.

(c) Any cotenant who enters the high bid or offer at any sale of one hundred percent (100%) of the undivided interests in any parcel of real property shall receive a credit for the undivided interest the cotenant already owns therein and shall receive a corresponding reduction in the amount of the total purchase price owed after deducting the costs and fees associated with the sale and apportioning the costs and fees associated with the sale in accordance with the orders of the court. The high bid or offer shall be for one hundred percent (100%) of the undivided interests in the parcel of real property sold, and the credit and reduction shall be applied at the time of the closing of the cotenant's purchase of the real property. When jointly making the high bid or offer at the sale, two or more cotenants may receive at the closing an aggregate credit and reduction in the amount of the total purchase price representing the total of such cotenants' undivided interests in the real property. Any credits and reductions allowed by this subsection shall be further adjusted to reflect any court-ordered adjustments to the share(s) of the net sale proceeds of each of the cotenants entering the high bid or offer, including, but not limited to, equitable adjustments to the share(s) of the net sales proceeds due to a court finding of the lack of contribution of one or more cotenants to the payment of expenses of the real property. (1868-9, c. 122, ss. 13, 31; Code, ss. 1904, 1921; Rev., s. 2512; C.S., s. 3239; 1949, c. 719, s. 2; 1985, c. 626, s. 2; 1987, c. 282, s. 7; 2009-512, s. 4.)

§ 46-28.1. Petition for revocation of confirmation order.

(a) Notwithstanding G.S. 46-28 or any other provision of law, within 15 days of entry of the order confirming the partition sale or real property, any party to the partition proceeding or the purchaser may petition the court to revoke its order of confirmation and to order the withdrawal of the purchaser's offer to purchase the property upon the following grounds:

(1) In the case of a purchaser, a lien remains unsatisfied on the property to be conveyed.

(2) In the case of any party to the partition proceeding:

a. Notice of the partition was not served on the petitioner for revocation as required by Rule 4 of the Rules of Civil Procedure; or

b. Notice of the sale was not mailed to the petitioner for revocation as required by G.S. 46-28(b); or

c. The amount bid or price offered is inadequate and inequitable and will result in irreparable damage to the owners of the real property.

In no event shall the confirmation order become final or effective during the pendency of a petition under this section. No upset bid shall be permitted after the entry of the confirmation order.

(b) The party petitioning for revocation shall deliver a copy of the petition to all parties required to be served under Rule 5 of G.S. 1A-1, and the officer or person designated to make such sale in the manner provided for service of process in Rule 4(j) of G.S. 1A-1. The court shall schedule a hearing on the petition within a reasonable time and shall cause a notice of the hearing to be served on the petitioner, the officer or person designated to make such a sale and all parties required to be served under Rule 5 of G.S. 1A-1.

(c) In the case of a petition brought under this section by a purchaser claiming the existence of an unsatisfied lien on the property to be conveyed, if the purchaser proves by a preponderance of the evidence that:

(1) A lien remains unsatisfied on the property to be conveyed; and

(2) The purchaser has not agreed in writing to assume the lien; and

(3) The lien will not be satisfied out of the proceeds of the sale; and

(4) The existence of the lien was not disclosed in the notice of sale of the property, the court may revoke the order confirming the sale, order the withdrawal of the purchaser's offer, and order the return of any money or security to the purchaser tendered pursuant to the offer.

The order of the court in revoking an order of confirmation under this section may not be introduced in any other proceeding to establish or deny the existence of a lien.

(d) In the case of a petition brought pursuant to this section by a party to the partition proceeding, if the court finds by a preponderance of the evidence that petitioner has proven a case pursuant to sub-subdivision (a)(2)a., b., or c. of this section, the court may revoke the order confirming the sale, order the withdrawal of the purchaser's offer, and order the return of any money or security to the purchaser tendered pursuant to the offer.

(d1) In the case of a petition brought pursuant to sub-subdivision (a)(2)c. of this section, and when an independent appraisal of the property being sold has not been previously entered into evidence in the action, and upon the request of any party, the court may order an independent appraisal prepared by a real estate appraiser currently licensed by the North Carolina Appraisal Board and prepared in accordance with the Uniform Standards of Professional Appraisal Practice. The cost of an independent appraisal shall be borne by one or more of the parties requesting the appraisal in such proportions as they may agree. Before ruling on the petition brought pursuant to sub-subdivision (a)(2)c. of this section, the court may in its discretion require written evidence from the appraiser that the appraiser has been paid in full for the appraisal. If based on the appraisal and all of the evidence presented, the court finds the amount bid or price offered to be inadequate, inequitable, and resulting in irreparable damage to the owners, the court may revoke the order confirming the sale, order the withdrawal of the purchaser's high bid or offer, and order the return to such purchaser of any money or security tendered by the purchaser pursuant to the high bid or offer.

(e) If the court revokes its order of confirmation under this section, the court shall order a resale. The procedure for a resale is the same as is provided for an original public sale under Article 29A of Chapter 1 of the General Statutes.

(f) An order confirming the partition sale of real property becomes final and effective 15 days after entry of the order of confirmation or when the clerk denies a petition for revocation, whichever occurs later. A party may appeal an order confirming the partition of sale of real property within 10 days of the order becoming final and effective. (1977, c. 833, s. 1; 1985, c. 626, ss. 3-7; 2001-271, s. 19; 2009-362, s. 4; 2009-512, s. 5.)

§ 46-28.2. When bidder may purchase.

After the order of confirmation becomes final and effective, the successful bidder may immediately purchase the property. (1977, c. 833, s. 3; 1985, c. 626, s. 8.)

§ 46-29. Repealed by Session Laws 1949, c. 719, s. 2.

§ 46-30. Deed to purchaser; effect of deed.

The deed of the officer or person designated to make such sale shall convey to the purchaser such title and estate in the property as the tenants in common, or joint tenants, and all other parties to the proceeding had therein. (1868-9, c. 122, ss. 13, 31; Code, ss. 1904, 1921; Rev. s. 2512; C.S., s. 3241; 1949, c. 719, s. 2.)

§ 46-31. Clerk not to appoint self, assistant or deputy to sell real property.

No clerk of the superior court shall appoint himself or his assistant or deputy to make sale of any property in any proceeding before him. (1868-9, c. 122, s. 15; Code, s. 1906; 1899, c. 161; Rev., s. 2513; C.S., s. 3242; 1949, c. 719, s. 2.)

§ 46-32. Repealed by Session Laws 1949, c. 719, s. 2.

§ 46-33. Shares in proceeds to cotenants secured.

At the time that the order of confirmation becomes final, the court shall secure to each tenant in common, or joint tenant, his ratable share in severalty of the proceeds of sale. (1868-9, c. 122, s. 31; Code, s. 1921; Rev., s. 2513; C.S., s. 3244; 1977, c. 833, s. 2.)

§ 46-34. Shares to persons unknown or not sui juris secured.

When a sale is made under this Chapter, and any party to the proceedings be an infant, non compos mentis, imprisoned, or beyond the limits of the State, or when the name of any tenant in common is not known, it is the duty of the court to decree the share of such party, in the proceeds of sale, to be so invested or settled that the same may be secured to such party or his real representative. (1868-9, c. 122, s. 17; Code, s. 1908; 1887, c. 284, s. 3; Rev., s. 2516; C.S., s. 3245.)

Article 3.

Partition of Lands in Two States.

§§ 46-35 through 46-41. Repealed by Session Laws 1943, c. 543.

Article 4.

Partition of Personal Property.

§ 46-42. Personal property may be partitioned; commissioners appointed.

When any persons entitled as tenants in common, or joint tenants, of personal property desire to have a division of the same, they, or either of them, may file a petition in the superior court for that purpose; and the court, if it think the petitioners entitled to relief, shall appoint three disinterested commissioners, who, being first duly sworn, shall proceed within 20 days after notice of their appointment to divide such property as nearly equally as possible among the tenants in common, or joint tenants. (1868-9, c. 122, s. 27; Code, s. 1917; Rev., s. 2504; C.S., s. 3253.)

§ 46-43. Report of commissioners.

The commissioners shall report their proceedings under the hands of any two of them, and shall file their report in the office of the clerk of the superior court within five days after the partition was made. (1868-9, c. 122, s. 28; Code, s. 1918; Rev., s. 2505; C.S., s. 3254.)

§ 46-43.1. Confirmation; impeachment.

If no exception to the report of the commissioners making partition is filed within 10 days the report shall be confirmed. Any party, after confirmation, shall be allowed to impeach the proceeding for mistake, fraud or collusion, by petition in the cause, but innocent purchasers for full value and without notice shall not be affected thereby. (1953, c. 24.)

§ 46-44. Sale of personal property on partition.

If a division of personal property owned by any persons as tenants in common, or joint tenants, cannot be had without injury to some of the parties interested, and a sale thereof is deemed necessary, the court shall order a sale to be made as provided in Article 29A of Chapter 1 of the General Statutes. (1868-9, c. 122, s. 29; Code, s. 1919; Rev., s. 2519; C.S., s. 3255; 1949, c. 719, s. 2.)

§§ 46-45 through 46-46. Repealed by Session Laws 1949, c. 719, s. 2.

Vision Books Order Form

Fax Orders:	1-980-299-5965
Phone Orders:	1-704-898-0770
E-mail Orders:	www.visionbooks.org
Mail Orders:	Vision Books, LLC P.O. Box 42406 Charlotte, NC 28215

Shipp To:
Name_____
Address_____
City_____State_____Zip_____
Phone_____Fax_____
Email_____@_____

Bill To: We can bill a third party on your behalf.
Name_____
Address_____
City_____State_____Zip_____
Phone   (   )   Fax_____
Email_____@_____

Pamphlet Number ($15.00 Each)	Qty	Total Cost
_____	_____	_____
_____	_____	_____
_____	_____	_____
_____	_____	_____
_____	_____	_____
_____	_____	_____
_____	_____	_____
Full Volume Set 1-92	92 Pamphlets	1,380.00

Free Shipping Shipping & Handling on Full Volume Orders
Add $1.00 Shipping & Handling per pamphlet $_____

Total Cost $_____

Thank You for Your Support. Management!

DID YOU ENJOY THIS BOOK?

Vision Books, LLC would like to hear from you! If you or someone you know has been fasely imprisoned, we would like to hear your story. If the 'North Carolina Criminal Law and Procedure' has had an effect in your life or if you have suggestions, we would like to hear from you. Send your letters to:

Vision Books, LLC
Attn: Staff Writers
P.O. Box 42406
Charlotte, NC 28215
Email: staff@visionbooks.org

Order Additional Copies:

Fax Orders: 1-980-299-5965

Phone Orders: 1-704-898-0770

E-mail Orders: www.visionbooks.org

Mail Orders: Vision Books, LLC
                      P.O. Box 42406
                      Charlotte, NC 28215

www.ingramcontent.com/pod-product-compliance
Lightning Source LLC
Chambersburg PA
CBHW051633170526
45167CB00001B/171